HOPE FOR YOUR FUTURE

HOPE FOR YOUR FUTURE

Theological Voices from the Pastorate

Edited by

WILLIAM H. LAZARETH

William B. Eerdmans Publishing Company

Grand Rapids, Michigan / Cambridge, U.K.

Wm. B. Eerdmans Publishing Co.
255 Jefferson Ave. S.E., Grand Rapids, Michigan 49503 /
P.O. Box 163, Cambridge CB3 9PU U.K.

Printed in the United States of America

07 06 05 04 03 02   7 6 5 4 3 2 1

Library of Congress Cataloging-in-Publication Data

Hope for your future: theological voices from the pastorate /
edited by William H. Lazareth.
p.   cm.
Includes bibliographical references.
ISBN 0-8028-4961-X (pbk.: alk. paper)
1. Eschatology.   2. Church renewal.
I. Lazareth, William Henry, 1928-

BT823.H66   2002
270.8′3 — dc21

2002019442

www.eerdmans.com

Contents

CONTENTS

Contents

CONTENTS

The Recovery of Theology
in the Service of the Church

The presupposition underlying this research project is that the so-called "crisis of the church" is neither organizational nor programmatic, but theological. The crisis *of* the church is simply the public face of the crisis *in* the church, which is essentially a crisis of faith.

The Crisis in the Church

There are many studies by social scientists of the phenomenology of this crisis. These studies have been useful and suggestive as to the dimensions and proportions of the problem, but they have seldom touched the heart of the matter. The heart of the matter is the loss of the church's identity as a theological community, occasioned by the distance at which the church lives from the sources of its faith and life. The heart of the matter, in the language of faith, is the apparent inability of the contemporary church to answer the question that Jesus put to his disciples long ago, "But who do you say that I am?"

The renewal of the church, now as always, is accomplished by the power of the Holy Spirit and is received as a gift of God. If history is any indication, however, the gift of renewal is most frequently given when the church places itself within the realm of possibility — that is, in the context of those means of grace by which, according to the Old and New Testaments, the Spirit works. Thus the renewal of the church begins, at least on the human level, with the recovery of those sources and practices that historically have enabled people to encounter and to be encountered by "the grace of our Lord Jesus Christ, the love of God, and the communion of the Holy Spirit."

The renewal of the church may be anticipated when witness is borne through preaching, teaching, pastoral care, and church administration to the gospel of what God has done in and through Jesus Christ. The persuasiveness of the Christian message, when accompanied by the power of the Spirit, is in the power of its articulation to render a more convincing account of the facts of life, to make more sense out of life, and to give more meaning to life than do other alternatives.

The church is often assisted but never renewed by such things as management skills, goal-setting processes, reorganization, public relations, or conflict management. The church waits most faithfully for the gift of new life when it recovers its identity as a theological community and attends to those sources and practices that are the promised means by which God creates, sustains, and preserves the church.

The Separation of Theology and Church

A significant part of the current crisis in the church is the hiatus between academic theology as an intellectual discipline and ecclesial theology as a confessional stance. The achievement of a high level of competence and specialization in theological education requires a certain degree of proficiency in rational analysis, as well as the mastery of languages, texts, ideas, cultures, and extensive bibliographies. It also requires the maintenance of a certain critical distance in order to distinguish the more from the less true. Bridging the gap between the academic study of theology and the confessional theology of the church, between the critical distance that rational analysis requires and the profound commitment that Christian witness requires, is not easy and is accomplished only with great skill.

Furthermore, there is a tendency on the part of many denominational theological seminaries, which live in proximity to secular institutions of higher education, to become centers of religious studies. Seminary faculty are increasingly educated in graduate schools of secular universities and are often called to teaching positions in denominational institutions with little knowledge of the theological tradition in which they are to teach. Seminary teachers increasingly write not for the church, but for other professionals in the "guild." Thus the primary purpose of the theological seminary — to prepare pastors for the theological vocation of preaching, teaching, and pastoral care — is undercut by the guild, the priority of which is not that of maintaining the identity of the Christian church.

As might be expected given these circumstances, there has been a sharp decline of the pastor-scholar both in seminary faculties and in the ministry of congregations. The movement from seminary faculty to the ministry of a congregation, and conversely from congregation to classroom, has all but ceased. The result is a relatively new phenomenon in American church life: the profound separation between serious theological work and congregational life.

The Trivialization of the Church

One of the legacies of continental Protestant Christianity is the subordination of questions concerning polity and program to convictions concerning the essence of the church. It began not simply with the question, "How can I find the gracious God?" or "What is the meaning of life?" but with questions concerning the nature of the church, such as "What is the essence of the true church?" and "What are the marks by which it may be recognized?" Questions about polity and boundaries were always secondary to the conviction that the church is the people of God, constituted by the Word of God. Other ecclesiologies, such as the Roman Catholic, Anglican, and representatives of the Anabaptist tradition, approach the essence of the church in other ways. But each would confess that the church, unique among all other constructs, is a profoundly theological reality.

The Protestant Reformers also had a clear understanding of the ordained minister. None would have suggested that the ordained ministry as such is essential to the church, only the Word of God heard in faith and obeyed in love. But they knew full well that the minister fulfilled an important office for the well-being of the church, namely that of preaching, teaching, and exercising pastoral care in the context of a Christian congregation. The task of the minister was the theological task of proclamation, explication, and application of the Word of God. The expectation was that, through such service, God would act to gather, establish, and empower the church. Once again, other ecclesiologies would confess that the ordained ministry is essential to the existence of the church. But all would agree that the minister's task is theological in nature, not merely organizational or primarily institutional.

A striking fact about the church in our time is that where ministers pursue their calling as church theologians with energy, intelligence, imagination, and love, the church lives . . . and where they do not, the church tends to be trivialized and languishes. A vital church possesses an institutional sense of self that distinguishes it from a civic club, social agency, political party, or self-help organization; and it does not confuse its minister with a social change agent, therapist, or entertainer. One might well document the fact that the crisis in the church parallels the loss of theological identity by the church and the shift in its understanding of the minister from that of pastor-theologian to that of chief executive officer. Hence the recovery of a substantive doctrine of the ordained ministry as a theological vocation, and a strategy for the formation and support of the pastor as theologian and scholar in preaching, teaching, pastoral care, and administration, are crucial for the renewal of the church and for the revitalization of contemporary Christian communities.

The Center of Theological Inquiry as Servant of the Church

The proposal to establish a center for advanced theological research was first advanced by President James I. McCord at a meeting of the Board of Trustees of Princeton Theological Seminary in 1962. "If the age in which we are living is one of transition and revolution, and if the shape of things to come cannot be predicted," he said, "surely the church ought to have some men and women who are giving intense thought at the deepest level to the church's theology, strategy, and mission in the age that is evolving."

After fifteen years of discussion and planning, a Center of Theological Inquiry was established in Princeton, New Jersey as a separate corporation, not under the control of any denomination or institution, to inquire at the post-graduate level into the relationship between theological and non-theological disciplines, including both the human and natural sciences; to inquire into the relationship between diverse religious traditions, particularly the Christian and non-Christian, Western and non-Western; to inquire into the present state of religious and quasi-religious consciousness in the modern world; and to examine other facets of religion in the modern world as may be appropriate to supplement these inquiries.

It was not intended that the Center should focus on religion in general or that it should undertake its task apart from the faith and life of the ecumenical church. To the contrary, the Center was intended as an expression of the claims and commitments of catholic Christianity to the uniqueness of Jesus Christ; the biblical concern for the redemption of individuals, societies, and the entire creation; and the service of God with the life of the mind. The assumption underlying its existence is that God is the source and author of all truth; that truth arrived at in any discipline is not inimical to faith in God; that where faith and reason seem to clash, either reason has been distorted or faith misunderstood and misrepresented.

Over 100 Protestant, Catholic and Jewish scholars, representing various non-theological as well as the traditional theological disciplines, have undertaken periods of residency at the Center to pursue their research projects. A like number have been involved in consultations, conferences, and seminars sponsored by the Center on such topics as theology and science, John Calvin and the visual arts, eschatology, globalization, and biblical authority. The Center seeks to fulfill its founders' vision by being a context in which people think ahead for the church in order to identify the ideas and issues with which theology will have to cope in the coming years, and to explore the resources upon which theology may call for so doing.

One issue yet to be addressed, however, is that of dissemination. The Center of Theological Inquiry is committed to the proposition that theology is not true to itself when it is simply an academic discipline, that Christian theology, being by definition incarnational, cannot be done in isolation from the church or the world. It seeks to foster interdisciplinary theological research whereby the faith of the church engages and is engaged by the various forces shaping the culture of which it is a part, including non-theological disciplines, such as science, and other philosophies of life and religious traditions.

How might interdisciplinary dialogue, such as that fostered by the Center, gain access to the mind and heart of the church, broaden its theological horizons, and inform its mission in the world? How is the church to recover its identity as a theological community of faith and hope as well as love? What can be done about the separation of theology and church? What role might the Center play in the renewal of the church in our time?

The Pastor-Theologian Program

Assisting us to address this current crisis in the church and in theology, the Lilly Endowment, Inc. made a major grant to the Center of Theological Inquiry in support of a new venture in ecumenical theological education. A *Pastor-Theologian Program* would seek to focus attention on the ordained ministry as a theological vocation and on the church as a theological community. We were acting on the conviction that in all denominations there are pastors of exceptional theological scholarship, who lack only the time, context, and encouragement for such pursuits, and that on their emergence as a formative influence the renewal of the church depended. They would be further equipped, while in the church's active service, to obey the apostolic admonition to be ready to answer all who ask about "an accounting for the hope" that gives life to the church (I Pet. 3:15).

The Center's grant proposal rested on the assumption that a ministry of theological substance is of crucial importance for the renewal of the church. It fully acknowledges the role and place of theological seminaries and divinity schools in preparing men and women for the ordained ministry, but it also contends that additional structures of intellectual development must also be in place if the pastor-theologian model of ministry is to be an instrument of the continuing reformation and renewal of the church. Participating pastors, as recommended by church and seminary leaders, would therefore be drawn ecumenically from congregations of various churches throughout the country.

"Reading the Bible in Faith" (1998-99)

It was further determined that the research of the first year of the program would focus on the theme of "Reading the Bible in Faith." Special attention would be given to the interpretation of two key texts: the binding of Isaac (Gen. 22) and the Passion of Christ (Matt. 26–27). The texts were chosen because they direct attention to theological issues that are crucial for the church's preaching and teaching in our time: theology of the cross, faithful suffering and death, obedience, the relation of the Old and New Testaments, and the identity, purpose, and action of the Triune God.

We believed that the church's current confusion is related to its loss of the capacity to read biblical texts such as these in profound engagement with church tradition. We hoped to help promote the recovery of practices of "Christian reading." Moreover, we expected that these conversations would generate a range of teaching and writing projects that could eventually be shared with one another and the wider public. That hope was eventually realized in publishing the first volume of this series: *Reading the Bible in Faith: Theological Voices from the Pastorate.*

"Theology, Science and the Future" (1999-2000)

It was subsequently decided that the research of the 1999-2000 academic year (explored in this second volume) would focus on the theme of "Theology, Science and the Future." Capitalizing on the general public's millennialist interest and concerns surrounding the year 2000, we concentrated theologically on these central issues: What can Christians hope for? How do signs of God's reign shape the church's faith and life today? Where can we find the power to prevail in a culture that faces unprecedented forces of both life and death? Our aim was to develop a realistic eschatology that was both doctrinally faithful and contemporaneously intelligible. The method was to explore the interrelation of the natural and social sciences with various biblical, theological, and ethical traditions.

During the ensuing period, the sixty-person group completed fifteen regional seminars, comprising three sessions of three days' duration each in different locations within five regional areas (Northeast, Southeast, North Central, South Central, Far West). All five groups expressed a growing sense of common purpose and mutual trust as the three parallel rounds of seminars progressed. Variety was provided by the circulation of eighteen academic resource persons (seminary and university professors). Thematic continuity was achieved through the critical group analyses of the provided ten common texts:

Donald Gowan, *Eschatology in the Old Testament.* T&T Clark, 1977.

Hans Küng, *Eternal Life.* Crossroad, 1991.

Walter Miller, Jr., *A Canticle for Leibowitz.* Harper, 1977.

Jürgen Moltmann, *The Coming of God.* Fortress, 1966.

John Polkinghorne, *The Faith of a Physicist.* Fortress, 1966.

John Polkinghorne, *Science and Theology.* Fortress, 1999.

John Polkinghorne and Michael Welker, eds., *The End of the World and the Ends of God.* Trinity, 2000.

Michael Welker, *God the Spirit.* Fortress, 1994.

Ben Witherington III, *Jesus, Paul and the End of the World.* InterVarsity, 1997.

Daniel Wojcik, *The End of the World as We Know It.* New York University, 1997.

The annual National Conference, held on March 23-26, 2000, integrated all the members of the regions with an international and interdisciplinary team of teaching professors who were completing their own three-year CTI Project studies on the same theme. These included Professors Larry Bouchard, University of Virginia; Donald Juel, Princeton Theological Seminary; Patrick Miller, Princeton Theological Seminary; Jürgen Moltmann, Tübingen University; John Polkinghorne, Cambridge University; Gerhard Sauter, University of Bonn; Janet Soskice, Cambridge University; William Stoeger, University of Arizona; Miroslav Volf, Yale University; Hans Weder, University of Zürich; and Michael Welker, Heidelberg University.

Expanding the Discussions

A complete roster of all clergy participants in the year's program activities is provided in the Appendix of this volume. By the end of June, each pastor-theologian had submitted a twenty-page research essay or project on a subject related to the year's general theme. Included in their number are the authors of the excerpted articles edited for publication in this volume.

Space limits obviously precluded the publication of all the material produced, and subject concentration understandably elicited a good deal of duplication. While these blocs of excerpted material are admittedly both short and taken out of context, they nevertheless contribute far more to a lively, multi-voiced discussion than would the total arguments of their authors' much longer original essays.

Additionally, each chapter here is opened with an editor's introduction that briefly integrates the theme-oriented excerpts with one another. Intentionally, the authors' diversity in style and structure has been retained. All authors were encouraged to "speak the truth in love" during frank exchanges, while analyzing both the problems and the opportunities they have experienced in exercising their holy calling in local congregations. They write primarily as pastors in dialogue with other pastors. In short, this format allows for more pastor-theologians to speak freely with one another, even if only partially here, in making their distinctive contribution to what is essentially an ecumenical group effort.

We publish this book, therefore, both as an ongoing record of the Center's stewardship, and as a cordial invitation for readers, especially other pastor-theologians in local congregations, to join us by interactive extension in this and other similar publications of annual discussions already projected for future years. We do so with deep gratitude to the Lilly Endowment, Inc. for its generous financial assistance and helpful staff support in our joint endeavor to strengthen outstanding pastor-theologians in their learned ministries for leading the people of God in the mission of the church of Jesus Christ in and for the world.

Wallace M. Alston, Jr.
Director, Center of
Theological Inquiry

William H. Lazareth
Program Associate,
Pastor-Theologian Program

PART ONE

BEYOND NIHILISM

CHAPTER I

Hope in Biblical Traditions

Introduction

The opening chapter presents some of the important biblical passages that deal with the "end" of the world, in both senses of temporal finitude and eternal fulfillment. The issues involved are of special significance for the dialogue between theology and science, since Christians confess belief in a Triune God who is the creator as well as the redeemer of the entire universe and its human inhabitants.

The dimension of Christian doctrine that concentrates on the final destiny of such "last things," whether in historical time or in God's purpose, is called "eschatology." It is integral to the central theme of hope and despair within the Holy Scriptures. In the Old Testament, it is closely related to the Messianic hope of the prophets; in the New Testament, it is a central subject of Christ's proclamation and parables about God's inbreaking reign, whether in its present or future dimensions. The gospel of Christ's death and resurrection decisively determined the hope of early Christians regarding their own resurrection, salvation, and final judgment.

A specialized genre of biblical eschatological literature has also been characterized as "apocalyptic." It refers to a cryptic revelation or unveiling of impending historical and cosmic events, often catastrophic and cataclysmic, that forecast the end of the present world and the coming of a new one. Daniel and Revelation are prominent examples of such biblical apocalypticism, both written in response to the severe oppression and persecution of God's people. Conflicting interpretations of apocalyptic imagery — literal, allegorical, or symbolic — have often divided Chris-

3

tians and their eschatological views of the future of nature and history over the centuries.

The opening collection of excerpts from five of the authors' essays introduces the reader to some key eschatological and apocalyptic passages in various biblical traditions. In the first essay, Jim Kitchens lauds the methodology of the pastor-theologian community as being made-to-order for working at achieving diversified unity on such issues through ecumenical and interdisciplinary dialogue. Adapting Polanyi's "society of explorers" as a model for faithful theological conversation, Kitchens witnesses to his own personal experience during two years of intensive interaction and growth within his seminar of pastoral colleagues. Personal commitment, team respect, mutual control, and concomitant responsibility were all essential elements of the group endeavor. The goal was to do communal theological reflection that intentionally seeks to follow the guidance of the Holy Spirit while meeting concurrent demands in pastoral preaching, teaching, and healing.

The next two articles analyze apocalyptic materials in Mark and Revelation, as canonically placed at the opening and closing of the New Testament. Douglas Dobson focuses attention on Mark 13's so-called "Little Apocalypse," and freely expresses his own academic "departure from most current scholarship." Whereas most commentators view Mark's material as pointing to some distant future, this author views it rather as extant apocalyptic material that was adapted by Mark to point imminently to the crucifixion of Jesus. Congruently in its setting, the passage is preceded by the self-sacrifice of a widow in the Temple as a parable of Christ's cross, even as the subsequent passage highlights the desire of the chief priests and scribes to have Jesus killed. Christ's atoning crucifixion is the "Apocalypse Fulfilled," the climactic end time of Mark's gospel of salvation.

Douglas Fletcher's study of "Heaven in Revelation" repudiates a popular view that the last book of the Bible is devoted to bizarre cosmic speculations. Instead, he presents the apocalyptic portrayal of heaven (21:1–22:5) as pastoral encouragement and hopeful counsel that is vividly depicted in religiously-coded imagery for a persecuted and suffering minority, which confidently fulfills identifiable Old Testament prophecies regarding (1) the creation story, (2) God's promises of blessing to Israel, and (3) the righteous judgment of Babylon. It is a book that affirms biblical faith and invites courageous obedience to the Lord God who acts creatively in covenantal fidelity throughout the trials and tribulations of human history.

Turning next to the resurrection of Christ as the salvific linchpin of New Testament eschatology, the excerpt of F. Harry Daniel compares Mark and Matthew in their "Gospel Endings of the Resurrection." Assuming both Markan chronological priority and the original ending of its terse resurrection account in the first eight verses of chapter 16, Daniel provides a close reading of the longer gospel conclusion that is found in Matthew. Analyzing the two authors' different settings, purposes, and resources, Daniel concludes that Matthew built on Markan foundations and then expanded description with consequences in ecclesial and missional coherence. His faith: Christ's resurrection event does not conclude on Easter, but lives on in "the close of the age" through the mission of a new people in a new age that has eternal significance. The risen Lord commissions his church to proclaim the victorious gospel, discipleship, and future hope of the inaugurated kingdom of God.

Laird Stuart complements this discussion with "The Witness of the Resurrection" in the eschatological message of the apostle Paul. His bold thesis is that "in the resurrection we witness a dialectic of continuity and discontinuity, which testifies to God's ability to create new life out of death and destruction, a creative act which belongs not to any inherent capacity of the natural world, but only to God." His attention centers on I Corinthians 15, where Paul affirms God's resurrection of the crucified Christ, through the operations of the Holy Spirit, with a spiritual and invisible body that is newly adapted to eschatological existence. Moreover, the faithful may now also hope for their own resurrection "in Christ," and by extension, that God's awesome power may finally insure as well the promise of a transfigured new heaven and new earth.

1. A Model for Faithful Theological Conversation

JIM KITCHENS

Davis Community Church
Davis, California

When it was suggested to us at Princeton in March that the audience for whom we ought to write this year's paper was our own regional group, I decided to stick with an intuition I'd had early in the year about what might be a fruitful topic for our discussion. In that light, I offer this paper as a response to a question I have asked myself more than once during the past two years: *What purpose do we in this program serve the church?* In other words, what is the value of our gathering as a collegium of pastor-theologians (other than the obvious values of beautiful setting, fine food and drink, and convivial friends)? Of what worth to our ministries, to our denominations, and to the church of Jesus Christ are our conversations? What good might emerge from the time we spend together and out of the relationships we have formed? What positive contribution might we make to the life of the church from this marvelous opportunity that has been afforded us?

Sometimes I dismiss these questions as no more than demons that emerge from the "shadow" side of my being just enough of a Calvinist for my theology of stewardship to make me worry whether we are producing enough return on the capital the Lilly Endowment has invested in us. But my guess is that I am not alone in thinking about these questions over the past two years. And my intuition is that these are, indeed, important questions for us to ask.

Just when I was about to conclude that my participation in the program was in fact selfishly motivated, Wallace Alston asked us to write about the ways the effect our participation had changed our ministries for the better. As I reflected on his request, I realized a number of changes in my life and work that I directly attribute to my being part of this program:

- a more thoroughgoing theological reflection in my preaching and teaching (a depth of reflection noted appreciatively by my parishioners).

- more excitement about inviting laypersons into shared discussions to reflect critically on the faith (and more eagerness in their response).
- a growing desire to engage pre-seminarians in our congregation in developing the habit of serious theological reflection prior to their entering seminary.
- a renewed interest in joining clergy colleagues in my presbytery in disciplines of regular theological reflection, resulting in the formation of a (forgive me, Robin Williams) "Dead Theologians' Society."
- a deeper sense of rootedness in the *fullness* of the Christian tradition as the necessary context for continuing engagement with those hot-button denominational issues that do not appear to be going away anytime in the foreseeable future.

What I would like to offer for our discussion is my sense that the work of the Hungarian-born scientist-philosopher Michael Polanyi on the methodology of science offers us, by way of analogy, some helpful insights into the methodology of theology. While Polanyi's sketch of the republic of science was based on what he knew best — how working scientists make new discoveries and share them with one another — he went on to extend his theory to account for the epistemology and the heuristic nature of all forms of human societies. Any such society, whether it be political, economic, or religious,

> derives its capacity for self-renewal from its belief in the presence of a hidden reality. . . . Any tradition fostering the progress of thought must have this intention: to teach its current ideas as stages leading on to unknown truths which, when discovered, might dissent from the very teachings which engendered them. Such a tradition assures the independence of its followers by transmitting the conviction that thought has intrinsic powers, to be evoked in men's minds by intimations of hidden truths. It respects the individual for being capable of such response: for being able to see a problem not visible to others, and to explore it on his own responsibility. Such are the metaphysical grounds of intellectual life in a free, dynamic society: the principles which safeguard intellectual life in such a society. I call this a society of explorers.[1]

I want to draw out some of what I think are Polanyi's implications for our understanding the theological community as a whole as such a "society of explorers" and for considering our pastor-theologian community (and within it the Western regional group) as one of the interlinking "local neighborhoods" within that organic society of mutual authority.

The Standing of the Pastor-Theologian

The faithful pastor-theologian enters the theological enterprise having made an a priori commitment to the truth of the reality s/he seeks to understand, that is, to God. We are not merely instrumentalists, developing theologies about God that have value simply because they are systematically consistent and elegant or even because they address a perceived human need. Instead, we are called to commit ourselves to — and be judged by — God, who is the object of theology's search for understanding. We submit ourselves to God in faith — in most cases more consciously than do most scientists to the object of their heuristic search — and pray that the insights that arise out of our experience of God's presence in the interpretative context of the church's theological tradition will give true insights into the nature of God and God's way with creation. Thomas Torrance talks about that submission when he expands on Polanyi's reference to St. Augustine:

> St. Augustine . . . was also fond of . . . the same passage from Isaiah: "If you will not believe, you will not understand." Again and again he emphasized that we must not seek to understand that we may believe, but must believe that we may understand. There is a deep reciprocal relationship between faith and reason, for "everyone who believes thinks, but thinks in believing and believes in thinking." But St. Augustine tends to connect faith with prior assent yielded to truth on the basis of authority, which gives access to understanding and is a necessary stage in reasonable inquiry.[2]

Such personal commitment — along with the willingness to make personal judgments about our insights and to believe passionately in them — is foundational to faithful theological reflection. According to Richard Gelwick,

> At every step (in the scientific process), there are questions of personal judgment that go beyond the rules. These are judgments that demand

insight and understanding. Two scientists could have a perfectly identical understanding of scientific laws and theories, but one may make a great discovery and the other spend his or her life doing ordinary research which conforms to current knowledge. The difference lies in the personal judgment of the scientist.[3]

Every pastor-theologian (indeed, every believing Christian) has been standing within "the society of explorers" to suggest new interpretive patterns that s/he believes to be a deeper and more profound interpretation of the theological tradition of the church. Every pastor-theologian, in our case, may be gifted by the Holy Spirit with insight that brings awareness of a new interpretative pattern arising from "data" that is already part of the church's accepted tradition. Such gifts may be recognized and rewarded by the community through a particular call to theological service in the church, so that some Christians gain a broader hearing in the church than others. But no one is drawn outside the circle of those who can potentially offer new, valuable, and true insight into the nature of God in the Christian community. By entering the field of theology as pastor-theologians, we become members in this society's system of mutual control and have a concomitant responsibility to be willing and faithful members of the theological enterprise.

Pastor-theologians bring a special sense of indwelling to the theological conversation with academic theologians. As theologians who indwell the Body of Christ as that body is incarnated in the life of a local parish, we bring unique insights into the nature of God to the roundtable of theological conversation. Not having the luxury of developing theology for its own sake, we bring the gift of doing theological reflection in the midst of the three-fold pastoral mission of preaching, teaching, and healing. Seeking to make sense of such "front-line" experiences of the Gospel's healing and saving power (and of the powers and principalities that resist that power), we have intuitive hunches about the way God works in the world that are not as readily available to those who have the (also noble) calling to academic theology. They need our corrective experience and insight as surely as we need theirs.

JIM KITCHENS

The Usefulness of the Pastor-Theologian Program

The Pastor-Theologian Program functions as one of those overlapping neighborhoods of interest within the organically linked theological society of explorers. It functions as a setting for mutual authority for those of us who are its members as well as for the church as a whole. It is one of those arenas in which we, in Polanyi's words, "keep watch over each other . . . both subject to criticism by others and . . . encouraged by their appreciation."[4] By the act of submitting our papers (literally) and our thoughts and commitments (implicitly) to one another, we agree to be gently corrected where our theological innovation doesn't quite ring true to the consensus of the group and to be encouraged by the affirmation of our colleagues that we may be "on to something" about the nature of God and of the church's existence. Each of us, I would be willing to wager, is not only a better but also a more faithful theologian for the parishes we serve because of our submission to one another's authority, an authority we trust to be reflective of the authority of the church's tradition and, finally, of God's authority.

The Pastor-Theologian Program is also, I would propose, an important link in the overlapping system of mutual control within the church as a whole. We in this group have a common call and competence in that we are committed to the concept of the pastor-theologian for a local congregation and in that we have all been blessed with the ability to wrestle deeply with the reality of God, whom we seek to know more fully through our common labors. But we also bear other markings and competencies that signify the *other* local neighborhoods to which we belong in the greater theological society of explorers. We are Presbyterians, Lutherans, Baptists, and Anglicans. We are Barthians, Tillichians, feminists, and process thinkers. We are deeply committed to liturgy, to Christian formation, to Bible study, and to ministries of social justice. Already we can begin to see the ways we are members of overlapping local neighborhoods that weave together the broader fabric of those within the Body of Christ for whom the guarding and the deepening of the church's theological tradition is a primary calling.

The Role of the Holy Spirit in the Theological Enterprise

Jesus, in his final conversation with the disciples in the Gospel of John, tells us that the Holy Spirit is "the Spirit of truth" who "abides" and will "be in" us and "guide us into all the truth." In this way, the Holy Spirit is that Polanyian "invisible guiding hand" that leads us into ever-deepening knowledge about the Triune God. The Spirit is the energizing force behind the sort of intuitive knowledge that Polanyi calls "tacit." It is the kind of insight that Polanyi acknowledges by his famous dictum: "we can know more than we can tell."[5] The Spirit enables us to begin to discern the emergence of deeper and more faithful interpretations of God and God's desires for us, to make passionate hunches, and to offer our insights to the mutually authoritative society of the church as a whole.

Of course, it is always crucial that, in our theological work, we heed Paul's insistence to "test the spirits" to come to a determination as to whether a proffered insight is in fact a truer understanding of the nature of God or is a well-intended but mistaken pattern of discernment. However, Polanyi also helps us to appreciate those who *do* miss the mark, even those heretics who have attempted to lead the church astray over the centuries. It is only as a society of explorers allows enough freedom among its members to allow for mistakes that it will also most fruitfully enable the discovery of true and faithful insights at the church's edge of understanding of God. As long as individuals are willing to submit to the system of mutual authority, the church as a society of explorers under the guiding hand of the Holy Spirit will remain faithful to God, who is its source and goal.

2. Mark 13: Apocalypse Fulfilled

DOUGLAS DOBSON

Holy Cross Lutheran Church
Salem, Oregon

A dialogue between science and theology on the issue of "last things" presupposes that each of the dialogists represents a coherent and generally accepted position within their respective fields of knowledge. While the scientific community may have reached some consensus as to what constitutes the appropriate language and content for such a discussion, in theological circles the "eschaton" remains a topic of great dispute. The reason, of course, is that there are several theological communities, all with very different allegiances and conceptions. Eschatology is but one more topic that goes looking for agreement within theological circles. The scientific community must wonder: Who is the real partner of the dialogue? Who can speak for the theological community when there is not one but several different voices?

I suspect that no such single spokesperson can or will ever be found. But even so, it is at least incumbent upon all theologians to try to find a common ground, a common place from which to speak. For Christian theology, that common ground will be the Bible and especially those parts of the Scripture that are eschatological in orientation.

One such piece has already come to the fore in our readings in this year's Pastor-Theologian Program. Several writers have commented on the so-called "little apocalypse" in the Gospel of Mark.[1] Since Mark 13 is one of the chapters under examination here, I propose to study it closely to see what it can contribute to the larger discussion.

Mark 13 is an exercise in time flowing backwards. It follows a path from a more distant future to the immediate present. Along the way there is also an important reference to the past. But the point of the chapter is to focus all concerns about time on to the event immediately to take place — namely, the crucifixion of Jesus.[2] There has been much debate and discussion about the meaning of chapter 13 and whether or not it is truly apocalyptic. But if one does not see the chapter aimed directly at the crucifixion and death of Jesus, one has not arrived at the heart of the matter.

Before commenting on the chapter directly, it is important to take note of the context. I do not intend to analyze exhaustively the chapters on either side of the thirteenth chapter, but merely look at the verses immediately surrounding it. Chapter 12 concludes with Jesus in the Temple watching people make their offerings. A poor widow puts two small coins into the treasury box and this prompts a comment from Jesus: "Truly I tell you, this poor widow has put in more than all of those who are contributing to the treasury. For all of them have contributed out of their abundance; but she out of her poverty has put in everything she had, all she had to live on *[holon ton bion autēs]*" (Mark 12:43-44).[3] Chapter 14 opens with a sense of great foreboding as authorities seek an opportunity to arrest and kill Jesus. Then in verse 3 begins the story of the woman who comes to Jesus with a jar of ointment. She anoints Jesus. After some complaining and scolding of her by those present, Jesus says, "Let her alone; why do you trouble her? . . . She has done what she could; she has anointed my body beforehand for its burial. Truly I tell you, wherever the good news is proclaimed in the whole world, what she has done will be told in remembrance of her *[eis mnēmosunon autēs]*" (Mark 14:6a, 8-9).

The immediate context of chapter 13, then, is its placement between two sections dealing with the death of Jesus. The poor widow gives her *biov.* Although this is generally translated as her "means of making a living" or what she "had to live on," and certainly does mean that, the word *bios* is also suggestive of her physical being, her individuated existence.[4] This widow is thus described as offering her entire existence — a parable for what is about to happen to Jesus. The opening of chapter 14 also carries forward this emphasis on Jesus' death. The chief priests and scribes are said to be desirous of his death, and Jesus himself acknowledges his approaching death by commenting on the woman's action as preparing his body for burial and saying that her action is a memorial of her. Thus chapter 13 finds itself firmly fixed on either side by allusions to Jesus' death.

The setting of the whole of chapter 13 is outside of the Temple with Jesus speaking about its coming destruction. At verse 3 the scene shifts to the Mount of Olives. Jesus alone is said to be sitting "opposite" the Temple, although his disciples are with him. There is more than a hint of antagonism in this as *katenanti* carries overtones of "opposition." In fact, we shall note how the controversy between Jesus and the Temple is carried out in the final chapters of Mark.

Before looking at chapter 13, we may say at the outset what is not to be found here. In fact, what must be stated clearly is that chapter 13 is not about the development of a moral cosmology. That view must be thoroughly and absolutely rejected.[5] Such an understanding merely imports into Mark an alien concern that cannot be substantiated from the text and that ultimately distorts the intention of the chapter. William Schweiker attempts to find a key to understanding the chapter in verse 27, where the "elect" are to be gathered. Schweiker equates the "elect" with the "good" and assumes that all who are not elect are therefore to be considered evil. And so, as Schweiker says, the chapter is about the differentiation of good and evil. The good are to find ultimate reward and the bad are to be punished. In Schweiker's view, Mark 13 thus serves to develop a moral cosmology and the church is cast in the role of the community of the righteous — that is, the good.

The problem with Schweiker's position, of course, is that there is absolutely nothing in the chapter to suggest that the elect are morally superior. In fact, such a view of the elect ignores some of the clearest conceptions of election in the Biblical tradition. The elect are those who *in spite of* their moral behavior are chosen by God and *not because of* such behavior. Many of the individual "heroes" of the Old Testament are dramatic examples of that. And more to the point, Jesus says it himself. When the complaint is made that Jesus eats with tax collectors and sinners, he responds, "Those who are well have no need of a physician, but those who are sick; I have come to call not the righteous but sinners" (Mark 2:17). The elect are not the morally pure. To suggest that they are, or that chapter 13 suggests that they are, is to misunderstand totally the issue with which Mark is dealing. Schweiker has thrown a veil over the chapter that needs to be torn open.

My suggestion begins with the assumption that Mark has adopted and reinterpreted apocalyptic language and imagery. Many scholars have commented on the wealth of such imagery in the first century.[6] Indeed, while the language in the chapter may be authentically from Jesus, Mark takes an additional step. As Mark makes use of the available language, he bends and shapes the images to focus them upon the crucifixion of Jesus. The crucifixion is the end time in Mark. It is also the beginning of the new age. This is why Mark can spend so little time on the resurrection. Important as the empty tomb may be, the cross nonetheless is the birth of the eschatological moment. The cross is the cataclysmic event that reveals the face of God. In stark and absolute horror, it is at the foot of the cross where one is invited to see the work of salvation. "For in those days there will be suffering, such as has not been from the beginning of the creation that God created until now, no, and never will be. And if the Lord had not cut short those days, no one would be saved" (Mark 13:19-20a). The "suffering" of which Jesus speaks is not the "end" in chronological time. There shall be suffering *after* this suffering. But this tribulation is the *kairotic* event of all time. It will be my task now to demonstrate how chapter 13 is directly aimed not at some distant future, but at the cross.

No modern scholar of whom I am aware has taken my point of view. R. H. Lightfoot[7] does at times, but he seems in the end unwilling to take the leap. Donald Juel, who is a strong advocate of Mark's theology of the cross, is nevertheless unwilling to see in chapter 13 anything but references to some future time of destruction and suffering that the church must undergo.[8] I must say that to argue a position, which seems universally rejected at worst or unrecognized at best by many fine scholars, leaves me more than a bit uncomfortable. But I, ever foolhardy, leap.

There is the most intriguing passage of chapter 13. What can be said of this statement in verse 30 that this present "generation will not pass away until all these things have taken place [*mechris hou tauta panta genētai*]"? Many commentators find it puzzling and inexplicable. One can only wonder why Mark would have included such a word from Jesus if he believed that Jesus' word had not been fulfilled. I take it that Mark is not a first-generation believer and that his work of writing the Gospel was undertaken precisely because the first generation (or at least many of that generation) has died. The point of the inclusion of this statement must be that from the perspective of Mark all these things have happened. One can hardly imagine Mark choosing to include a statement of Jesus that proves Him to be either a liar or wrong about so important a matter.

The exact timing of the crucifixion is beyond the knowledge of Jesus or anyone else, he says (13:32). Only the Father knows. The disciples are not to trouble themselves with trying to determine when the *kairos* is *(pote ho kairos estin)* (v. 33). Instead, Jesus tells them three times in the remaining verses of the chapter that they should stay awake. These words, of course, prepare us for the scene in the next chapter when Jesus takes his disciples to Gethsemane. Three times he comes to Peter, James, and John and finds them sleeping after telling them to keep awake. Thus chapter 13 begins by pointing the reader to the more distant future, and it concludes with a focus on the moment at hand. This is what I meant with the suggestion that time flows backwards in the chapter. We see predictions of the future destruction of the Temple and the persecution of the church, the coming of the great suffering (which I believe is the crucifixion) and a call to present alertness. In the normal course of time, these things are in reverse order of their occurrence.

Chapter 13 of this most fascinating of the Gospels is easily misunderstood. William Schweiker, interpreting it as he says "from a literary perspective," sees it as a text "about the coming of the Son to inherit his kingdom."[9] In this Schweiker is correct. He reminds us that the Son of Man passage in Daniel 7:14 announces that "To him was given dominion and glory and kingship." But he fails to recognize that if chapter 13 points toward this, it is at the cross where the inscription proclaiming him king is placed. Pilate, the soldiers, the chief priests, and the scribes all hail him (though mockingly and ironically) as king.

Chapter 13 is not a distraction from the rest of the Gospel. It is not a little apocalyptic essay about morality that imposes itself in the story at an inconvenient moment. It is not even a "long pause . . . for warnings and promises about the future."[10] The chapter is far more integral to Mark's purposes than that. One thinks of a favorite expression of Jesus throughout this Gospel: Let anyone with ears to hear listen!

If I am correct about Mark 13, there remains one fair question unanswered: What difference does this make to the discussion between science and theology? Perhaps nothing. On the other hand, it may also serve as a good reminder that, in ways that are fundamental to its texts, theology must insist that time cannot be measured by simple arrows.

The arrow of time is indeed an important issue to be discussed. Time moves forward. But there is a reality that is not subject to the measurement of time as chronological. "Eternity" or the divine has a way of ripping open the heavens and coming into the present world. It reveals itself in ways that are not obvious but can be approached only through irony or by way of opposites, such as Jesus "opposite" the Temple. The great and glorious kingdom comes in a cross and death. These are not matters that can in any way be measured by instruments. Yet as theologically aware persons we must insist on their reality. Even as St. Paul would argue, this is great foolishness (1 Cor. 1:18-28). The cross is foolishness. I am sure that Mark agrees. Yet there may be no other way besides this way of foolish speech to identify a reality that surpasses the one that is scientifically measurable. I can only imagine that science must have a struggle with such a claim. But then again, if I understand Mark 13, it is this strange and mysterious and in the end salvific activity of God that measures us, not we who measure God. God's instrument is a *stauros* — a desolating sacrilege, a tree of life.

3. Heaven in Revelation

DOUGLAS FLETCHER

Westlake Hills Presbyterian Church
Austin, Texas

It is not uncommon in a situation of grief for a family to turn to its pastor and ask: "What is heaven like?" Behind the question is hope and the presumption that a pastor can offer not merely a comforting but also an authoritative description of the promise of heaven. Questions about heaven for pastors also arise when people ask about the meaning of Christian affirmations such as the closing phrase of the Apostles' Creed, "the life everlasting." What does it mean to affirm the life everlasting? Is it wrong to wonder what heaven is like?

An examination of the picture of heaven in Revelation 21:1–22:5 yields an extraordinary sense of the richness of Scriptural references and echoes. These references seem to operate with three filters in mind: (1) the filter of the creation story; (2) the filter of God's promises to Israel; and (3) the filter of heaven in discontinuity with Babylon.

Reading Revelation 21 and 22
through the Creation Account in Genesis

Revelation 21 begins with the creation of a new heaven and a new earth. The phrase can be seen as a direct allusion to the first creation of "heaven and earth" and as a signal to the reader that images of this new creation are to be related to the first creation (cf. 1 Enoch 91:6: "and the first heaven shall depart and pass away, and a new heaven shall appear"; and 2 Pet. 3:10-13).

The work of the second day of creation, the separation of the waters, does not apply to this new creation, for "the sea was no more" (Rev. 21:1). This intriguing phrase seems best and is most often interpreted in relationship to the Genesis account and suggests that chaos, represented by the symbol of the sea (cf. Rev. 13:1), is no longer held at bay or existing at the boundaries of creation but is, in fact, gone.[1]

There are also, in Revelation 21, symbols of the reverse of the curse of the fall. In Genesis 3:8, prior to the fall, God is described as walking in the garden; in Revelation 21:3, God dwells among mortals. Moreover, the curse of original disobedience is set aside as death, which is the culmination of that curse, no longer has power (21:4).

From the throne, the connection of the picture of Revelation to the creation story is reemphasized with the words "It is done! I am the Alpha and the Omega, the beginning and the end" (21:6). Water flows from "the spring of the water of life," a more theologically oriented description of waters than the river in Eden (Gen. 2:10). In fact, Revelation's description of the river locates the river's source as it springs from the throne of God and the Lamb (Rev. 22:1).

The tree, which was the source of temptation and curse, which had been in the middle of the garden (Gen. 3:3), is replaced by two trees of life, one on each side of the river of the water of life, and these bear fruit each month, recalling the fruitfulness of Eden and the curse of toil for Adam. As if the images are not sufficiently suggestive, Revelation 22:3 makes the point abundantly clear and gives it greater breadth: "Nothing accursed will be found there *any more*."

As in the garden of Eden, the relationship of the humans to God is central, but in Revelation that relationship is described in the language of worship, reminiscent of the structure of creation in Genesis 1 with its Sabbath rest. The mark on the foreheads of the servants in heaven (Rev. 22:4) recalls and functions as a counterpoint to the mark placed by God on Cain (Gen. 4:15).

The description of the new heaven and the new earth closes with a recalling of the first day of creation, when God made light and separated the light from the darkness. In Revelation there is no creation of light, for the glory of the Lord is the light. The use of the image of light in Revela-

18

tion draws in not only the creation story but all Scriptures that resonate with that story, such as 1 John 1:5: "God is light and in him there is no darkness at all." The description of heaven draws together the uses of the image of light.

It is impossible to read Revelation 21 and 22 without hearing echoes of the creation story in Genesis. Both the similarities and differences are instructive. There is a reclaiming of the purpose of creation and its elements, and the dimensions of continuity are profound. We hear affirmed the goodness of creation as God does it again. However, the author of Revelation does not feel bound merely to recreate the Garden. The new creation is more fruitful and glorious than the first, without even the possibility of chaos, and without a need for created light.[2]

Reading Revelation 21 and 22 through God's Promises to Israel

The opening chapters of Genesis are not sufficient for fully describing the imagery of heaven in Revelation. There is a second stream of interpretive resonances that relate to the promises to Israel. In fact, the language of a new heaven and a new earth in Revelation is actually taken from the prophet Isaiah: "For I am about to create new heavens and a new earth; the former things shall not be remembered or come to mind. But be glad and rejoice forever in what I am creating; for I am about to create Jerusalem as a joy, and its people as a delight" (65:17-18). In this passage, Isaiah connects creation imagery with Jerusalem rather than with the Garden of Eden. The result is that the promises to Israel are on the same footing as the structure and order of creation.

The echoes are especially strong of Isaiah and Ezekiel in Revelation 21 and 22. Isaiah wrote that in the heavenly Jerusalem, "no more shall the sound of weeping be heard" (Isaiah 65:19; see also Isaiah 25:8, "Then the Lord will wipe away the tears from all faces," and 35:10), and Ezekiel prophesied, "My dwelling place shall be with them" (37:27; see also Zechariah 2:10-11 and Leviticus 26:11-12). The river of life also echoes Isaiah: "Lo, everyone who thirsts, come to the waters" (Isaiah 55:1; see also John 4:13 and 7:37), and being brought to a high mountain follows the prophecy of Ezekiel (40:2). The open gates of the city are suggested in Isaiah 60:11 and the trees in Ezekiel 47:7. That there is no temple in the city is a part of the radical newness, of the dwelling of God with the people.

The description of the walls of the city is influenced by Exodus (28:17-21) as well as Isaiah (54:11-12). That the names of the apostles of Jesus are on the foundations shows that the design of heaven itself is impacted by God's work through human history.

The river through the holy city is suggested by Psalm 46, Ezekiel 47:1, and Zechariah 14:8 with its "living waters." Inasmuch as the water springs from the throne, there may be an echo of Zechariah 13:1: "On that day a fountain shall be opened for the house of David and the inhabitants of Jerusalem, to cleanse them from sin and impurity." Heaven is christologically centered. The water of life has come from the (blood of the) Lamb (conversely, in Revelation 16:4, springs of water become blood as from one of the bowls of the wrath of God).

While the leaves of the tree of life, which are for the healing of the nations, do not have direct Scriptural referents, they reinforce in a profound way that heaven is not merely the culmination of the creation but also of the work of God in human history.[3]

It was Old Testament prophets who connected the faithfulness of God with Jerusalem at the center of the new creation. That prophets of Israel had sustained hope through adversity with the remembrance of this promise would not have been lost on the first readers of Revelation. The picture of heaven in Revelation includes the history of God with the children of Israel and with the Church, and that makes the new creation different from the first.[4] Most significantly, that new creation cannot be conceived as a promise to individuals but as faithfulness to a community. And Revelation locates the Lamb at the heart of that city.

Reading Revelation 21 and 22 in Discontinuity with Babylon

The images of heaven in Revelation need to be read against the backdrop of the creation account in Genesis and the promises of God to Israel and the Church. However, the picture of heaven in Revelation also needs to be read contextually in relationship to the city of Babylon. The impact of the persecution of the Church and the martyrdom of Christians was to enhance the contrast of the Kingdom of God to the kingdoms of this world. Heaven in Revelation is set in contrast and opposition to Babylon: "The woman you saw is the great city that rules over the kings of the earth" (Rev. 17:18).

Babylon (Rome) is described extensively in Revelation 17 and 18. It is a great whore "seated on many waters" (17:1), interpreted in 17:15 to mean "people and multitudes and nations and languages," an obvious contrast to the New Jerusalem, where there is no sea. Babylon is filled with those "who committed fornication and lived in luxury with her" (18:9) such as have been explicitly excluded from the New Jerusalem (21:8).[5] It is a city of extraordinary wealth: "Alas, alas, the great city, clothed in fine linen, in purple and scarlet, adorned with gold, with jewels and with pearls" (18:16), which will not last (18:19). Babylon is a whore (17:1); the New Jerusalem is a bride (21:2).

The contrasts are striking: because it is the work of God, the New Jerusalem comes down from heaven (21:2), while Babylon is "thrown down" (18:21). The New Jerusalem is adorned for her husband (21:2); Babylon "glorified herself" (18:7). Jerusalem will be God's people (21:3); Babylon will be judged by God (18:8). Babylon's tears will not be wiped away, but she will receive "a like measure of torment and grief" (18:7), "as they wept and mourned" (18:19). On Babylon's forehead was written a name, "Babylon the great, mother of whores and of earth's abominations" (17:5), while the Lamb's name would be on the foreheads of his servants (22:4).

Both cities are fabulously wealthy, but their wealth is different. Babylon's wealth was from commerce; the New Jerusalem's is an inheritance (21:7). An inheritance was the most respectable way to develop wealth and is an image used throughout the New Testament (Matthew 5:5; 19:29; 25:34; Mark 10:17; Romans 8:17; 1 Corinthians 15:50; Galatians 4:7; 1 Peter 1:3-7). Revelation 21:9-10 closely parallels 17:1-3 and allows no doubt that the New Jerusalem is being contrasted to Babylon.

In Revelation, glory and honor are brought in, but not wealth. The city has no need of such tribute. The catalogue of wealth in the New Jerusalem in 21:15-21 is the most extensive picture of heaven's wealth. It would be wrong, however, to judge it simply as the imaginings of a wishful thinker. Instead, the picture draws together images from the Old Testament and contrasts them to Babylon. As Robert Royalty writes, "It is important that Babylon and the New Jerusalem are set in contrast to each other, for without the wealth of Babylon, the wealth of heaven and the

New Jerusalem would look decidedly different."[6] Moreover, wealth imagery is found throughout the New Testament (cf. 1 Timothy 6:17-19; 2 Corinthians 4:7-12 and 6:10; 1 Peter 1:3-4). It is hardly appropriate to single out Revelation.

In its opposition to Babylon, and in remembrance that Cain was the founder of the first city (Gen. 4:17), the New Jerusalem holds out God's power to take a city, an image of corruption, and make it God's own, according to Royalty: "This new creation signifies, then, that God *reverses* what had been the instrument of revolt in order to make of it the work of reconciliation."[7]

Revelation's picture of heaven is often characterized as taking a step into speculation that invites readers to launch into their own imaginings of heaven. On the contrary, what we see is reflection on the promise of heaven through the filters of creation, God's promises, and human achievement. First, Revelation draws from the stories of creation in Genesis and suggests that this new creation deeply affirms the goodness of the first, but is also its culmination. Second, the picture draws from Scripture's own images of the New Jerusalem suggesting the profound faithfulness of God to the promises to Israel and the Church. Heaven itself is marked with that history and with the grace of the Lamb at its heart. Finally, Revelation contrasts the power of God and God's glory to the pale imitations of human construction, which will not endure.

Rather than inviting a departure from the text of Scripture, Revelation offers a picture carefully constructed from great Biblical themes. The picture itself points us to faith's affirmations, not to other pictures. It invites our awe at God's creative work, the faithfulness to God's promises, and the power above every power.

It also invites our faithfulness. "Those who conquer will inherit these things" (Rev. 21:7). Interpreters largely agree that these words are hortatory. The picture of heaven in Revelation is not speculative theology, but the pictorial representation of a thematic integration of Biblical themes. The picture of heaven is drawn to inspire confidence and courage on earth in God's sovereign power. Rather than inviting our speculations, it invites us to live out its hope.

4. Gospel Endings of the Resurrection

F. HARRY DANIEL

Second Presbyterian Church
Little Rock, Arkansas

Only eight verses to stem the chaotic tide of death, defeat, and despair engulfing Jesus, the disciples, and the women? That is the counterweight Mark uses to bring the second Gospel's witness to the resurrection to an end. That Mark crafted this ending is suggested by three pieces of corroborating evidence: the overwhelming textual evidence that the Gospel ended at 16:8, the existence of additional though somewhat artificial endings in the textual tradition, and the confirmation of both Matthew and Luke that their copies of Mark ended at 16:8 (Markan priority is assumed). Many analyses of the Gospel itself arrive at the same conclusion — an uncomfortable conclusion for some. While most current interpreters now accept this conclusion, Mark's ending is often treated as inadequate, with Matthew considered to be the primary witness.

The evaluation may be couched in terms such as "These two Gospel writers found Mark's conclusion to be indecisive, since it does not include appearances of the risen Lord," and this is often followed by a list of other items Mark should have included. Is that a helpful way to understand these two Gospel writers' intentions? Or could the issue be addressed differently? Perhaps they are building on Mark's foundation having grasped clearly Mark's narrative intent and recognizing its integrity. It may be argued that they have in fact read Mark 16:1-8 carefully and constructed their narratives based on his ending. Regardless of how we understand their narrative expansion of Mark, we need to address the integrity of Mark's ending. And it can be argued that the intensity of Mark's presentation of the Passion narrative threatens to overwhelm the Gospel's ending. But does it? An answer requires retracing and rediscovering how Mark's narrative does its work.

A close reading of 16:1-8 begins first with an observation: the simplicity and brevity of the text are deliberate. But what do these verses conclude? To answer that question requires a brief look at the Gospel's plot. Then the reading of Mark's conclusion is undertaken not as an isolated passage but in the narrative texture of the Gospel, since the interpretation of any particular text in a Gospel is not confined to that text alone; other texts need to be brought into the conversation.

Mark is a Passion-dominated Gospel. The cross is both destiny and goal. Already by 3:6 there is a plot "to destroy him," which includes a very strange, unlikely group of co-conspirators. The critical motion of the narrative is a gathering, absorbing, consuming plot of misunderstanding and destruction. First, this is centrally highlighted by three predictions of pain and death in 8:27–10:52, a section which also re-defines discipleship as Passion-filled, and then reaches a climax with a detailed, agonizing account of Jesus' final days ending in crucifixion in chapters 11–15. But the pathos is tempered by the promise of resurrection in the three Passion predictions, though it is consistently understated (the same five words) while the description of Jesus' pain-filled approach to death increases in vivid detail. In fact, the third Passion prediction (10:33-34) with its elaborate detailing of the events leading up to Jesus' death and its brief reference to resurrection bears a striking resemblance proportionally to chapters 14, 15, and 16. Clearly the pathos of the Passion on Friday with its pain, death, and loss is tempered by the rending of the temple curtain and the poignant, revealing confession of the centurion who correctly identifies Jesus at the moment of his death. And it might be tempered also by the presence of the women who may not be a final example of discipleship failure but profoundly the hint of resurrection hope. The women provide the narrative continuity between the Passion narrative and the conclusion in the tomb with Mark listing the names in each context (15:40, 47 and 16:1).

Matthew

Matthew responded to Mark's intense, terse narrative creatively. It is not that he found it indecisive; rather, he found it intriguing and chose not to negate it, but build upon it. While Mark's narrative brings the women to the threshold of a new world, Matthew walks through Mark's open door, newly awakened to a now-opened world illuminated by resurrection; and he explores its dimensions and aspects in its narrative, retaining two of the names of the women and the words of proclamation: "He is not here, he is risen."

Matthew has read Mark carefully. Clearly he understands Mark 16:8 as a profound response to the proclamation of resurrection but a response remaining somewhat ambiguous. The women have been confronted by what they cannot understand or control, a God of enormous worth, power, and being. Mark is content to leave the experience of resurrection at that level, having carefully bound this God to Jesus and the cross. But Matthew knows that this same God is available and accessible and is now in this world in a powerful, compelling fashion, and from his presence enormous consequences, responsibilities, and tasks flow. Thus he shifts the energy of Mark's descriptive encounter toward spelling out the consequences in a positive manner. Hence the possible negativity of 16:8b disappears; though the word *phobos* is kept, it is interpreted differently. Matthew narrates no rebuke of the women by the risen Lord when he appears to them and restates the command to "Go" in 28:10 that would have been likely if the last phrase of Mark 16:8b had been retained. Their flight has been re-described as "running to proclaim."

Matthew also narrates as well as rewords the description of the women's intense response. Fear is experienced, but it is the fear of encounter with the powerful Lord (compare 14:26), and accompanied by joy (2:10; 13:20, 44; 25:21, 23) that, with one exception (13:20), renders an occasion of powerful encounter with Jesus or experience of the kingdom of heaven. A quest with its powerful finding is reaching completion. The women are frightened, surprised, but also delighted, and now the risen Jesus himself meets them. While omitting all but one word of Mark 16:8b, interestingly, Matthew does introduce a negative note into the final scene on the mount: "some doubted." But at the tomb and going to carry out their commission, the women testify to the power of the resurrection on both counts: the empty tomb ("he is not here") and the appearance of the risen one ("suddenly Jesus met them"). Their response here in encounter builds on their initial fear and joy, for now they worship him.

The appropriateness of their responses stands in striking contrast to the panicked fear and sordid scheming of 28:4-5, 11-15. Matthew carefully crafts the starkness of the contrast, and he has edited Mark's ending to remove any possibility of misunderstanding the women's response. They dissipate the strength of the alternative explanation of the empty tomb, for they knew why it was empty and they saw Jesus. Matthew's narrative is not as awkward as some suggest. He is grounding the resurrection in the testimony of the women, as did Mark, though in an entirely different manner. They witnessed the empty tomb, were met by the risen Lord, carried out their commission, and have begun to live lives of discipleship without permitting the world of death to dictate the circumstances. Theirs is a rebirth of faith in the light of the resurrection. No doubt here. This is no fraud (27:64).

For Matthew, the women are enduring to the end (compare 10:22). Mark's narrative presentation has been persuasive for Matthew. Nothing need be said at the awesome place of resurrection, but there must be an obedient response to the appearances of the risen Jesus. Commissioning requires response, and response for Matthew always involves obedience to spoken words, especially teaching and being taught. The risen Jesus in verses 9-10 repeats the words of commission spoken by the angel at the tomb. Only the angel, Jesus, and the priests speak at all in the entire chapter. In fact, the last words of the Gospel are the direct discourse of the risen Lord, commissioning the disciples to go, instructing them to respond by teaching and baptizing, and making promises of the greatest import for Matthew and his church.

Matthew has imagined what ongoing Christian life would look like in response to the resurrection. Jesus, liberated by God from the power of history and death, is still the Christ who bears the marks of history (conveyed by his name Jesus in the angel's message) and death ("the crucified"), but who also is risen and now present in the midst of history and death. What was not hoped for is given nonetheless, and consequences flow mightily. Teaching, in the style and manner of discipleship, is of the essence; hence the careful structure of Matthew's Gospel and the commitment to teaching future generations made on the mountain. Earlier in this Gospel, Jesus' ministry has been described by three verbs: teaching, preaching, and healing (4:23; 9:35). In the mission discourse in chapter 10, the disciples are commissioned to preach and to heal (verses 7-8). But only in Matthew 28:20 are they commissioned to teach. The presence of the risen Lord changes life radically: not only is a unique benefit given, but a special obligation is also imposed.

Yet Matthew also knows that the conflict generated by alternative worldviews will last until the end of time. Their conflict will be resolved only then. Time experienced here and now is conflicted time, but it is altered time as well, for now it is time with a presence: that of the risen Lord. Now those promises in 1:23 and 18:20 take on a wholly new, temporal setting. God with us in Jesus is now a permanent presence.

Disciples are called to lives devoted to labor-intensive and loving service, committed to teaching the kingdom. They will lead conflicted lives in a conflicted world. The conflict will not be easily resolved but ongoing. As the reality of the resurrection intrudes into the world of the cross and death in 27:51-53, so the reality of opposition and confrontation intrudes into the new world of resurrection in 28:11-15. The denial of resurrection even appears on the mount in the contrasting verbs in verse 17: "worshiped, but some doubted." So the conflicted life of the disciples and the church will be until the end.

Matthew coins a phrase unique to his Gospel — "the close of the age" *(tēs sunteleias tou aiōnos)* — to describe this conflicted environment. The phrase occurs in 13:39, 40, 49; 24:3; and as the very last words of the Gospel in 28:20. The parable of the wheat and the tares (13:24-30) and its explanation (13:36-43) paint a dark, despairing, destructive picture of struggle "until the close of the age." This darkness and destruction is deepened in 24:3, where the disciples ask Jesus to describe the events leading up to the close. The description that follows is brutally explicit (24:19, 22, 29, 36-38, 42, 50). But in the light of the resurrection, more can and must be said. All those terrifying days with the heavy emphasis on the process of ruin are also days filled with the presence of the risen Lord: "behold, I am with you until the close of the age." The process of ruin is offset by the powerful God who is not duty-bound to destroy, but who loves the creation and is present in it. The anguish of chapters 13 and 24 is balanced by the presence, possibility, proclamation, and teaching of chapter 28. Conflict remains and is to be endured, but the outcome is clear.

For Matthew, Jesus' suffering and death on the cross is an apocalyptic event, as is his resurrection. On the former occasion, Matthew inserted vivid language describing the impact of Jesus' death: temple destruction, earth pain, resurrected saints, and a spoken confession of faith by a gentile. Now in the latter, he rewrites Mark's narration of the opened tomb by adding vivid language about an angel splendidly attired who descends, rolls back the stone effortlessly, and jauntily sits on the rock, and who in the meantime reduces the guards to abject fear. The shaking of 27:54 returns, but whereas the wounded earth was responding there, here the shaking is caused by the intervention of God's emissary, who overwhelms the opposition. The irony is impressive: the living act like the dead (28:4) and the dead one is alive. As angelic messengers always do when they approach the addressees, the first words are "Be not afraid," spoken not in the tomb but out in the open. This is a commissioning in the Old Testament sense of the genre. Resurrection news is task-oriented.

Conclusion

Closure: "a bringing to an end; conclusion."

Premature: "occurring, coming, done too soon or before the proper time."

Human beings craft endings: a perceived end makes a segment of life a story, with its moments given significance. Endings provide boundaries that make time comprehensible,[1] stimulating hope, challenge, or inspiration. In the Gospel endings crafted by Mark and Matthew, the God whom Jesus trusted responds to an ending, conceived by the human actors as *the* end. But perceiving the reality of God remains both painful and joyful in the face of all such endings, which are and must remain provisional in the light of Jesus' resurrection.

For Mark the women are impressed, becoming aware of the awesome presence of God in Jesus, but they possess no ideas yet with which to grasp it, no concepts to circumscribe it. Their shaky, tense, ecstatic experience of the firstness of the resurrection is clear.[2] What it means is not. Mark's last word *gar* ("for") expects more. This is an ending in awe of the resurrecting God who alone crafts the end. Mark knows to wait. The future is only partially determined by human endings. This is an end time to be followed by other, redeemed, redeeming time. For Matthew this divine ending to Jesus' story consists of recognition and fresh cognition. There is presence for the living of these last days in which new life is created, life shaped and nurtured by the faithful church, the church faithfully teaching the words and deeds of Jesus.

Both are explicit: any human attempts to replace "an" with "the" before "end" founders on the God who gives life to the dead and brings into existence things that do not exist. The end is not ours — any human's — to say.

Jesus is not here in this humanly crafted ending, but in this new beginning. He is free to be present in all human endings and he will be at the end what he always was. When is an ending not the end? When one Gospel ends in the middle of a sentence: "for . . ." When another Gospel ends with a promised presence in these times: "behold, I am with you all the days until . . ." Any closure is premature.

5. *The Witness of the Resurrection*

LAIRD J. STUART

Calvary Presbyterian Church
San Francisco, California

The purpose of this paper is to juxtapose the prospects for destruction, which we face both on an individual and on a cosmic scale, with the testimony to God's creative power manifest in the resurrection of Jesus Christ and the promised resurrection of others. The thesis is that in the resurrection we witness a dialectic of continuity and discontinuity, which testifies to God's ability to create new life out of death and destruction, a creative act that belongs not to any inherent capacity of the natural world but only to God.

In a variety of ways, our lives are faced with the prospect of destruction. Most of us do not spend much time contemplating destruction, but on occasion the prospect confronts us. It occurs when someone dies, especially if it is someone who is close to us. The finality of death leads us into a frightening, disturbing encounter with the prospect of destruction.

The prospect of destruction comes to us in a less immediate but nevertheless enticing form in many popular movies. We have had in the past five years a host of movies about the end of the earth or the threatened end of the earth. Whether the earth and our civilization are threatened by hostile alien invaders or by asteroids, the point is made — the earth and all of us upon it could be destroyed. Destruction on a personal or cosmic scale is a frequently imagined possibility in a number of video and computer games.

More remote from most people, but still present with us, are the projections of scientists regarding the end of the universe. William Stoeger writes, "From all the indications we have from the neurosciences, biology, physics, astronomy and cosmology, death and dissolution are the final words."[1] He goes on to explain the view, widely held among scientists and others, that the universe will eventually be destroyed in one of two ways. Either it will evanesce, continue to expand to a point at which it will cease to be able to bear life, or it will contract, continuing to expand until gravitational forces create a contraction, which will end in what is called "The

Big Crunch." Somewhere along the line in this contraction, the universe will no longer be able to support life. Evidently there is more evidence for the former possibility at this time.

Stoeger also reviews other possibilities for destruction, at least the destruction of our earth. There is evidence of enormous destruction caused by the impact of asteroids and comets on this earth in the past. It is possible there could be other collisions, perhaps involving the sun, following the pattern of other stars. As it expands, as part of a long and dramatic process of dying, the sun will eventually come close enough to the earth to scorch all life upon earth. Another possibility for destruction is the collision of what are known as neutron stars. These are extremely dense stars. In some instances, two of these stars have been found to be in orbit around each other. If the orbits decayed and the stars spiraled into each other, it would create enough radiation to be lethal to all life within 1,500 to 3,000 light years of earth. Scientists have calculated that we might expect three such mergers in our own galaxy every 100 million years. Two such systems are within the lethal range. Finally, if a massive star within several light years from earth were to collapse and form a black hole, it would release what Stoeger calls an "incredible number of hyper-energetic neutrinos" which would kill many species on earth through cancer and genetic mutations.

Examining the prospect of resurrection, on the other hand, brings fewer insights from scientific research and more from the Bible. A major issue for Paul was the expectation in Jewish eschatology that the resurrection of the dead, whenever it occurred, would involve a physical and visible body. He needed to be able to assert not only the reality of the resurrection of the dead, but also the resurrection of a spiritual and invisible body. This was especially true, of course, if he wanted to hold out any possibility of a resurrection that would occur upon death. As Gordon Fee expressed it, Paul understood a denial of the resurrection would mean a "denial of any continuity between the present and the future" of each believer, and that the precise "point of continuity lay with the body" — the resurrected body.[2]

In I Corinthians 15:35 Paul acknowledges the question "How are the dead raised? With what kind of body do they come?" Paul expresses frustration with the lack of faith suggested in such questions by beginning his answer with the exclamation "Fool!" He begins his explanation by using an analogy to sowing. First, without explanation, he states that when we sow something it must die before it grows. Evidently this means that the seed that is sown dies or changes before it becomes a plant. He continues by explaining that it is not the body, the full-grown plant, that is planted, but a seed from which the plant grows. He writes that God gives to each seed the body God has destined or chosen for it. Furthermore, Paul writes that there are different kinds of flesh, for humans and birds and fish, for instance. There are also different kinds of bodies, heavenly bodies and earthly bodies.

Next, Paul moves into his discussion of our resurrected bodies. In verse 42 he writes, "So it is with the resurrection of the dead." Clarence T. Craig points out that Paul deliberately sets up his case by referring to "the resurrection of the dead" instead of the resurrection of the body or the flesh.[3] Paul then moves into his four part comparisons:

> What is sown is perishable, what is raised is imperishable. It is sown in dishonor, it is raised in glory. It is sown in weakness, it is raised in power. It is sown a physical body, it is raised a spiritual body. (15:42b-44a)

Much has been written about Paul's use of the words *sōma, psychikon,* and *pneumatikon.* Clearly Paul is drawing a distinction between the physical body and the spiritual body, and describing how the same life is given two bodies. As mentioned, he is working to address those who believe a resurrected body must be visible and physical. He is also working to affirm that the resurrected life is the same as the previous life, as it was for Jesus. So Paul is working precisely at the interface of continuity and discontinuity.

In affirming God's ability to give us a spiritual body, Paul intends to indicate that we have a body under the operation of the Holy Spirit.[4] In other words, by using the term we translate as "spiritual body," Paul is not so much drawing attention to its nature or substance as he is drawing attention to its origin and source. It comes into being by the work of the Holy Spirit. As Gordon Fee suggests, it is spiritual not as in "immaterial" but spiritual as in "supernatural." It is a body under the domination of the Holy Spirit and "adapted to eschatological existence."[5]

Although Paul refers to a spiritual body, there is a continuing debate over the very substance or matter of this body. Hans Conzelmann refers to W. G. Kümmel's assertion that the resurrected body does not consist of spirit.[6] Fee agrees with Kümmel, saying that the resurrected body is not "composed of spirit."[7]

What is agreed upon is that the resurrected body to which Paul is referring is created by the Holy Spirit. It is not a physical body. It is under the operation of the Holy Spirit. It is real. It is alive, but it cannot be seen.

In these verses is the crux of Paul's case. He has affirmed the reality of a resurrection of the dead, and he has described the resurrected body as something other than a physical and visible one. In so doing he has employed the dialectic of continuity and discontinuity. As Orr and Walther put it, "The apostle affirms a doctrine of continuous creation,"[8] although it is a continuity that works through discontinuity.

Paul continues his case by drawing a comparison between Adam and Christ. Adam, the first man, was a living being but he was made of dust. Christ, the last man, the last Adam, is a life-giving life. Christ is a spirit and a man of heaven. Just as God is able to create these two lives, Adam and Christ, Paul is saying, God is able to create two lives for each of us, an earthly life and a spiritual life, a life in this world and a life in heaven. The two lives are different, discontinuous, but they are different forms of the same person so that the self is continuous in discontinuous bodies.

Paul moves on by saying the perishable cannot "inherit the imperishable" (15:50). Our earthly body cannot inherit or generate the heavenly body. It is God who gives us the imperishable body, and it is God who wins the victory over death.

Paul is working around the boundaries of great mysteries. He is giving an explanation of something he has come to believe. He is trying to answer a question with as clear and intelligible an answer as possible. This is the only place in the New Testament where there is such an attempt. There are other references to the resurrection, but this is the sole effort to offer an explanation.

Paul clearly believes that there is a resurrection, not only for Christ but for others as well. The resurrection is the result of God's work. There is nothing inherent in human nature or nature itself that could accomplish such an event. In the process of resurrection, the dialectic of discontinuity and continuity is displayed. Again, the body of this life perishes and a new body is provided by God. The position is summarized by Paul in Philippians 3:21: Christ "will transform the body of our humiliation that it may be conformed to the body of his glory, by the power that also enables him to make all things subject to himself." There are discontinuity of body and continuity of self.

Christoph Schwöbel writes, "The *theological* content of the *christological* story is the key to its *eschatological* significance."[9] It is the work of God in the life of Christ, specifically in the resurrection of Christ, that gives the eschatological significance to the life of Christ for us. God created the resurrection of Jesus Christ; God can create resurrection for each of us. By extension, God's creative abilities can even by the same powers evident in resurrection insure a new heaven and a new earth. It is our belief in the resurrection and our belief in the kingdom of God that together form the basis of our theological response.

The resurrection demonstrates God's ability to create new life through the dialectic of discontinuity and continuity. The kingdom of God refers in general to the new kingdom, the new heaven and the new earth God will create in the future. It will be the kingdom in which the resurrected live. As Schwöbel points out, in the kingdom of God there will be no temples and churches, because there will be no distinction between the church and the world. The imagery of the kingdom of God, complex as it is, nevertheless signals God's desire to apply to the whole of creation the same creative abilities that make resurrection for Christ and individual persons possible.

The core of our theological response to the prospect of destruction, therefore, has two elements. The resurrection demonstrates the ability of God to create new life in the presence of destructive powers. The kingdom of God projects that ability onto the whole of creation. What are suggested in these two beliefs are both the awesome power of God and the equally awesome loyalty of God to individuals and to creation itself.

There are a variety of implications of this for pastoral ministry. First and foremost, it provides us with a fundamental strategy for dealing with concerns regarding destruction, whether it be destruction of an individual life, destruction of the earth, or even destruction on a more cosmic scale. It leads us to biblical descriptions of the resurrection both of Christ and of others. While it does not provide us with a description of what specifically might happen in the face of the destruction of the earth or the universe, it gives us a foundation for hope based on the creative powers at God's command.

CHAPTER II

Theological Views of Christian Hope

Introduction

Eschatological themes have always played a prominent role in the history of Christian thought. Once the cyclical views of time in Greek religion were replaced by the linear thrust of Hebrew revelation, Isaiah could prophesy about the histories of Judah and Jerusalem: "In the days to come. . . . He shall judge between the nations. . . . they shall beat their swords into plowshares, and their spears into pruning hooks; nation shall not lift up sword against nation, neither shall they learn war any more" (2:2, 4). Moreover, ever since Christ first proclaimed the good news of God ("The time is fulfilled, and the kingdom of God has come nearer"; Mark 1:15), his followers throughout the ages have been hopefully wondering: Within us, or in our midst? During our lifetime, or in the distant future? On earth, or only in heaven?

One powerful voice in the ongoing deliberations has been "The Vision of God in Thomas Aquinas," as here described by Ken Williams. At heart is the promise of human beatitude for resurrected believers of endless growth and eternal joy in the face-to-face knowledge and love of God. Thomas's vision of eternal life is based on the infinite reality of God as the universe's Creator and Perfecter. As God's grace fulfills nature, so the knowledge and love of God directly actualize human nature in its eternal glorification.

In developing Luther's conviction that "Things above Us Do Not Concern Us," Virgil Thompson cautions against faithless anxiety or undue preoccupation with eternal life. It is all in God's hands, not ours. The Christian's calling is to trust God in confident and hopeful anticipation.

We are freed in Christ to cultivate peace and justice on earth ("beneath us") as we await the fulfillment of God's promised salvation ("above us"). In a "theology of the cross" that celebrates Christ's divine victory hidden amidst human defeat within a fallen world, an eschatology *sub contrario* depends not on sight, but on our faith alone.

"Kierkegaard Goes to the Eschaton" is an excerpt from Rush Otey that contends that in the modern age, interdisciplinary discussions are more in the theological than the biblical fields. Søren Kierkegaard, for example, responded to the nineteenth-century scientific and materialistic worldview of his time, and its philosophical companion Hegel, with a call for an existential "leap of faith." This leap is absolute and unmediated by culture or science. In affirming that "subjectivity (not subjectivism) is truth," Kierkegaard warned against basing one's life on scientific "proofs" that reduce life to only the physical and the quantifiable. Since eternity intersects time paradoxically in Jesus Christ, we must also have the courage to believe in the face of the absurd.

John Christopherson's excerpt introduces "God's Relation to Nonbeing in Paul Tillich's Thought." The root metaphor "nonbeing" stands for the existential encounter with nuclear annihilation, concentration camps, AIDS epidemics, and ecological plunder so rampant in twentieth-century life. Tillich's corollary response is "eschatological panentheism," a condition wherein all things in history find their solutions in depth within the eternal life of God's saving Spirit. "Eschatological" relates the temporal to the eternal, dealing not so much with the future of the last things as with the ever-present and ultimate fulfillment of all things. "Panentheism" rejects any pantheism that identifies God with the world; it affirms rather "the presence of the Spirit of God under the conditions of existence, breaking through the alienated structure of existence and restoring its essential structure." The cross of Christ reveals the good news that the divine penetrates and rejuvenates human life at its worst to its own "new being" in Christ.

Finally, Randy Cooper illumines the eschatological faith of William Stringfellow in "Amidst the Melancholy of These Days." This civil rights legal activist and lay theologian wrote confidently of the second coming of Christ by joining his New Testament peers (in the book of Revelation) in eagerly awaiting the Final Day. Anticipating the complete redemption of "the whole of creation," Stringfellow considered reductionistic scientism and creationism, for example, to be among the demonic "principalities and powers of this fallen age" that compete with the lordship of Christ for human loyalty. The disciplines of physics and astronomy "are inclined to a vainglory, in which they presume sovereignty over humanity and over the creation." However, the same can be true of theology; all rational discourse is prone to idolatry. Both disciplines have often dismissed the apocalyptic book of Revelation as "quaint" at best and "crazed" at worst. Rather, as Hauerwas also contends, it is "the right mode of narrative for persons struggling as Christians to live in the kind of world in which we live."

6. The Vision of God in Thomas Aquinas

KEN WILLIAMS

Rockland Community Church
Golden, Colorado

In this essay, I want to explore how Thomas Aquinas conceived the promise of everlasting life in earlier chapters of the *Summa*. Thomas developed his entire theological project around this everlasting vision of God in knowledge and love (often called "the beatific vision" or the vision of the blessed): "For now we see in a mirror, dimly, but then we will see face to face. Now I know only in part; then I will know fully, even as I have been fully known" (I Cor. 13:12).

Surprisingly, Thomas develops his conception of the beatific vision in the first pages of the *Summa*. The twelfth question deals with how we know God, and it consists of thirteen articles, most of which deal with this everlasting vision of God in knowledge and love.

In the first article, Thomas asks whether any created intellect can see the essence of God. His response is pivotal to everything that follows. God is supremely knowable: as the infinite Act of Existence, God is also the infinite Act of Understanding. Yet "what is supremely knowable in itself may not be knowable to a particular intellect, on account of the excess of the intelligible object above the intellect; as, for example, the sun, which is supremely visible, cannot be seen by the bat by reason of its excess of light."[1] Just as a bat is blinded by the sunlight, so is the human intellect "blinded" by the infinite intelligibility of God.

Because the human intellect can understand so little about God, some have concluded that it cannot ever hope to see the essence of God. Thomas disagrees, because he believes that human beings are created to know and love God. "For there resides in every man a natural desire to know the cause of any effect which he sees; and then arises wonder in men. But if the intellect of the rational creature could not reach so far as the first cause of things, the natural desire would remain void."[2] The ultimate beatitude of human beings consists in the use of their highest function, which is the operation of the intellect. If we cannot know the essence of God, then we will never be able to attain beatitude or the highest good.

The second article is more technical and thus harder to understand. Having established the conviction that the human intellect can know the essence of God, Thomas asks whether the essence of God is seen by the human intellect through a created image or likeness. Thomas operates with a realistic conception of knowledge and understanding. Two things are required for sensible and intellectual vision: the power of sight and the union with the thing seen. "For vision is made actual only when the thing seen is in a certain way in the seer."[3] When we see a stone, a likeness of the stone is in the eye. Likewise, when we understand the nature of a thing, there is a union between the power to understand (the agent intellect) and an image (which is received into the passive intellect) of what is understood. "The knowledge which we have by natural reason contains two things: images derived from the sensible objects; and the natural intelligible light, enabling us to abstract from them intelligible conceptions."[4] As Robert Jenson puts it, "two things are required for seeing: . . . the power of sight, and the union of the seen reality with sight, for there cannot be the act of sight unless the reality seen is somehow in the one who sees."[5]

According to Thomas, the human intellect is a created participation in the infinite understanding of God: "for the light of natural reason itself is a participation in the divine light."[6] For the intellect to be able to understand the essence of God, there has to be a union between the power to know and the reality of God. "Therefore, in order to see God, there must be some similitude of God on the part of the visual faculty, whereby the

38

intellect is made capable of seeing God."[7] Since a created likeness of God falls infinitely short of what is required, God bestows the light of glory upon the intellect, raising it to the level where it can know the essence of God.

This happens only through grace. By its own natural powers the created intellect cannot know the essence of God. It is only by the light of glory infused or poured into the intellect that human beings can see and know the essence of God. "Hence it is necessary that some supernatural disposition should be added to the intellect that it may be raised up to such a great and sublime height."[8] This illumination of the intellect is called the light of glory. "By this light the blessed are made deiform."

Thomas is reserved in describing what the light of glory is like. He describes it as "the infusion of gratuitous light."[9] It is a created participation in the infinite reality of God. When he asks whether those who see the essence of God are able to comprehend God, he answers the question by making a distinction. On the one hand, no created intellect can comprehend the infinite reality of God: only God can fully comprehend God. On the other hand, the blessed can attain God and thereby comprehend God. "And in this way comprehension is one of the three prerogatives of the soul, responding to hope, as vision responds to faith, and fruition responds to charity."[10]

In this technical discussion it is easy to lose the way and fail to understand the overall point that Thomas is trying to make. He is discussing the conditions for the beatific vision, for everlasting life, for seeing God face-to-face. Human beings are the subjects of this act, while God is the object. By God's power and love, human beings are raised to a higher level of being, the level of grace and glory. Yet humans are not so overwhelmed with God's grace and glory as to be no longer independent creatures of God. "The creature remains, though raised to greater likeness to God by the *lumen gloriae;* the human personality is not extinguished, for its identity with God is not effected by a fusion of substance, but by a complete identity in knowledge and love."[11] There is a basic unity between grace and glory: the light of grace is the seed of which the light of glory is the flower.

Many people think that Thomas stresses knowledge at the expense of love, but the relation between the two is more nuanced than most people think. In article six, Thomas asks whether some of the blessed see the essence of God more perfectly than others. Thomas answers this in the affirmative by saying that "one intellect will have a greater power or faculty to see God than another."[12] The difference has to do with love and desire:

> Hence the intellect which has more of the light of glory will see God more perfectly; and he will have a fuller participation of the light of glory who has more charity, because there is more desire; and desire in a certain degree makes the one desiring apt and prepared to receive the object desired. Hence he who possesses more charity, will see God the more perfectly, and will be the more beatified.[13]

In *The Compendium of Theology*, Thomas's language is livelier. As the One who is the infinite fullness of joy, God wants to share his joy with us forever. "Full joy," Thomas writes, "can be gained from no creature, but only from God, in whom the full plentitude of goodness resides."[14] This fullness of joy must be understood not only from the side of God, but also from the side of the person who experiences it. "As we have shown, in the vision of the divine essence, the created spirit possesses God as present; and the vision itself sets the affections completely on fire with divine love."[15] This vision of God, whose very essence is beauty and goodness, "cannot be gazed at without love. Therefore perfect vision is followed by perfect love." This joy is "what crowns human beatitude."[16]

Before I offer an assessment of Thomas's understanding of the beatific vision, we must remember that the *Summa* was never finished. In some ways scholars have to speculate about how Thomas would have developed his eschatology in the light of his work as a whole. For example, some scholars think that he placed more emphasis on the role of affectivity as he worked his way through the *Summa*.[17] If this is true, we wonder how this might have changed his understanding of everlasting life.

First, Thomas's vision of everlasting life is based on the infinite reality of God. As the infinite Act of Existence, the One who is the perfect plentitude of goodness, understanding, and love, God is not only the Creator of this vast universe, but its end and goal as well. Our hope in everlasting life is completely dependent upon the infinite reality of the One who has given us the gift of life, who knows each of us by our names, who guides and directs us through our earthly journey, who comes to us through his Word and Spirit, and who promises us the gift of everlasting life through Jesus Christ.

Some conceptions of God, ancient and modern, are too small to guarantee the promise of everlasting life. The same cannot be said about the Triune God described in the many writings of Thomas Aquinas. At first, Thomas's description of God can seem to be rather austere, but eventually this sense of austerity gives way to a breathtaking view of the infinite greatness of God.

Second, there is Thomas's nuanced understanding of the relation between knowledge and love. There are plenty of passages in the *Summa* that seem to indicate that Thomas was a rationalist, albeit a Christian rationalist, at heart, but there is a remarkable balance between the intellect and the will in his writings. On one level, knowledge comes first, but on another level love comes before knowledge. For example, he restates a familiar theme of the *Summa* in his discussion of charity:

> The operation of the intellect is completed by the thing understood being in the intellectual subject, so that the excellence of the intellectual operation is assessed according to the measure of the intellect. On the other hand, the operation of the will and of every appetitive power is completed by the tendency of the appetite towards a thing as its term, wherefore the excellence is gauged according to the thing which is the object of the operation. Now those things which are beneath the soul are more excellent in the soul than in themselves, because a thing is contained according to the mode of the container. On the other hand, things that are above the soul, are more excellent in themselves than they are in the soul. Consequently it is better to know than to love the things that are beneath us; . . . whereas the love of the things that are above us, especially God, ranks before the knowledge of such things.[18]

Human knowledge either brings things up (material things) or down (God) to our level; human love is a movement toward and a resting in the thing that is loved. Love moves us out of ourselves toward the object loved; even more, it effects a unity between the two. This is why love of God is more important than knowledge of God in this life.[19]

In the next life, God will raise the blessed through the light of glory so that the blessed will see God face to face. Whatever else the beatific vision is, it is a matter of endless growth in knowledge and love. A static understanding of the beatific vision must be avoided at all costs. This endless life of knowing and loving God directly will never be boring —

that is at least the hope that we have in Christ. Still, every preacher and every theologian struggles to articulate properly this great mystery of our faith.

Third, Thomas shows a masterful and balanced approach to the relation between nature and grace. His followers have not always found such a happy balance. One of the age-old controversial questions of Thomistic theology involves the natural desire to see the essence of God. Two extremes must be avoided. The first extreme is that if we are created to know God, then the vision of God is somehow owed to our created natures, which undercuts the radically gratuitous character of God's grace. The other extreme is to sever the relation between nature and grace by denying that there is any connection between our natural desire to know God and the gift of the beatific vision.

7. "Things above Us Do Not Concern Us" (Luther)

VIRGIL F. THOMPSON

Bethlehem Lutheran Church
Spokane, Washington

Supposedly, when the three-story universe went out the window of the cultural imagination under the pressure of modern science, heaven went with it. From a scientific point of view, the probability of heaven is not much improved in the present day. As William Stoeger has observed, "From all the indications we have from the neurosciences, biology, physics, astronomy and cosmology, death and dissolution are the final words. There is not a scientifically supportable foundation for the immortality of the soul, the resurrection of the body and the person after death, a transformed new heaven and new earth."[1]

Heaven's problems are not limited to its perceived incompatibility with modern-day scientific convention. Theology has itself been critical of heaven, or at least of certain conceptions of heaven. Jürgen Moltmann rather poignantly addresses the problem of heaven from the point of view of theology: "The thought of death and a life after death can lead to fatalism and apathy, so that we only live life here half-heartedly, or just endure it and 'get through.' The thought of a life after death can cheat us of the happiness and the pain of this life, so that we squander its treasures, selling them off cheap to heaven. . . . The notion that this life is no more than a preparation for the life beyond, is the theory of a refusal to live . . . a religious fraud . . . religious atheism."[2]

Given the strength of the scientific evidence and the theological dangers, it might seem that Christian preachers would be well advised to close the book on heaven and move on to more promising pursuits. Where God still clings to our culture, claims Steiner, "He is a phantom of grammar, a fossil embedded in the childhood of rational speech."[3]

And yet while the fate of heaven may seem sealed in the tomb of dearly departed Christian hopes, reports of its demise may prove greatly exaggerated. Despite the heavy weight of scientific evidence to the contrary, the hope of heaven appears, at least in my little corner of the world, to have a secure hold on the human imagination. In fact, if the statistics of George Gallup are any indication, hope of heaven among my immediate neighbors in faith does not represent an isolated aberration, but to the contrary, a commonplace of contemporary cultural beliefs. According to a recent survey, for example, seventy-nine percent of Americans agree that "there will be a day when God judges whether you go to heaven or hell."[4] Accordingly, one might safely infer that at least seventy-nine percent of the population still believes in heaven.

The eschatological claims of faith, as for example Paul demonstrates in dealing with the crisis in Corinth, function de-constructively as well as constructively. To the point, allowing science to establish the criteria for determining the credibility of eschatological claims has led to speculation not grounded in the theological and biblical tradition of the faith. The eschatological claims of the faith themselves call into question the speculative approach to the subject matter of eschatology.

Theologians and scientists can debate endlessly the nature and scope of God's eschatological purposes without ever getting any closer to knowing what God has actually in mind. Christian hope is not built on speculation concerning what God may or may not do up there in the wild blue yonder beyond history. Rather, Christian hope is established in and by what God has done in history. To say it more specifically, Christian eschatology is not based on speculation about what is possible or likely given this or that view of God, given this or that view of the nature of matter. Speculation of that sort has provided very little basis for any sort of consensus about what humans might legitimately hope.

Luther would contend that this should come as no surprise. God, he contended, hides in our speculation. He refuses to be found where we want to find him. God will be found only where he reveals himself for our salvation, in the word of his promise, spoken in the message of the death and resurrection of Jesus Christ. As Paul put it, "For the message about the cross is foolishness to those who are perishing, but to us who are being saved it is the power of God. For it is written, 'I will destroy the wisdom of the wise, and the discernment of the discerning I will thwart.' . . . For since, in the wisdom of God, the world did not know God through wisdom, God decided, through the foolishness of our proclamation [of the cross], to save those who believe" (I Cor. 1:18-19, 21).

Christian eschatological hope is built upon the preached promise of Jesus' death and resurrection. That is the datum on which eschatological hope hinges. It may be freely admitted that if the preaching and the historical datum that justifies it prove not to be true, then Christian hope is in vain. Responding to the crisis of eschatological hope in Corinth (see I Cor. 15:12), Paul did not direct the attention of the congregation to speculative propositions, what God might or might not do to answer faith's doubt. Rather, he directed the attention of the congregation to the reality of God's activity in history, specifically to the historical datum of Christ's death and resurrection. "If the dead are not raised, then Christ has not been raised. If Christ has not been raised, your faith is futile and you are still in your sins. Then those also who have died in Christ have perished. If for this life only we have hoped in Christ, we are of all people most to be pitied" (I Cor. 15:16-19).

The Hope of Heaven in Luther's Perspective

While the biblical tradition speaks about the hope of heaven in two modes, heaven above and heaven to come, it prefers, for reasons that we shall now explore, to speak in a primary way of the heaven to come. According to Gerhard Forde, "the reason for preferring the 'to come' idea is to convey something about the relation between this world and the other world. The idea of a world to come implies that it is something absolutely new, something that like all future events rests solely in the hands of God."[5] There is nothing humanity can do to help or hurry the coming of God's saving rule or kingdom. As Jesus taught his disciples, no one even knows when the kingdom will come; "about that day and hour no one knows . . . only the Father" (Matt. 24:36). It will come as a thief in the night (Matt. 24:43). The whole matter is out of human hands. It comes from above. The only thing that believers can do is wait and pray, "Thy kingdom come. . . ." It is to say, as Luther explains in the Small Catechism, "God's kingdom comes without our praying for it, but we ask in this prayer that it may come also to us."

Just as the saving kingdom of God comes solely by his action without human help, so also it rests solely upon his promise. What guarantee does faith have that the kingdom will actually come? Faith is not without a foundation. It has the testament of the Lord himself. As he declared to the disciples at the Last Supper,

> "Take, eat; this is my body." Then he took a cup, and after giving thanks he gave it to them, saying, "Drink from it, all of you; for this is my blood of the covenant, which is poured out for many for the forgiveness of sins. . . . I will never again drink of this fruit of the vine until that day when I drink it new with you in my Father's kingdom." (Matt. 26:26b-29)

Of this promise, Forde declares, "Even though we cannot yet see it, we can hear it coming in the Word, we can feel it, touch it, taste it in the sacraments. That world which is beyond price, beyond our ability to earn by works, which is entirely unnecessary and thus absolutely free comes to you here and now to make you new and set you free."[6] Not only do these words, along with the words of baptism and the preaching of the good news, sign and seal the promise, but in fact they bring about what they promise. When the promise elicits the believer's faith, trusting God to be God, then here and now human life is restored to what God intended that it should be all along. The creature is free to live by faith in God the Father, Son, and Holy Spirit, trusting the promise of life to come beyond death, and here and now attending to the down-to-earth affairs of this life, caring for the creation and the neighbors with whom it is shared.

Of course, as the old priest in George Bernanos's story admits, people will still have "their own worries to grapple with, just the same."

Hunger, thirst, poverty, jealousy — we'd never be able to pocket the devil once and for all, you may be sure. But man would have known he was the child of God; and there lies your [eschatological] miracle. He'd have lived, he'd have died with that idea in his noddle. . . . That wouldn't have stopped the labourer ploughing, or the scientist swotting at his logarithms, or even the engineer making his playthings for grown-up people. What we would have got rid of, what we would have torn from the very heart of Adam, is that sense of his loneliness.[7]

The eschatological act of God in Christ restores the believer to the life of this world with hope for the life to come, and with trust in God as God for life here and now. Believers, by faith in the promise of God, get back their down-to-earth lives, restored to the affairs of this life in manageable proportion. The believer is no longer compelled to use this life to prove himself or herself worthy of God's heavenly reward. As Mark Mattes puts it, "what is eschatologically miraculous is God's doing for us what it is not possible for us to do, that is, to create new, non-self-justifying beings of faith."[8]

An oft-repeated story reports Luther's response to a question inquiring what he'd do if he knew the world was coming to an end.[9] He would, he said, "go out into the garden and plant a tree." The story nicely illustrates how faith lives by hope of heaven to come. Because the coming kingdom of God's salvation rests solely in the promise and power of God alone, and for that reason is as sure as sure can get, Luther is persuaded not to leave this world (where else is there to go?). Neither does he despise the world, but he "enters into it all the more fully and takes up its concerns and tasks all the more seriously."[10] Confident that the end is the means employed by God to bring about the new creation — new heaven and new earth — the believer is free to go about doing the things human beings have been created to do. Instead of using the good God-given gift of human reason to speculate what God may or may not be up to out there in the wild blue yonder, the believer uses reason to manage the down-to-earth affairs of this life. Taking God at his Word, the believer trusts that God being God will be able to keep the promise regardless of how impossible or fantastic it may seem, based upon what we have seen of life so far. For his part, the believer is content to live down to earth, working, waiting, and praying.

This is what Luther meant when he said, *"Quae supra nos nihil ad nos"* — those things above us are of no concern to us. Human reason, set free from the anxious aspiration to inquire of the what, when, and how of the things above, may now be employed in salutary fashion toward the things below, toward the things of this earth. It may be used to care for creation and the neighbors with whom we share it. Trusting God to take care of the things above us, as he has promised to do, we are free to cultivate peace and justice, love and joy, here and now, as creation awaits the fulfillment of God's promised salvation.

We may not be able to answer the crisis of death — neither in its personal nor in its cosmic dimension — but we can live here and now by faith that we have a God who has promised to answer death with the life to come. In the words of Johann Anselm Steiger, "When the whole world starts staggering and falls into chaos, then this is cause for faith in a radically counter-factual way, to see the new creation anticipated. In the apocalyptic end of the world the believer sees the blooming of the new world. . . . The logic of the faith, which is completely incommensurable with the wisdom of the world, draws a new rhetoric and dialectic after itself."[11] Luther articulates the point nicely in what one might call eschatology *sub contrario:*

> For who has ever heard that it means the trees are budding and blooming when the sun and moon lose their shine, heaven and earth crash, the people shake and tremble, air, water and all creatures are positioned as if everything now wanted to go to the ground? If that means it is beginning to get green and become summer, then it is a strange language and a new grammar. I think it should much more mean the opposite, that a rough, cold dead winter is coming, which ruins all fruit and whatever grows there. But Christ is a different master, who can speak differently of things and comfort better than we. He makes out of the unfriendly sight a pleasant, comforting picture and makes out of the rhetoric a beautiful, delightful interpretation and interprets it in this way, that when I see the sun and moon dark, the water and wind roaring, and both mountain and valley knocked down, I should say, "God be praised, it will now be summer."[12]

We may not be able to bring in the kingdom, but we can tend the down-to-earth affairs of this life in the time that we have been given. The point to see is that hope of heaven, understood in the way we have been here making the case, does not drive a wedge between this life and the next life, does not lead one to abandon this life in pursuit of the life to come, does not lead one to despise this life for the sake of that which is to come. In fact, as Luther made the point, "From this we see that Christ is not sitting idle above in heaven but he is fighting without ceasing with our enemies and taking them captive so that they cannot harm us."[13]

Heaven so conceived, far from being an escape from life, is seen to be for the redemption of the earth. Understood in this way, hope of heaven can be seen to give us back this life as we were meant all along to have it. As Forde explains, "It is an act of hope to [tend your vocational affairs — the affairs of marriage, family, politics, business, profession, and so forth] — when you think the end is near. It is hope based on the trust that God will not deny his creation; that the world to come does not mean the destruction of what is good in this world, but its fulfillment."[14] To hope is to enter into the struggle for life, good and just, against the odds, against the forces that oppose it, to enter into the "travail of creation," as Paul put it. Just so, the hope of heaven gives us to work and wait.

8. Kierkegaard Goes to the Eschaton

RUSH OTEY

*First Presbyterian Church
Pensacola, Florida*

*Teach me, O God, not to torture myself and not to make a
martyr of myself in suffocating reflection, but to take deep and
wholesome breaths of faith!*

a prayer of Kierkegaard

The initial intention of this paper was to review various commentaries on the book of Revelation in order to discern any interactions between biblical scholarship and twentieth-century science on the theme of apocalyptic eschatology and the New Creation. How are biblical studies entering the dialogue between science and Christian faith? Is it important that biblical scholarship take notice of developments in cosmology as expressed in theories of indeterminacy, quantum physics, black holes, and entropy theory — all of which have occurred since Einstein?

In the first place, I discovered that there are many more works on Revelation than I anticipated, probably because of market-driven publishing to capitalize on the end of the millennium. More significantly, there is little evidence from the commentaries that biblical scholars, particularly those who represent mainline seminaries and divinity schools, are building bridges to or even taking notice of developments in the natural sciences. The bibliographies given in the commentaries make scant reference to physical science, though other modern disciplines (such as political and social sciences, linguistics, and historiography) are called upon extensively. The chief reference to science as related to eschatology found in current commentaries is the listing of Carl Sagan's *Cosmos* and Jonathan Schell's *The Fate of the Earth* in the bibliography of Eugene Boring's commentary in the *Interpretation* series; others, such as the volume from *The New Interpreter's Bible,* have no such listings. The interdisciplinary discussions are occurring in the field of theology rather than biblical studies. To the extent that the preaching and teaching of the church are informed and even shaped by biblical commentaries, this is noteworthy, and raises many of the issues considered in the first year of the Center of Theological Inquiry's Pastor-Theologian Program.

How is Scripture authoritative when its worldview is radically different from the worldviews of the twentieth and twenty-first centuries? If preaching is done "with the Bible in one hand and the newspaper in the other," what does the preacher make of current scientific eschatologies where the end of all things, if not the process of the ending, is certain? If the purpose of a commentary is simply to attempt to convey what the Scriptures probably meant to the initial hearers in their own time and place, so what? Commentators who consider Genesis have long been taking note of scientific theories in their work; perhaps there is more comfort with origins rather than destiny. Biblical commentaries unabashedly and appreciatively make use of archeology, historiography, political and economic studies, and linguistic analysis, but is there room for physics and astronomy? Is God an archaism, an illusion, a filler of gaps? Is God necessary in understanding what may happen to creation at the end? Is the divorce between religion and science in fact growing, despite the good efforts of those considered in the Center for Theological Inquiry's projects? Is the dialogue between faith and science simply an effort of the faithful to legitimate ourselves, or is there a similar effort in the scientific community? Do changes in scientific theory necessitate a re-reading of Scripture, and if so, is this happening in biblical scholarship related to eschatological texts? When it comes to eschatology, are the "pre-critical" commentaries of, say, the early desert Fathers as valid for the life of the church and the proclamation of the gospel as more recent efforts?

John Polkinghorne, in *Science and Theology: An Introduction,* delineates six varieties of interaction between science and theology: conflict, independence, dialogue, integration, consonance, and assimilation.[1] With regard to eschatology, modern biblical scholars generally have pursued the path of independence, which Polkinghorne observes is the stance of treating science and religion as "quite separate realms of enquiry in which each discipline is free to pursue its own way without reference to, or hindrance by, the other."

While both science and theology seek truth, there are inherent dissimilarities between science and theology that, if not resulting in irreconcilable differences, at least make consonance a highly problematical goal. Science and theology have different purposes and fundamentally varying perspectives. The aim of science is primarily descriptive; the purpose of theology includes prescriptive and promissory elements. The perspective of science may or may not include transcendence and purpose; Polkinghorne demonstrates that, as a result of quantum physics, there is room for unpredictability and freedom within scientific theories of creation and eschatology. However, this is not necessarily the result of a divine hand at work. It seems to me that at the end of the day, Polkinghorne builds his case for God on a restatement of the arguments from design (the "anthropic principle"), arguments that at least since the time of Kant are difficult for many scientists and theologians to endorse. In his *Critique of Pure Reason,* Kant concluded that "the utmost that the argument can prove is an *architect* of the world who is always very much hampered by the adaptability of the material in which he works, not a *Creator* of the world to whose idea everything is subject." Polkinghorne writes more as a person of faith than a pure scientist. This may be his great contribution, but his irenic perspective will continue to be suspect in the scientific community.

Further, there is the matter of prediction. Science attempts to make predictions based primarily upon the limit of empirical study, even when it is acknowledged that the scientist inevitably makes decisions within the process of inquiry that direct and interpret the results of the process. The predictions of science by definition are subject to revision; they are hypothetical and theoretical. Theology, on the other hand, shapes considerations about the future from the standpoint of revelation and promise. The church is in error when it employs apocalyptic texts such as Revelation to develop specific timetables for the end, for this is an adulterous mixture of its own tradition with the scientific method. In doing this, the church demonstrates a pathetic zeal to be acceptable in the eyes of the world. Even scientists at their best do not always claim certainty in their models for the end of all things — will it be the Big Bang or the Big Crunch? And when? During the past year, I came across a cartoon in which a scientist says, "In five billion years, the world will end." A student, obviously anxious, asks, "Did you say billion or million?" "Billion," comes the reply. To which the relieved student says, "Whew! I thought you said million!"

Let us imagine that, through the lens of the Hubble telescope, astronomers forecast with great degree of unanimity that on May 17, 2005, an asteroid will strike the earth and the earth will become without form and void, disintegrated. One might arrive at one of the following interpretations: (1) The asteroid is fulfilling the mysterious, creative purposes of God. Science and Scripture agree that one day all things will perish. All previous timetables were wrong, but ultimately this matters little, since God is Alpha and Omega. (2) The asteroid is a historical accident, similar to a boulder that tumbles down a mountainside and strikes a school bus full of children, but God can and will work beyond the accident. There will be a new creation in which there is no more suffering, despite the suffering of anticipating and enduring the blow of the asteroid. (3) The asteroid is like the Beast in Revelation, clearly in opposition to God and wreaking great havoc, but ultimately not victorious over the will of God. The faithful must stand fast in their confession of the Lamb, to the point of death. Faithfulness is the key to suffering and to human existence. (4) God will intervene and the asteroid will miss the earth. (5) The asteroid is a punishment for sin. Evil will perish, but the faithful will be carried to God's presence. (6) Everything, including the asteroid and all history and all discussion and theology and faith, is pointless and meaningless. There is no God; there is no purpose. (7) "I would rather stake my faith on the one empirical constancy in the history of this entire enterprise:

apocalyptic predictions always fail!" (Stephen Jay Gould, professor of paleontology at Harvard, in *New York Times*, October 23, 1997).

The Church has forever been engaged in a struggle to be "in but not of the world." At many points, but particularly with regard to the subject of eschatology, the proclamation of the Church questions and often even directly opposes the prevailing wisdom of culture. Faith is "the assurance of things hoped for, the conviction of things not seen" (Heb. 11:1). Preaching is keeping alive a "prophetic imagination," in the words of Walter Brueggemann. It is indeed "foolishness to the Greeks." (Peter Berger provides a helpful discussion of this "cognitive deviance" or "defiance" in *A Rumor of Angels.*) There were many times during the past two thousand years when the demise of the gospel appeared to be at hand. One arrives at a decision of "Either/Or" in this matter of the end of all things: either one trusts where reason cannot promise, or one subscribes to a doom of incalculable sadness and retreats into resignation or hedonism or pointless tinkering, all of which capitulate to cultural and admittedly temporal norms. The issue is death, whether personal or cosmic. Either death is all there is, or there is a God who resurrects. While there are important considerations and relationships between creation and eschatology, there are more important ones between Easter and eschatology. It is here, I believe, that the first and second years of the Pastor-Theologian Program must be joined. Was there supreme, ultimate, irrevocable reconciliation through the death of the Messiah or not?

It is here that Revelation, the final book of Scripture, has been and always will be in tension and conflict with any secular eschatology, be it political, scientific, environmental, or human in its inception. Whatever else it is, Revelation is Christocentric. Thus, while it may be at first glance embarrassing, it is finally of little importance for the Church that Biblical commentaries do not interact with quantum physics or other contemporary scientific theories. Without Christ, it is highly ironic that persons should gain a sense of peace and comfort from science — for example, that there should be a sense of renewal from vacationing under the summer stars. If Steven Weinberg is correct that all is pointless, there is no comfort there — only cold terror.

The novelist Saul Bellow mused in unforgettable language in *Herzog:*

> But what is the philosophy of this generation? Not God is dead, that point was passed long ago. Perhaps it should be stated Death is God.

This generation thinks — and this is its thought of thoughts — that nothing faithful, vulnerable, fragile can be durable or have any true power. Death waits for these things as a cement floor waits for a dropping light bulb. The brittle shell of glass loses its tiny vacuum with a burst, and that is that. And this is how we teach metaphysics on each other.[2]

During the course of the past year, I kept seeking and waiting and yearning for a breakthrough, a consonance of theology and science. While there is indeed more congruence of method (inquiry, humility, metaphorical and "model" language, trial and error, freedom/indeterminacy, progressive learning/revelation, the "Protestant principle"), and there are, as shown by Polkinghorne, many more possibilities for dialogue and cooperation than fundamentalists of either discipline would admit, there is finally the irreconcilable discrepancy between the futility implicit in secular eschatologies and the redemption promised in Christian faith. The believer (scientist or pastor-theologian) must choose how to proceed (or not), how to live (or not). At this point, even Weinberg is an existentialist! As the recently deceased Tom Langford of Duke Divinity School once said, "The existentialists finally require one to respond to essential questions."

A familiarity with or subscription to the predictions of Nobel laureates in physics is not necessary for the Church to be the Church any more than public opinion polls regarding Roman rule or a foreknowledge of Copernicus, Galileo, Newton, or Einstein was available to John of Patmos. Still, the issue now is whether to keep going in face of eventual certain death. Upon what premise and promise do we live and move and have our being?

Revisiting Kierkegaard

The Danish theologian Søren Kierkegaard (1813-1855) responded to the scientific and materialistic worldview of his time, and its philosophical companion Hegel, with a call for a "leap of faith." There are places where Polkinghorne is openly critical of Kierkegaard's tendency toward subjectivism. Yet Polkinghorne says in *The Faith of a Physicist*, "Our rational inquiry must not blind us to the awe-inspiring and ineffable mystery of

God to which religious experience bears testimony. Kierkegaard said, 'May we be preserved from the blasphemy of men who "without being terrified and afraid in the presence of God . . . without the trembling which is the first requirement of adoration . . . hope to have direct knowledge.""[3] Ultimate truth involves a leap of faith.

Kierkegaard warned against basing one's life upon scientific "proofs," for this approach reduces life to the physical and the quantifiable: "If . . . faith begins to cease to be faith, then proof becomes necessary so that the man who has lost his faith may still enjoy the approbation of the bourgeois."[4] Science had even then become unconcerned with the questions of how to live. In *Concluding Unscientific Postscript*, Kierkegaard even predicted that "in the end all corruption will come about as a consequence of the natural sciences." Science, he insisted, "by pretending to explain the miracle of qualitative change only throws dust in our eyes. It pretends to be on the point of explaining everything," but finally suffocates and defrauds human beings "not only of the wonder which is the starting point of religion, but of the possibility which makes spiritual life possible."[5]

For Kierkegaard the key is not consonance or mediation, but paradox. In Christ, eternity meets time. Relativity is lost through the deep certitude of passion and total commitment. What Kierkegaard calls for above all else is the courage to believe in the face of the absurd. As Warren Groff and Donald Miller summarized it, "Such courage stands before truth nailed on a tree, which neither compels nor coerces, which allows neither idolatry nor indifference. It is a courage that knows how quickly faith becomes idolatrous, trying to possess what can only be shared, trying to turn 'crucified Truth' into dogma or institutional establishment."[6]

Polkinghorne follows Kierkegaard more than he admits. For Kierkegaard, what is necessary is not a blind leap of faith, for few were as well educated and as articulate as he; in his examinations at the University of Copenhagen, he was "summa cum laude" in physics and mathematics as well as philosophy.[7] His point is that faith is never provable, easy, or even probable. There is no gradual accumulation of rational proofs for God's existence, or for the resurrection, or for the new creation. One performs a willed act of faith despite fear, doubt, and sin. The leap is not out of thoughtlessness or out of ignorance, but out of volition. The leap is sheer and unmediated by culture or science, and is not made by quantitative discoveries or changes in theories. It is (and here

Polkinghorne is not really in disagreement) made from doubt and para-dox.[8] Kierkegaard's understanding of necessity and possibility is a precursor not only to Berdyaev, Barth, and Niebuhr (crisis theology born out of dialectic and paradox), but also to Polkinghorne's eschatological categories, including continuity/discontinuity.

But Kierkegaard cautions against always taking refuge behind the paradox in one's own existence and in the life of the Church. How is one to live in the face of death, whether one is persecuted by the Romans, ostracized by the cultural elite of Denmark, or viewing an oncoming asteroid through the Hubble telescope? Does one finally trust more the continuity or the discontinuity? Are human beings to be living forward toward the death of Creation or toward the New Creation? The eschatology of Revelation, which proclaims the ultimate victory of the Lamb, cannot be squared with the eschatology of Weinberg, which posits nothing beyond the destructive continuities at work.

Justo Gonzalez provides a memorable metaphor:

> When we leave our driveway, we determine which way to turn on the basis of where we are going, in other words, the future is the cause of our decision. . . . A good analogy for all of this is my father-in-law's way of reading a mystery book by beginning at the end. From the point of view of purely efficient causes, that is a crazy way to read a book. But it is probably much closer to the way the book was written. Most likely, the author decided on the solution long before the first word of the book was ever written. The entire book, from cover to cover, makes clearer sense when you read the story, not simply as the result of dozens of separate events that unfold in chronological order, but rather as the result of that final event, which pulls all the rest to itself. . . . In summary, the future guides both our present activity and our reading of the past.
>
> This is one reason why the book of Revelation is so enthralling. . . . The Book is mysterious, paradoxically enough, because it declares what the early Church announced openly: that when the final trumpet sounds, loud voices in heaven will proclaim, "The kingdom of the world has become the kingdom of his Messiah, and he will reign forever and ever" (Revelation 11:15). . . . When we read from this end, we can look at the present time, when the beast holds sway and is worshiped by the peoples, tribes, and nations, in a different way.[9]

The Church lives or dies by the *faith* that in Christ is revealed, given, promised the way all things shall go. Although eventually the tomb will receive creation and all therein, in Him all things hold together and shall be made new. That is surely a leap of faith, but not a vain one, when the alternatives are considered.

9. God's Relation to Nonbeing in Paul Tillich's Thought

JOHN R. CHRISTOPHERSON

The Christus Collegium
Montana State University at Bozeman, Montana

Paul Tillich's position on "nonbeing" is what he refers to in his most mature work, the magnum opus of his *Systematic Theology,* as "Eschatological Panentheism."[1] In the largesse of this rather formidable formula, Tillich demonstrates himself to be the master of correlation: addressing the fearful questioning of the breathless human spirit as it faces nonbeing as expressed in the horizontal, temporal question of "the end" (eschaton) together with the vertical, divine answer of reassuring grace — where time takes on a spatial metaphor — that "all things" *(ta panta)* are in God (panentheism). This formula of "Eschatological Panentheism" seeks to address how the questions of the "when" and "where" of the dimensions of history can find their answer within the multidimensional unity of all life; that is, eternal life in the all-encompassing dimension, or womb, of God's saving Spirit.

According to Tillich, the *eschatological* part of this formula "deals with the relation of the temporal to the eternal."[2] As with his discussion on the doctrine of *creatio ex nihilo,* Tillich again uses the ontological term of "relation." Thus, we would argue that Tillich's understanding of eschatology has not so much to do with a focus on "last things" *(ta eschata)* looming out there somewhere in the future as it does with the relatedness of God "in all times and in all places." Tillich writes,

In order to emphasize the qualitative connotation of *eschatos* I use the singular: the *eschaton*. The theological problem of eschatology is not constituted by the many things which will happen but by the one "thing" which is not a thing but which is the symbolic expression of the rotation of the temporal to the eternal. . . . The eschatological problem is given an immediate existential significance by this reduction of the *eschata* to the *eschaton*. It ceases to be an imaginative matter about an indefinitely far (or near) catastrophe in time and space and becomes an expression of our standing in every moment in the face of the eternal, though in a particular mode of time.[3]

But what is this "one thing" of which Tillich speaks, that towards which all of history points as it stands under the negativities of existence and therefore under the ambiguities of life? According to Tillich, the answer is the Kingdom of God.[4] And the central manifestation of this Kingdom — which includes life in all of its realms or dimensions — is the person of Jesus the Christ. In him "the kingdom of God is at hand" (Mark 1:15). In relation to Jesus the Christ, "the great Kairos," time is fulfilled (Galatians 4:4). And at the foot of the Cross of Christ, time reaches its depth moment, its fullness of being "in spite of" nonbeing.[5] The Cross marks the interstice where being and nonbeing come together, as the "one point in the center."[6] Here "being and nonbeing hang together," according to Heidegger. And thus for Tillich, God and nonbeing are to be thought together on the basis of Christ and his Cross. The Crucified One is the way God's power of being is perfected. At the heart of God, from all eternity, there is a cross:[7]

It is the greatness and heart of the Christian message that God, as manifest in the Christ of the Cross, totally participates in the dying of a child, in the condemnation of the criminal, in the disintegration of the mind, in starvation and famine, and even in the human rejection of Himself. There is no human condition into which the divine presence does not penetrate. This is what the Cross, the most extreme of all human conditions, tells us.[8]

In the best of times as well as the worst of times, God is present as "the creative depth of every moment," the *nunc aeternum*. The eternal is not a future state of things. It is always present.[9] Therefore, against any dualistic tendencies, Tillich writes, "The divine life participates in every life as its ground and aim. . . . God does not sit beside the world, looking at it from outside, but he is acting in everything *in every moment*."[10] And against any tendencies toward Pantheism or Idealism, Tillich does not push ahead "the hands of time." The tolling of the death bell is still heard. Nonbeing as well as the coming kingdom is at hand. For to speak of God's Kingdom being at hand means that it is here and not here. The threat of nonbeing, of "not having any time left," still remains. That is to say, the Kingdom of God has a fragmentary, "now, not yet" character. It does not come "in an equal rhythm but is a dynamic force moving through the cataracts and quiet stretches."[11] And so in the great words of the hymn of old, Tillich continues to pray with all of creation: *Veni creator spiritus.*

We move then to an issue which has been presupposed in our previous discussion; namely, Spiritual Presence and how this informs what Tillich means when he speaks of the *panentheistic* part of his formula: eschatological panentheism.

> What then is spirit? For Paul, for the Christian Church, it is the presence of God under the conditions of existence, breaking through the alienated structure of existence and restoring its essential structure.[12]

For Tillich, the Spirit or Spiritual is first of all to be understood as the Spirit of God, the divine ground of being or power of meaning, who as the power of life is revealed in life, though fragmentarily, as the "eternal possibility of resisting nonbeing"[13] that conquers the threat of nonbeing in the New Being of Jesus the Christ — giving life, and hope, and spirit to humankind in time and space. In very Pauline fashion, Tillich says, "Spirit is the power of God in us."[14]

Tillich's thought becomes very pastoral and healing at this point. He begins with an ontological theme of unity: "[Spirit] is at home everywhere."[15] That is to say, all dimensions of life, even expressions of nonbeing such as illness and death, are "held together," are unified by the healing power of Being Itself, by God's Spirit. There are no dimensions outside the all-encompassing dimension of the Spirit. Thus, Spiritual Presence is that "depth dimension" in which "all dimensions are rooted and negated and affirmed."[16] This offers humankind the courage to be.[17] For "the Spiritual Presence acts upon [creation and history] *in every moment. . . .* [And] no human form of life and thought can be shut off from the Spirit."[18] "[Humankind] is never left alone."[19] And this is good news for us "pilgrims on earth" who live under the constant threat of nonbeing. Tillich writes with the Psalmist, "God is our dwelling place."[20]

> Time creates the present through its union with space. In this union time comes to a standstill because there is something on which to stand. Like time, space unites being with nonbeing, anxiety with courage. . . . To be means to have space. . . . But to be spatial also means to be subject to nonbeing.[21]

This is known *en Christo* — in the personal life, the Spirit of Jesus the Christ. And so throughout the history of creation we see the power of God's Presence as Spirit, even in the midst of the "dark places of the earth." It is the same Spirit who "brooded over the waters" of chaos in Genesis; the same Spirit who "stood watch by night," deep down in that manger of straw at Bethlehem; the same Spirit who promises to be with us even "to the close of the age" — whether by cosmic crunch or the ennui of entropy; gathering all times and places into God's bosom as "Thy kingdom come on earth as in heaven."

> All acts of man's spiritual life are grasped by the Spiritual Presence. In biblical terms, there is no temple in the fulfilled Kingdom of God, for "now at last God has his dwelling among men! He will dwell among them and they shall be his people, and God himself will be with them."[22]

We move now to a metaphor that is found throughout Tillich's thought (more implicitly perhaps than explicitly), one that better helps us to envision God's relation to creation and nonbeing over against Panentheism: "the womb of God." For example, Tillich muses:

> When God created the potentiality of the atom within himself he created the potentiality of man, and when he created the potentiality of man he created the potentiality of the atom — and all other dimensions between them . . . pregnant with infinite tensions.[23]

Further, Tillich writes: "We are continually dependent on the origin [God]; it bears us, it creates anew at every moment, and thereby holds us fast."[24] "God is the continuous, carrying ground of the world."[25] Here, in the highly symbolic, poetic language of nonbeing as seen from the inside of God, Tillich is able to speak of God's immanent relation to the world — not only as a fellow sufferer, but deeper still, as one who "labors and travails" (Isaiah 53:11).[26] "The center of our whole being is involved *in* the center of all being; and the center of all being rests *in* the center of our being."[27] Here is the full sense of *en* in Tillich's Pan-*en*-theism. "What happens in time and space, in the smallest particle of matter as well as in the greatest personality, is significant for the eternal life. And since eternal life is participation in the divine life, every finite happening is significant for God."[28]

For Tillich, "'in' is the preposition of participation."[29] And it needs to speak at once — in order to be adequate theology — of both God's immanence and transcendence to creation. "God is beyond essence and existence, in that he is the ground of both and as such related to them both, not in the form of identity but in the form of participation."[30] Thus, for Tillich, the Holy as Being Itself is "beyond" the tragedy of essence and existence and yet "this does not mean *without* it."[31] There is always "room in the inn" of Being Itself for creation, for God's risking a dynamic creation of freedom.

Spirit on the one hand *drives* being out of itself, and on the other serves to *unify* the multi-dimensionality of life, moving ever "downward" and "upward" and "forward" toward the time and place when "God is all in all" (I Cor. 15:28) — as the "unconscious desire to return to the mother's womb."[32] We see here something of the medieval mystic's *exitus-reditus* theme, the "coming out of the center of the totality and [being led] back to it,"[33] the eternal movement of a "going out and returning"[34] — or the eternal purging of nonbeing from being, that is, the "essentializing" of all things within the womb of God — a *continually new creation* out of the old *(aufgehoben)*.[35]

> The new comes to birth in history. What is the new? In one respect it is the restoration of the old — not simply a restoration, however, but the elevation of the old to something new, to a new creation.[36]

Here is Tillich's image of the "unity of God. In communion of the Holy Spirit."[37] But it is not an image of community that might be characterized by a static "animal blessedness." Instead it is dynamic, alive. "But now the question arises: How can the fulfillment of the eternal be united with the element of negation without which no life is thinkable? . . . This leads to the fundamental assertion: The Divine Life is the eternal conquest of the negative; this is its blessedness."[38] And so, Tillich concludes Volume III of his *Systematic Theology* where he began, with an exposition of Romans 11: "O the depth of the riches and wisdom and knowledge of God! . . . For from him and through him and to him are all things" (vv. 33, 36).

Conclusion

Nonbeing reveals what God is being about in the world. The ends of the world always end in God. This is our "blessed assurance" that "all will be well." And at the heart of this eternal blessedness, for both the divine and the human, Creator and creation, is the claim that "blessing rests upon sacrifice."[39] "[God] takes the negation [of nonbeing] upon himself."[40]

For Tillich the Being of God's love, made known in the power of the New Being of Jesus the Christ over nonbeing, never ends: "Love never ends."[41] But love is real only if there is the "serious otherness of nonbeing,"[42] giving meaning to the sense that nothing lasts forever. And since nonbeing is centered within the very womb of God, nonbeing can never finally be bounded:

> "The meaning of creation is revealed in its end. . . . The end of [creation] leads back to its beginning."[43]

10. "Amidst the Melancholy of These Days" (William Stringfellow)

RANDY COOPER

First and Trinity United Methodist Church
Henderson, Tennessee

See to it that no one takes you captive through philosophy and empty deceit, according to human tradition, according to the elemental spirits of the universe, and not according to Christ.

Colossians 2:8

Christ Will Come Again

There is a prevailing view in our day that the universe as measured, known, and imagined contains all that ever was, now is, or will one day be. This view is born of a tragically common understanding that the universe is a closed system where, if there is a living God, God cannot act mightily in history to bring time and history to their fulfillment.[1] Within this view, there is no hope of the creation's consummation when in God's time God comes to reign in glory. William Stringfellow rejects such an understanding of the creation by writing confidently of the Second Coming of Christ and by joining his New Testament peers in eagerly awaiting the final day.[2]

To live in hope of the return of Christ is to affirm that Jesus Christ is lord of time and history, that Christ is sovereign of the whole of creation. Biblical eschatology does not regard the final consummation as "some fantastic disjuncture but as a happening profoundly implicated in the whole of the history of this world (Mark 13:32-37; Luke 21:10-28)."[3] This eschatological hope does not anticipate a complete discontinuity with history, but rather the complete redemption of time and history.

Christians and others who "suffer" the spiritual gift of discernment are able to behold signs or tokens[4] of the Resurrection within the life of the world as promises of a final consummation on the Day of the return of Christ:

Biblical politics has to do with acting now in anticipation of the vindication of Christ as judge of the nations and other principalities, as well as persons. So here and now biblical people live and act, discern and speak, decide and do, in expectancy of Christ's promptness. The excited imagery in Revelation of the Second Coming of the Lord, with midair apparitions and other marvels, may have caused some to dwell upon the texts literalistically — to fix upon the wonders rather than upon the excitement of hope.

But we can be saved from so demeaning the Second Coming of Christ if we see that, for all its mystery, the Second Advent is faithful to the mission of the First Advent, and is no disjuncture or disruption. On the contrary, it is the consummation of all that has transpired in Christ's ministry in this world, from the homage of Creation rendered to the Christmas Child, through the undoing of death's temptations in the desert, to the secret of every parable and the authority of every healing and exorcism, unto the day alone on the Cross condemned by the principalities and powers, abandoned by everyone, consigned to death, until the Resurrection. Biblical living is watchful for that consummation but does not strive to undo the power of death, knowing that death is already undone and is in no way whatever to be feared and worshiped. Biblical living originates in this consolation.[5]

Indeed, our expectation of the return of Christ is heightened by our witness to the presence of the resurrected Christ in the death-dealing events of the world that are powerless to defeat God's final purposes. Christians live in the joyful affirmation of that ancient proclamation of faith: Christ has died; Christ is risen; Christ will come again.

Reflection upon Eschatology and Science

In his introduction to a book of selected Stringfellow writings, Bill Kellerman notes that Stringfellow began in his later works to substitute "the whole of creation" for "the world." Such a change no doubt reflected Stringfellow's primary concern to implicate the powers and principalities in the full range of their presence in the life of the world.[6] Any consideration of the creation as including the known universe would have been secondary in his mind, the times being what they were.

Yet times have changed. Creation is now a word laden with polyvalent meaning. One cannot speak of the creation without pictures provided by the Hubble telescope coming to mind. To speak of the creation nowadays is to include galaxies, black holes, and quantum theory, along with life in this world. Thus the question: Can one properly employ Stringfellow's language and theology to address issues that arise in the meeting of science and eschatology? Simply put, does his theology help to further the conversation?

The Principalities of Science and Theology

Curiously, in our studies of the past year we pastor-theologians have not applied the language of powers and principalities to our study of science and eschatology. This is quite amazing, when one considers the influences upon the human mind and the human community of the various and sundry principalities arising within these two disciplines. Yet what better language do we have than this biblical language, which names the legions of powers that demand our attention and, in their fallenness, compete for our loyalty? How else can we speak truthfully about science and theology if we do not employ the language of our biblical faith?

We readily behold the principalities in the closed worlds of scientism and creationism, in the agnostic proposals of the likes of Carl Sagan, and in the rightly criticized spread of scientific reductionism beyond scientific inquiry. Yet as we consider science in these and other manifestations, there continues the belief, "inculcated profusely in the culture, that science is morally neutral or, to put it in some traditional theological terms, that science as a principality somehow enjoys exemption from the fall."[7] Biblically, we are naive to suppose that physics and astronomy and their sister disciplines are any less fallen than other principalities within the pantheon of science. The world of physics is not morally innocuous, and astronomy, like all disciplines, suffers the loss of its vocation to glorify the living God. Moreover, these disciplines in their present ascendancy are inclined to a vainglory in which they presume sovereignty over humanity and over the creation.[8] They seek to become an overarching worldview in which their story becomes the only truth by which we live. Stringfellow's theology serves to remind us that we Christians have no need to compromise the truth that science has come under the dominion of death as much as has any other principality within the creation.

Lest we assume a libelous spirit in this observation, let us readily confess that we can make the same observation for theology. We only need to consider the heretical, Gnostic eschatologies that draw their life parasitically from the gospel — and that are found all too often in the basements of congregations, hoping to find their way upstairs into the pulpits and pews of our sanctuaries — to recognize that theology is a fallen principality within the life of the church and world. Or we can consider the dearth of eschatological hope in many congregations and reach much the same conclusion. We are able to confess that theology suffers the onslaught of death as much as does science.

Yet Jesus Christ has died for all the creation, including those principalities that have come into being under the governance of God. Pastors, theologians, and scientists can share the common confession of the loss of our respective vocations while also working in our particular fields in the confidence that the truth we seek is for the glory of God. Theologians who seek to glorify Jesus Christ will speak a word that opens our eyes to the Word of God in the groaning creation. Whether they know it or not, scientists will have the same vocation, a vocation to understand the creation within the purview of the cruciform gospel of Jesus Christ.

As a pastor, I cannot presume to participate in the advanced, theoretical discussions between science and eschatology. At best, I can listen in on the deliberations and make occasional comment. Perhaps a more humble proposal, appropriate to my vocation, can be as follows: Let the sciences of the stars be taught in such a way that a student, child or adult, will cry wonder and glory to the God of the creation. And in all church-related educational institutions — elementary, secondary, or university — let science be as doxological as any other discipline. Indeed, let theology be edified by the knowledge that science presently offers to the world, for such knowledge will one day be welcomed into the holy city and become part of its glory.[9] Projects worthy of our best efforts might include: How might a class be taught to a college student that leaves her filled with the desire to praise God? And how might a congregation develop a theology that opens Christians' eyes to the presence and vitality of the Word of God within the creation? Such projects would fall well within the scope of us pastors who serve as resident theologians within our congregations, where scientists and educators are called to life in the Body of Christ.

Eschatological and Apocalyptic Language

We mainline Protestants have been robbed. We have allowed the more conservative traditions to steal our language from us. We have read Hal Lindsey and been amused. We have judged the theology found in the "left behind" series of novels to be poor science fiction. We hear the less educated make statements about the faith that we in our sophistication would not make. In seeing the many abuses of eschatology, we have ceased with the use thereof, failing to utilize the eschatological language of our biblical and ecclesial traditions.

That being the case, it may be more accurate to say that the conservatives have taken nothing from us that we have not first laid aside. For two hundred years we have doubted whether apocalyptic and eschatological language bears truth. We have viewed such language as mere poetry. We have adopted the modern worldview that God cannot or will not act within the history of the world in any final way. We wonder if we can use eschatological language in a modern, scientific world.

Yet as Janet Soskice has reminded us, the liberal anthropology we have inherited undermines eschatological language more than does the science we have developed.[10] John Shelby Spong could not be further from the truth when he says Christianity must change or die. The faith and church are alive and quite well in other parts of the "modern" world. We are closer to the truth if we say that we have often doubted the truth of eschatological language and promises.

If Stringfellow's theology contributes nothing else to the discussion between science and theology, his theology beckons us to a way of speaking our faith. He calls us to use the language that is rightfully ours. His own way of speaking as a Christian is partial antidote to the sickness in our churches. Stringfellow, it is said by Stanley Hauerwas,

> was positioned in such a way that he could see how apocalyptic language was working to help us understand the way the world is. Stringfellow did not want to translate the language he used into some other language in order for it to be understood; instead, he wanted to help us see how apocalyptic language narrates our world in a manner that helps us not to be seduced by the world's ways of doing good. Stringfellow understood, we believe, that apocalyptic is the right mode

of narrative for persons struggling as Christians to live in the kind of world in which we live.[11]

If at times Stringfellow was accused of being limited by such language or even labeled "quaint" in his thinking,[12] he did not mind. He knew that we are equipped by apocalyptic language to proclaim that all creation languishes in death, and we are further equipped by the eschatological promises of God to proclaim that it shall not always be so. Finding our apocalyptic and eschatological voices is a crucial issue facing mainline churches. Such language endows us with the biblical promise that God will not remain sidelined or excluded from the life of the creation.

CHAPTER III

Eschatological Hope Today

Introduction

Theology is an ever-changing discipline that reflects upon Scripture and tradition while inevitably, if not intentionally, reflecting its own finitude and sinfulness. This truism is highlighted by the reflections that emerge in a millennium year, when whole cultures were caught up in the encounter of memories and expectations, the interaction of the perennial and the novel. The ambivalence of combining human optimism and pessimism pales in our meditation of Christian hope, a unique gift of the Holy Spirit, which coherently unites elements of both continuity and discontinuity with the inaugurated eschatology of its origins.

In our own day especially, the intersecting forces of theology and science reflect a new mood of tempered rationality and chastened realism. On the astrophysical front, all the available evidence and extrapolations point to a remote future catastrophic end of the universe, whether in the dying gasps of an expansive "Big Bang" or as the contracting spasms of an implosive "Big Crunch" — despite all our successful interplanetary travel and unprecedented medical research breakthroughs. On the theological front, doctrinal norms and ecclesial commitments are being taken more seriously for our earthly direction and discipleship. The euphoria of the 1960s (e.g. in the messianic optimism of Jürgen Moltmann's *Theology of Hope* and a myriad of liberation theologies) has been forced in less than a half century to contend once again with global poverty, environmental crises, and the retribalized resurgence of ethnic strife and inhuman genocide. Just what are the realistic signs of the church's "living hope through the resurrection of Jesus Christ from the dead" (1 Peter 1:3)?

Allen McSween calls for a renewed wrestling with "the Bible's Master Story." Moving beyond, but not without, the fragmentation and even deconstruction inherent in the historical-critical analysis of all written texts, the church can also learn anew from recent popular infatuations with extreme apocalypticism. People hunger for a sense of meaning and purpose grounded in God, a more compelling vision of biblical hope that encompasses creation, redemption, and sanctification in Trinitarian plenitude. Such a hope will be based on the promises of God, take seriously the reality of death, involve the renewal of the whole creation, and lead believers into ethical action along with ecclesial praise.

"The Cross as an Eschatological Act of God" is Richard Floyd's exposition of the gospel that the "new creation" in Christ is "from God, who reconciled us to himself through Christ, and has given us the ministry of reconciliation" (II Cor. 5:18). The earliest church interpreted the Christ-event as an act of the God of Israel and the fulfillment of the eschatological mission and message of the Old Testament. The God who acted in the exodus of Israel and the resurrection of Jesus is the Lord of history as well as eternity. The New Testament fulfills the Old in all its essential eschatological features, most paradoxically in the resurrection of the crucified Jesus. All the various proleptic christological titles ascribed to Jesus witness to the integral interrelation of the crucifixion, resurrection, and the promise of the coming of God in the glory and fulfillment of a new creation. That the resurrected one is also the crucified one is emblematic of the Christocentric realism of authentic Christian hope: God achieves a very costly victory.

John Rogers's excerpt on "Our Hope for Years to Come" advocates "a genuine alteration of human concern from the self and its powers to God and his providence." This is posed as the ultimate answer to our "warring madness, ecological neglect, and technological meltdown" in the repentant repudiation of our "self-reliance, self-sovereignty, and self-confidence." It was the optimistic message of the eighteenth-century Enlightenment, not the Holy Scriptures, that rational and autonomous human beings are uniquely endowed and destined to realize "liberty, equality, and fraternity" in the advancing moral progress of an enlightened humankind. Rather, true eschatology means our trust that "in the crucifixion and resurrection of Jesus Christ, we have seen God's victory over the powers of evil, sin, and death." Now, the disillusionment of the early twenty-first century provides new opportunities for the church to proclaim hopefully the faithfulness of God and our appropriately grateful response in acts of justice and mercy in community life.

This "Eschatological Transfiguration of the Moral Life" is also the focus of the concluding excerpt by Joseph DeRoulhac. Again, eschatology is interpreted holistically, "not simply as the last things or the destiny of all things, but as illuminating the inner meaning of all time and space." Christians are to begin to experience the fullness of life here and now. We are to anchor our moral action in God's final end for creation. DeRoulhac argues that through our moral action, "human beings create time and space for God to accomplish the divine end for human existence amid the frailties of creaturely existence and the vicissitudes of history." Such a transfigured ethic will concentrate on trust and will be radically contextual in nurturing covenantal relationships. Marriage, for example, may then be viewed as a covenant of fidelity in which God is invited to come into the partners' life together and to fulfill the divine end for it. "As beings created in the image of God," DeRoulhac writes, "people have the privilege of participating with God in the divine drama of new creation."

11. The Bible's Master Story

ALLEN C. McSWEEN, JR.

Fourth Presbyterian Church
Greenville, South Carolina

"In its eschatology, mainstream Protestantism has suppressed the blood, the chaos, and the terror of the Apocalypse; and these have leapt out like the bogey from under the bed. If the mainstream churches cannot give a satisfactory account of the End, is it surprising that many people will choose to go elsewhere where those needs can be met and addressed?"[1]

James Moorhead

After all the hoopla, the year 2000 arrived and nothing happened. The much-hyped "millennium bug" proved as harmless as a housefly. Books warning of massive catastrophes, many claiming to be based on "Bible prophecy," now sit on the deep-discount shelves of bookstores. Did we "dodge a bullet" by careful and at times expensive preparations, or was the "bullet" loaded in the chamber of our consciousness merely by the overactive imagination of media that thrive on sensationalism and by apocalyptic groups that thrive on catastrophe mongering? Either way, the calendar turned to 2000 and not even our computers hiccupped.

But what may have happened in a way too subtle to be measured at the moment is that through the flurry of apocalyptic speculations surrounding the year 2000, Christian eschatology was rendered even more questionable in the minds of many. If so, that would be a great loss in a time when an authentic biblical vision of hope is desperately needed. If we as pastor-theologians in the mainline traditions are to help articulate for our people a more faithful vision of Christian hope, we need to enter into a constructive and critical dialogue with the apocalyptic theology that is widespread today. The first step in that task will be to seek to understand its appeal. We will then be in a better position to critique its inadequacies and build upon its strengths as we attempt to offer a more adequate expression of Christian hope. Such will be the task of this paper.

What Can We Learn from Contemporary Expressions of Apocalypticism?

A. We learn that people have a tremendous hunger for a sense of meaning and purpose grounded in God. The spiritual emptiness of the modern world portrayed in the dominant media and experienced in secular culture is everywhere evident. We cannot live without a deeper sense of meaning and purpose than any form of materialism offers. In particular, scientism and technology cannot provide the overarching and undergirding meta-narrative that could order our exponential increase of knowledge into a coherent whole. In the words of Neil Postman,

> Like the Sorcerer's Apprentice, we are awash in information, without even a broom to help us get rid of it. The tie between information and human purpose has been severed. . . . [We have no] transcendent nar-

72

ratives to provide us with moral guidance, social purpose, intellectual economy. No stories to tell us what we need to know, and especially what we do *not* need to know. . . . What we are facing, then, is a series of interconnected delusions, beginning with the belief that technological innovation is the same thing as human progress . . . which is linked, in turn, to the most serious delusion of all: that it is possible to live . . . without a transcendent narrative . . . one that tells of origins and envisions a future; a story that constructs ideals, prescribes rules of conduct, provides a source of authority, and above all, gives a sense of continuity and purpose.[2]

As pastor-theologians we have a vital role to play in enabling people to appropriate for themselves the great master story, the "transcendent narrative," rendered in the Bible. The great story of the Ends of God gives meaning and purpose to the stories of our lives and the universe.

B. We learn that people long for authentic hope — and long for it so desperately that they will accept almost anything that seems to offer hope and meaning in the midst of events that threaten to overwhelm them. What is offered in the apocalyptic movements of today is a counterfeit hope. But the fact that it is so attractive indicates that we have failed to present a biblical view of hope that is able to grasp people's attention, move their hearts, and motivate their actions. We must find new, compelling ways to affirm the triumph of God's love in Jesus Christ. We need to articulate a biblical vision of hope that speaks not of the destruction of creation, but of its transformation and redemption.

C. We learn that we have a great deal of work to do in enabling ourselves and others to understand the whole of God's revelation in Scripture far better than we do. A large part of the appeal of popular apocalypticism is that it appears to be biblical. It seems to take the Bible literally. As pastor-theologians we need to be able to demonstrate a way of taking the Bible seriously (perhaps we should even say "literally") that recognizes that the various forms and styles of literature in Scripture need to be interpreted in accord with the "rules" for understanding each particular literary form. Just as one does not read a love letter the same way one reads an essay on eschatology, so different styles of literature have their own "rules of engagement." We need to help our people understand better the genre of apocalyptic literature in order to show how its symbols function apart from a literalistic "prophetic timetable."

Throughout the fall of 1999 I sought to do that in sermons, a retreat, newsletter articles, and Sunday School classes, with what, I hope, were positive results. This paper grows out of the outline I used for a retreat and a class on apocalypticism.

D. We learn that we need to articulate a more compelling vision of biblical hope that takes seriously the goodness of creation, God's liberating work in history and beyond it, and the biblical promises of the redemption of all things in Christ. Since theology, like nature, abhors a vacuum, it should not surprise us that the "eschatological vacuum" in the mainline churches has been filled with all kinds of apocalyptic hot air. People are hungry as never before for a faithful and hopeful articulation of the goal for which all things were made and toward which, by the sovereign love of God, all things are moving.

What Might Such a Vision of Hope Look Like?

A. It will be based on the promises of God, not our predictions or scenarios of the future. The difference is subtle but deeply significant. Adherents of "Bible prophecy" will argue that their prophetic scenarios are indeed the revealed promises of God. And yet there is a strong tendency to rely more on the predicted scenarios of the future than on the One behind them "whose ways are not our ways and whose thoughts are not our thoughts." Everything that really matters hangs on the faithfulness of the God who promises a new creation, not our cleverness in deciphering "prophetic texts." Donald Juel sums up the matter well:

> The reality and finality of death cannot be dispelled by arguments. Only God can raise the dead. Death's hold on our imaginations will yield only to God's action that is available to us now only in the form of a promise. The promise assumes the form of discourse that we normally call proclamation or preaching through which God actually gives life and gives birth to hope. Such hope springs not from interpretive schemes but from a word that must be spoken to us from outside — finally, from God. That such words are spoken and do give life is reason for confidence that death and futility are not the end. That such words can be spoken in ordinary human systems of signs is an indication that the world subject to futility is still vulnerable to . . . a God who raises the dead.[3]

Christian hope is not based on predictions of the future, but on trust in the surprisingly sovereign God of Exodus and Easter who has called and claimed us as his own and who will not abandon us in life or death. Our hope is not grounded in a system of doctrine, however biblical it may claim to be, but in the commitment to creation and the human enterprise within it of the One who has promised to "make all things new," and who has already begun that renewal in small, but far from insignificant ways, in our own lives and in the life of the world. Over against apocalyptic scenarios of the future, Christopher Morse rightly affirms:

> What faith professes to hear in the gospel testimonies [of the future] is not a prediction of the inevitability of destruction, but a promise, as only God can keep, that even when the worst things come upon us that can possibly happen, they will not be able to prevent Christ's coming to us in redemption, an ultimate reclaiming from all harm.[4]

B. It will be a *modest* hope that does not seek to know more than what God has chosen to reveal to us. It will not ignore Scripture's own clear warning that it is not for us to "know the times or seasons" of the End time. Jesus says plainly that "the day and hour" of the End is revealed to no one, not even the Son, but to the Father only. Reinhold Niebuhr was right in warning Christians not to attempt to say too much "about the furniture of heaven or the temperature of hell." We hope for more than we have yet experienced based on our trust in the faithfulness of God. "What no eye has seen, nor ear heard, nor the heart of man conceived, what God has prepared for those who love him" (1 Cor. 2:9).

C. It will be a *Christ-centered* hope shaped by the gospel narratives of his life, death, and resurrection, not by highly subjective interpretations of apocalyptic images. Death for us as individuals and for the universe as a whole is the ultimate limit of any hope not grounded in the sovereign Creator and Lord of life. Christian hope is essentially hope in the resurrection — the resurrection of Jesus, of all who are incorporated into his resurrection life, and of the universe that ultimately will be "set free from its bondage to decay and obtain the glorious liberty of the children of God" (Rom. 8:21).

This Christ-centered hope is based not on our wishful thinking or apocalyptic fantasies, but on what God has already done in Jesus Christ and is already doing in our lives. We discern the outline of the future by tracing the promises of a faithful God through Scripture and into our own lives today. What God has done and is doing keeps our hope grounded in the realities of redemption. And because that redemption is incomplete in all of us, it keeps us straining forward for that which we can see and greet only from afar, the "city whose builder and maker is God."

D. It will be a hope that takes the reality of death seriously, but takes even more seriously God's lordship over death. The traditional understanding of the "immortality of the soul," still prevalent today, serves, often unwittingly, to deny the stark reality of death, and thus tends to devalue the preciousness of bodily, physical life in this world. Yet Scripture attributes immortality to God alone and nowhere ignores or disguises the reality of death. Death is real and, to all human perceptions and powers, final. But beyond the final frontier of death is the all-encompassing love of God, "the Father Almighty," who in the resurrection of the beloved Son, Jesus the Christ, enacts and demonstrates God's promise to maintain his relationship to all on whom he has set his eternal love. In the words of the German theologian, Christoph Schwöbel:

> The Christian hope based on the death and resurrection of Christ does not deny the finitude of all created beings but transcends it. The hopes of the finite to participate in eternal life are not based on its own nature but *exclusively on God maintaining his unconditional creative relationship to what he has created even beyond death* [emphasis mine]. While taking the threat of utter futility seriously, Christian hope is nevertheless left neither to the noble resignation of tragedy nor the joyless mirth of farce. The Gospel of Christ promises a continuity that is maintained beyond the discontinuity of the death of finite life, a continuity that is already promised in the proclamation of the Gospel and in the celebration of the sacraments.[5]

E. It will be a hope for the transformation and renewal of the whole creation, not merely the salvaging of human "souls." The biblical hope is for "a new heaven and new earth," for creation renewed, not destroyed. The emphasis in Scripture and creeds on the "resurrection of the body" can save Christian hope from a gnostic flight from the material and lead to a deeper appreciation for God's will and power to redeem the whole created order. We do not have language with which to describe such a transformation. We can no more fully conceive of the world to come than an unborn child in the womb can envision life in this world. What we have are rich, inspired metaphors of banquets and garden cities and age-old enmities reconciled as lions lie down with lambs and snakes no longer bite. To the list of metaphors from the Old Testament, Paul adds his own in 1 Corinthians 15 — the image of a seed that germinates in a surprising way. Just as a hard, black watermelon seed is vastly different from the plump, juicy melon that comes from it and yet is organically related to it, so in the resurrection of the dead the new embodiment that comes from God is vastly different from the body that has died and yet is still the same personal reality. For Christian hope, the essential emphasis is on a renewed embodiment in which to love and be loved eternally.

F. It will be a hope that leads to *action in the present,* not despair or resignation. If visions of apocalyptic destruction tend toward resignation in the face of historical evils, the biblical vision of the "new creation" and the reconciliation of all things in Christ can and does lead to constructive action in the present, even in situations that, humanly speaking, appear hopeless. Hope in the triumph of God's love in Jesus Christ empowers Christians to bear witness in the present to the future that is promised. In that task, liturgy and social action are inseparably joined as the adumbration and celebration of the promised reign of Christ.

G. It will be a *lyrical* hope that can and must be sung. Walter Brueggemann, among others, has pointed to the "lyrical pluralism of hope" found in Scripture. Biblical hope is not rooted in prophetic scenarios or apocalyptic timetables. It centers in the Triune God whose powerful promises are remembered with gratitude, embraced in faith, and affirmed in hopeful action. Authentic hope is thus better sung than argued.

If we do not or cannot provide a more compelling vision of Christian hope and a more meaningful theological framework within which to make sense of life, death, and destiny, we should not be surprised if, in the words of James Moorhead, "many people will choose to go elsewhere where those needs can be met and addressed." Thus we have serious theological work to do. The rich biblical images of hope, when taken seriously and articulated faithfully, can and do provide the sense of meaning and purpose to the human drama in creation without which human life loses its coherence. Our task as pastor-theologians is to articulate, celebrate, and live out as faithfully as by God's grace we can the eternal hope that is ours in Christ, who makes all things new. To him be the glory, now and forevermore.

12. The Cross as an Eschatological Act of God

RICHARD L. FLOYD

First Church of Christ in Pittsfield
Pittsfield, Massachusetts

*The theological character of the christological story is the key to
its eschatological significance.*

Christoph Schwöbel

The cross of Jesus Christ stands over the future and provides the key to understanding both "the end of the world and the ends of God." I use the
phrase "the cross" as Paul did, as shorthand for the whole decisive act of God
by which God defeated sin and death through Jesus Christ. "The cross" used
this way includes the resurrection but keeps before us the crucial truth that
the risen Christ is the crucified Jesus. The cross understood this way is our
best model for viewing the future as one of discontinuity and continuity,
both for personal existence and for human history. The promise of the Gospel is that the faithfulness of God as one who loves his creation transcends
the discontinuities of death and futility. It is in this identity of God that hope
for the future lies. And for the church this hope is not an abstraction.

Already the pattern of discontinuity and continuity is experienced by
Christians in their justification, where the sinner is made discontinuous
with his or her own sinful actions and assured the continuity of God's
graceful relationship based on God's steadfast love and mercy and not on
the sinner's past. The church then experiences in its own life the pattern
by which it looks in hope to the future. Christoph Schwöbel is surely right
when he writes, "The total dependence on God's creative love which is
the ground of liberating hope for the future is already the foundation of
the church in faith."[1]

Early Christology Is Eschatological

The earliest church interpreted the cross and resurrection of Jesus to be
an act of the God of Israel, and the fulfillment of the hoped-for future de-

scribed in the eschatological texts of the Old Testament. What prepared these Jews to accept a crucified God, and how did that acceptance change their understanding of the very identity of God?

Richard Bauckham has recently made the argument that the way biblical and post-biblical Israel understood the identity of Israel's God had two key features: (1) God as the creator of all things, and (2) God as the sovereign ruler over all things. In addition, God is identified by his acts in Israel's history, especially in the Exodus, and by his character description given to Moses: "Merciful and gracious, slow to anger and abounding in steadfast love and faithfulness" (Exod. 34:6). The acts of God and the character of God together identify God as the one who acts graciously towards his people.

This God, then, by his very identity, was expected to act in the future. Second Isaiah, for example, expects a new exodus, which will show decisively God's identity as creator and ruler of all things. "In the eschatological exodus," according to Bauckham, "he will prove to be the God of all people, Sovereign and Savior of all, in a way consistent with his identity as the gracious God of his people Israel."[2]

The first Christians, who had experienced this new exodus in Jesus, understood that God was continuing the story, and "a new narrative of God's acts becomes definitive for his identity."[3] The God who acted in the Exodus had now acted again in the cross and resurrection of Jesus: "The new story is consistent with the already known identity of the God of Israel, but new is the way he now identifies himself finally and universally, the Creator and Ruler of all who in Jesus Christ has become the gracious savior of all."[4]

When the church included Jesus, a human being, humiliated and exalted, into the identity of God, they were saying something radically new about the identity of God. Nevertheless, the novelty of God crucified did not betray the identity of the God of Israel. On the contrary, as the early church examined the Scriptures, they could find consistency in the novelty. They found the God of Israel and the God of Jesus Christ to be one and the same God.

In the dying and rising of Jesus, God had done a new thing that could be adequately described only in the language of Old Testament eschatology. It was the restoration from exile, the new creation, the healing of the rift between God and Israel and more. Paul Van Buren once described Christian use of the Hebrew Bible as "reading someone else's mail." He has recently written, "that thesis needs to be qualified by the recognition that in fact the church never read the scriptures with a sense that it was reading someone else's mail, and that is because Peter and his fellow discoveries of the gospel read them as their own Jewish mail, albeit with eyes made new by the desperate need, on that 'first day of the week,' to understand the crucifixion of Jesus of Nazareth as the King of the Jews."[5]

So the various writers of the New Testament made new use of familiar eschatological materials to express their belief that in the dying and rising of Jesus Christ, Israel's hopes for an ideal future had arrived, or at least begun. For example, in Mark, our earliest gospel, there are clearly eschatological features in the story of the crucifixion of Jesus: "darkness came over the whole land" (Mark 15:33; see, for comparison, Jer. 4:23); "the curtain of the temple was torn in two, from top to bottom" (Mark 15:38). In the crucified and risen Jesus, the hopes and expectations of Israel were now embodied and accompanied by cosmic signs and wonders appropriate to the coming of God's future.

The reversal of fortune is another common Old Testament eschatological theme taken up by New Testament writers. Donald Gowan writes that "God's promise to make right all that has gone wrong with this world and human life is the essence of Old Testament eschatology."[6] The dying and rising of Christ mirrors the Old Testament eschatological hope for a restoration or a new Creation. We see a good example of this when Paul speaks about "the God who calls into existence things that are not" (Rom. 4:17). Another example is how the restoration texts in Second Isaiah are read by the church to refer to the cross and resurrection of Jesus rather than to the return from exile of their original context. We have only to think of the use of Isaiah 40 in the Advent portion of Handel's *Messiah* to see a powerful example of how the eschatological materials were reused to refer now to Jesus and the reversal of fortune that his coming promises.

These new uses of old eschatological texts help us see that the gospel of Jesus' cross and resurrection was understood eschatologically from the beginning. They can also help us to see that many of our modern problems with the idea of resurrection lie in our attempts to understand the resurrection as an individual and non-eschatological act. But to the Jews of that time, the resurrection of an individual was both unprecedented and unexpected. That the crucified Jesus was resurrected could mean to them only the coming of God and with him the general resurrection of the last days (i.e. Daniel 12). Jürgen Moltmann writes,

Jesus' resurrection from the dead was never regarded as a private and isolated miracle for his authentication, but as the beginning of the general resurrection of the dead, the beginning of the end of history in the midst of history. His resurrection was not regarded as a fortuitous miracle in an unchangeable world, but as the beginning of the eschatological transformation of the world by its creator. Thus the resurrection of Jesus stood in the framework of a universal hope of eschatological belief, which was kindled in that resurrection.[7]

Among the earliest Christological titles were those with a future orientation — for example, Christ as the "first fruits of them that sleep," "the pioneer and perfecter of our souls." These descriptive titles looked ahead to God's new future, now inaugurated in the rising of the crucified, but not merely as the continuation of the past. Rather, God's future was understood as a new Creation, as new as the original Creation was in comparison to the primordial chaos it replaced, and as new as the rising of the crucified Jesus. Referring to the various proleptic Christological titles, Moltmann says,

> That means that the crucified Christ was understood in the light of his resurrection and that his resurrection was understood in the light of his future in the coming God and his glory. Therefore his historical crucifixion was understood as the eschatological kingdom of glory in which the dead will be raised. The "future" of which the first real anticipation was seen in his resurrection was not understood as future history and thus as part of transitoriness, but eschatologically as the future of history and thus as the pledge of the new creation.[8]

So for the earliest church, resurrection of the crucified Jesus was neither primarily an anthropological nor a soteriological symbol; rather, it disclosed the identity and character of God. God is the righteous one. His righteousness will ultimately be victorious over the forces of unrighteousness, over injustice and sin. That the cross should be the instrument of this victory was surely new content in their understanding of the identity of God, but it did not contradict the identity of the God who had acted in the past and whom they had always expected to act again.

RICHARD L. FLOYD

The Identity of the Crucified

There was then great significance in the identity of the crucified one. It was not just any man who was raised. It was a man condemned by the religious law of his people and brutally executed by the civil law of Rome, the great earthly power of the time. These features are not incidental to the *kerygma*, as if the raising of any person would have had the same significance and the same subsequent gospel. No, the fact that the one raised was crucified as a powerless victim, abandoned by his friends and even by the one he called Father, demonstrates God's faithfulness and solidarity with all who are powerless and abandoned in this world.

The identity of the God disclosed in the cross resonates with the identity of the God of the prophets who sought righteousness for the poor, the oppressed, and the powerless. The cross discloses anew God's righteousness in a world of unrighteousness suffering. Moltmann writes:

The question of whether there is a God or not is a speculative question in the face of the cries for righteousness of those who are murdered or gassed, who are hungry and oppressed. If the question of theodicy can be understood as a question of the righteousness of God in the history of the suffering world, then all understanding and presentation of world history must be seen within the horizon of the question of theodicy. Or do the executioners ultimately triumph over the innocent victims? Even the Christian Easter faith in the last resort stands in the context of the question of the divine righteousness in history: does inhuman legalism triumph over the works of the law and of power? With this question we go beyond the formal statements about the proleptic structure of eschatological faith to the matter of Christian faith itself.

We must not only ask whether it is possible and conceivable that one man has been raised from the dead before all others, and not only seek analogies in the historical structure of reality and in the anticipatory structure of reason, but also ask who this man was. If we do, we shall find that he was condemned according to his people's understanding of the law as a "blasphemer" and was crucified by the Romans, according to the divine ordinance of the *Pax Romana*, as a "rebel." He met a hellish death with every sign of being abandoned by his God and Father. The new and scandalous element in the Christian message of Easter was not that some man or other was raised before

82

anyone else, but that the one who was raised was this condemned, executed, and forsaken man. This was the unexpected element in the *kerygma* of the resurrection which created the new righteousness of faith.[9]

Here the biblical affirmation that God cares for the poor and oppressed is given a dramatic new emphasis in the cross. God's steadfast love and mercy engage the suffering world as never before, and at great cost to God. If the raising of a man inaugurates the new eschatological age, then the raising of this man, the Crucified One, provides new content to what sort of future it might be and what sort of God is bringing it about.

How does a divine act that accepts death as the very means of redemption alter expectations for God's future? What is new about eschatology because of the cross? As we have said, the cross provides the key to understanding the identity and character of God for the future as well as for the present and the past. It does so by providing new content about the identity of God. The early *kerygma* stressed the new idea that God raised the crucified Jesus, and in so doing, defined himself as the God who raises the dead. In Moltmann's words, "The subject of the action was God, the object of the suffering was the executed Jesus, and the event was regarded as an eschatological event."[10]

This has radical implications for the way the church views both its own life and its relationship to the world. The eschatological understanding of the cross provides the critical principle that de-centers our preoccupation with both individual and corporate concerns. It also calls into question any ideology that would use the gospel to further its own ends. Anthony Thiselton has written,

The cross is a scandalous reversal of human expectations and values. . . . In the theology of the Fathers, as in that of Paul, the message of the cross challenged the corporate constructs, expectations, and wish fulfillments of communities or of individuals as a scandalous reversal of human expectations and values. Far from reflecting pre-existing social horizons, the cross and the resurrection gave birth to new horizons, which in turn effected a cross-contextual liberating critique and individual and social transformation. This is a far cry from the notion that communities can only project their own images onto texts, thereby to construct their meanings.[11]

The cross provides the church with an anti-ideological bias that protects the gospel from being blown about by any number of contemporary cultural winds or co-opted by any number of alternative faiths, religious and secular.

The cross also protects the church from both utopianism and cynicism, because it keeps in view that the resurrected one remains the crucified one. Thiselton points out how the resurrection appearances function first of all to establish *continuity of identity* between the crucified Jesus and the transformed, exalted, Lord Christ. That continuity of identity is an important principle for the church as well: the community that rises with Christ also dies with him. As Thiselton puts it, "If the Christian *kerygma* announces that the new humanity shares in this resurrection, continuity-contrast-confirmation, we need not be surprised if the earliest texts also trace the same pattern of transformation and continuity in the experience of the earliest witnesses who proclaim it."[12] So Peter denies Jesus, and in so doing, shares in the "failure" of the cross. Apostleship then entails weakness and suffering as well as resurrection, the restoration of a broken relationship.

13. Our Hope for Years to Come

JOHN B. ROGERS

Covenant Presbyterian Church
Charlotte, North Carolina

After the reading of the law and the prophets, the rulers of the synagogue sent to them, saying, "Brethren, if you have any word of exhortation for the people, say it."

Acts 13:15

That was how the elders of the synagogue at Antioch issued the invitation (plea?) to Paul and Barnabas on that Sabbath Day. It was the time in the service for the sermon — the exhortation — and the community sought a word of encouragement. What was their future to be? Facing the erosion of their status in the Roman Empire, fearing for the fate of Jerusalem, the prospects were not encouraging. And although they could not have foreseen the long and tragic road ahead for their children's children, their forebodings were well founded. What word did Paul and Barnabas have that would undergird them as they sought to live their faith in God's righteous rule and providence, come what may? "If you have such a word for the people," they said, "now is the time for it" — the time *(chronos)* for it in the order of worship, and the time *(kairos)* in our life together.[1]

The church today needs such a word as much as did the synagogue at Antioch. For us, the prospective ending of the human world epoch on a cosmic scale will eventually result from either the expansion of the universe (the "Big Bang" become a whimper) or its contraction (the "Big Bang" reverses into the "Big Crunch"), unless in the meantime we do ourselves in through warring madness, ecological neglect, or technological meltdown. If anybody has a word of encouragement, now is the time for it.

For such a word to be truly encouraging requires a genuine alteration of human concern from the self and its powers to God and his providence, from self-reliance to reliance upon God, from self-sovereignty to the sovereignty of God's steadfast love and invincible grace, from self-confidence to trust borne of a new confidence in and involvement of God's creative and redemptive work.

Because human life is more than a biological episode, it is not possible, from a Christian perspective, to speak in any ultimate sense about human existence, or about a human being, without reference to God. If there is one constant theme throughout the Bible, patristic Christianity, and the subsequent history of Christian thought, it is that God's business with Creation embraces the whole of Creation — the world at every level, existence in every form. To confess God as "Creator of heaven and earth and of all things visible and invisible," in the words of the Nicene Creed, is to acknowledge that Creation is God's intentional project and is wholly dependent upon God's constant creativity. This, practically speaking, is what "creation from nothing" means. Creation is an ongoing business, with possibilities and capacities built into the entire enterprise. The providence of God means God's production of such an enterprise, and God's provision for its continuance — including the possibility that it might go well or go awry.

Furthermore, such provision involves the preservation and suste-nance of the entire project within the given limits of finite space, time, and order, and its ultimate consummation and redemption in God's own "good time." This confession recognizes and acknowledges God's sover-eign providence in God's appropriate relation to every conceivable level and category of Creation: nature, history, and the life of the spirit — these all depend on God's constant creativity for their existence, and for the fulfillment of the *given* possibilities.[2]

All the meanings and values that may be achieved in human life stand within an inexorable, inscrutable givenness. Human beings are God's creatures. Human existence roots in God's intention. Our lives un-fold and our projects take place before God and under the sway of God's will and purpose. Our destiny is shaped by God's steadfast love and invin-cible grace. The same love and purpose that give us being and sustain us in existence (besetting us behind and before, as Psalm 139 expresses it) move in, with, through, and among us toward the fulfillment of God's de-sign for his world and his children.

Now if that sounds all too familiar, all too traditional, all too unsatis-factory as we preach and teach and make our Christian witness in today's scientific and increasingly secular culture, consider what, of itself, the world has to offer. Sir John Polkinghorne has observed,

> On a cosmic scale, the history of the universe is a gigantic tug-of-war between the expansive force of the Big Bang, driving the galaxies apart, and the contractive force of gravity, pulling them together. These two effects are so evenly balanced that we cannot tell which will win.
>
> Accordingly, two alternative scenarios must be considered. If ex-pansion prevails, the galaxies now receding from each other will con-tinue to do so forever. Within each galaxy, gravity will bring about con-densation into enormous black holes which will eventually decay into low grade radiation through a variety of possible physical processes. On this scenario, the universe ends in a whimper. If, on the other hand, gravity prevails, the present expansion of the galaxies will one day be halted and reversed. What began with the Big Bang will end in the Big Crunch, as the whole universe collapses back into a singular cosmic melting pot.
>
> Neither of these catastrophes will happen tomorrow; they lie tens of billions of years into the future. Nevertheless, one way or the other,

the universe is condemned to ultimate futility, and humanity will prove to have been a transient episode in its history.[3]

Life evolves toward greater complexity and capacity, but nature is neither self-contained nor self-explanatory. History is a record of tragedy and triumph, of agony and glory, but history's meaning does not emerge from history's flux. Nature reaches its climax in humanity, and humanity flowers in personal relations and in community, but the final meaning of human life does not await us at the end of a process of development. Death waits at the end. We are finite and therefore are not self-sufficient, self-explanatory, or self-fulfilled.

Whatever of hope nature, history, or the human self may offer in a proximate or penultimate sense, in this let us rejoice and be glad. What continued scientific inquiry into the mysterious universe might encounter as "signals of transcendence," in the words of Peter Berger, let us by all means welcome for further exploration. However, any ultimate claim for the human prospect, the human possibility, the human future must be grounded in an ultimate reality — in the eternal God himself. Cosmic death and human death pose equivalent questions of what is God's intention for his creation and his children. What is at issue — the substance of our hope for years to come — is the faithfulness of God.

At its best, Christian faith stands for and works toward the highest and fullest development of the human self, for the fulfillment of God's design in human life and history. The Christian gospel, when rightly proclaimed, emphasizes that human beings, in relationship with God and one another, should experience genuine spontaneity of love and trust, and that they must come to know the meaning of justice, mercy, and community (Micah 6:8). The Christian ethic is an ethic of responsibility that puts concern for persons foremost because of the abundant revelation of God's concern for all of his children. It aims at the transformation of culture through the mind and will and heart of Jesus Christ.[4]

Christian faith is marked by high hopes and great expectations. It is confident of God's loving purpose for the human family and of God's ultimate victory over all that would obstruct and defeat the fulfillment of human life. It points to the sovereign grace of God, God's intent and concern made operable in the complex web of personal life and human community that moves in and among us and draws us into its mysterious working.[5] God's grace goes before us in all our crises, preparing our hearts for faith:

Through many dangers, toils, and snares I have already come . . .

Grace sustains us in all our doings, revealing nature and history as arenas of God's sacramental presence and providence:

'Tis grace has brought me safe thus far . . .

And grace enables us, with power and hope, for life's journey through death to destiny:

And grace will lead me home.

The essential quality of Christian living is a calm confidence in God's presence and action in life, giving meaning to all we can do with God's gifts and securing the values we have come to cherish through God's love. Faith is the acceptance of our being at God's hands and the dedication of our powers for service to God and humanity in this atmosphere of love and grace into which we have entered and which is already triumphantly manifest in Jesus Christ. This is the mode and manner of life that looks toward the full maturity of every individual life and of the total human community — never through cheap grace or indulgent love, never in disregard for the divine demands of justice, truth, and righteousness, never by a magical sleight of hand, and thus never without ordeal and judgment for unrighteousness — but always in the sovereign, eternal power of God, who is not defeated by human rebellion, not appeased by human "sacrifice," not impressed by human boasting, and who, out of a good and unswerving purpose, will bring his kingdom to its consummation and us to our true completeness.[6]

This is what eschatology means, and has meant from the beginning: that the justification and vindication of our lives — their meaning and value — are not in our hands, but in God's hands; not in good fortune or bad, but in God's kingdom of love and righteousness. In face of death — our own death and the death of the universe — our hope is not in some immortality we possess as natural endowment, nor in some moral ingenuity or achievement whereby we avoid a divine apocalyptic judgment that engulfs the earth. Rather, we trust that in the crucifixion and resurrection of Jesus Christ we have seen God's victory over the powers of evil, sin, and death. We claim the promise that because Christ lives we shall live also. And we rest in the assurance that our lives, and the lives of all of God's children, are "hid with Christ in God" (Col. 3:3).

Our ultimate confidence is not in ourselves, nor in nature, nor in history with its countless human achievements, but in God — who has made us for himself and "on purpose," and who will not leave his work unfinished. Through the divine initiative of love and grace and the faithful lives and intelligent actions of devoted women and men, God will yet bring to pass the consummation of his purposes for humankind — "the communion of saints" — in which God's children will find their human possibilities fully realized, in faith, in love, and beyond all hope.

So we believe, and so we pray:

> The Lord is good;
> > his steadfast love endures forever,
> > and his faithfulness to all generations.

(Psalm 100:5)

14. Eschatological Transfiguration of the Moral Life

JOSEPH DeROULHAC, JR.

*First Baptist Church of Redlands
Redlands, California*

*Eschatology sets beginnings under a promise that has ruptured
the chain of cause and effect and broken open a future that has
liberated freedom from the paralysis of the past.*[1]

Paul Lehmann

Christian eschatology explicates not simply the eschaton, that is, the last things or the destiny of all things, but it also illuminates the inner meaning of all time and space.[2] Eschatology opens us to the possibilities of the present and gives new meaning to our past. A realistic future hope empowers us to live fully and freely in the moment, allowing neither the hurts of the past nor apprehension and fear of the future to thwart our resolve and ability to seize the present as the arena of divine blessing and providence. The eschatological thrust of the Hebrew and Christian scriptures orients us in time and space, enabling us to experience the fullness of life here and now.

While everyone's outlook on life is shaped by some eschatological sensibility — either explicit or implicit — not all eschatological perspectives nourish the courage needed to confront creatively and compassionately the evil in this world and promote the good of all Creation. Many visions of the final end obscure the deeper possibilities of the present, deny the past of any real meaning or significance, and empty the future of any real hope. Apocalyptic scenarios, whether religious or secular, that announce the destruction of all that is have difficulty articulating the ultimate value of what has been and presently is. Such views pose a particularly acute problem for ethics. If what we do has no ultimate bearing, why strive for moral excellence? Moral courage in the face of evils that threaten to overcome us issues most readily from the hope that what we do matters in the eternal scheme of the cosmos. That moral reflection intricately bound to the eschatological emphasis of the Hebrew and Christian scriptures proffers such courage by anchoring moral action in God's final end for Creation.

An eschatological perspective on the moral life differs markedly from the wisdom traditions of the Ancient Near East and the classical traditions of Ancient Greece that typically establish moral norms from empirical observation. From the standpoint of eschatology, the moral life is not simply about what I am doing, but about what God is doing. As H. Richard Niebuhr argues, moral action is best understood as the fitting response to what God is doing in our world.[3] An eschatological grounding or morality allows us to explore what God is doing and how this relates to our own action. Moral action is understood not as the following of precepts or principles, but the opening of our lives and worlds to God's destiny. This transfiguration of the moral life arising from Hebrew prophecy and the teachings of Jesus helps us perceive the fullness of time and the importance of the moment for the cause of God in Creation.[4]

This paper explores how the eschatological understanding of the Hebrew and Christian scriptures helps us understand more clearly the relationship of God's end for Creation to the daily moral action of human beings. The argument will be made that through moral action human beings create time and space for God to accomplish the divine end for human existence amid the frailties of creaturely existence and the vicissitudes of history. Covenant faithfulness unlocks, for us, the inner dynamics of moral action and relates it to the end for which God creates the universe.

Toward a Transfigured Ethic

What does an ethic transfigured by the Bible's eschatological vision look like? First and foremost, this ethic always gives priority to the action of God in the world. This ethic will not assert itself as a means of accomplishing God's intention for Creation, but as the opening for God to come more fully and freely into the concerns and struggles of people in the here and now. This transfigured ethic recognizes that the *means* of God's end for the world will embody the *end* itself and that God's action defines the value of our lives and endeavors.

A transfigured ethic will concentrate upon trust. The issue will not be what course of action will be most effective or strategic, but how can one give God the most freedom and room to work for redemption and reconciliation. This ethic will be radically contextual, seeking to understand in each situation how God calls people to trust divine power and compassion. General rules may be formulated, but must never be seen as recipes. They are but examples of how people can open their lives, relationships, and endeavors to God's coming. Moral action in this sense cannot be separated from the spiritual intent of the heart, for the trust extended to God will be the avenue by which God will most fully and freely bring into actuality the ends of Creation in people's lives and the world.

The keynote of this transfigured ethic is faithfulness, the very basis of covenant relationships. As one seeks to understand what trusting God entails, covenant faithfulness will be the central focus — covenant faithfulness to God and all of Creation. This world was created for covenant faithfulness and through such faithfulness the end of God for our lives and world is fulfilled. As people relate to one another and to all Creation, trust in God is displayed by people's willingness to be faithful — to trust God to fulfill the promise of all their covenant relationships.[5] In this way, relationships with God and with all others are made integral, giving the moral life coherence and force.

Consider the issue of marriage. Marriage can be viewed from many different vantages — economic, social, and romantic perspectives, just to name a few. Marriage can also be viewed eschatologically from the vantage of a transfigured ethic. Marriage covenants can be conceived as the creation of time and space for God to accomplish in the hurts and hopes that couples share together over a lifetime the very ends for which God created them. Such eschatological understanding radically changes one's whole perspective on marriage. Relationships are enriched and cherished in new ways and new possibilities are explored and affirmed. Considering the social norms and expectations that shape marriage in a given society, a transfigured ethic will concentrate on how faithfulness is best expressed in the particular context of one's marriage, trusting God to fulfill the promise of this particular covenant. God is thereby given the opportunity to come into this covenant relationship in a new way, working for the divine end — the promise — of the marriage.

From this perspective, marriage is not simply two people seeking to be faithful to a covenant they have made to one another and to God, but the invitation for God to come into their relationship, the special time and space they have created together, and fulfill the divine end for it. The eternal goodness, wonder, joy, and love flowing from this relationship are not the work of the marriage partners but of God, who comes into the time and space they create to fulfill the promise of their relationship.

How faithfulness is expressed in different circumstances will require growing creativity and experience as well as trust. While the adjudication of conflicting loyalties will be a daily challenge, a transfigured ethic will take chances and be bold, exploring how people stand faithfully even in the most difficult circumstances. Since God's end involves the reconciliation of all Creation, Jesus' insistence that his followers love their enemies is critical.[6] Jesus' emphasis on faithfulness even to one's enemy demonstrates that every relationship has moral relevancy. Moreover, the difficulty of this moral mandate prevents people from ever believing God's final end for their lives has been realized this side of God's new heaven and new earth. But this mandate also spurs people to be ever ready for those occasions when God can come and do some new thing in their lives.[7]

Walter Wink recounts the story about a woman in bed being awakened by an intruder kicking open the door of her bedroom. In the fright of the moment, the woman, seeking to make personal contact on a more human level with her intruder, asks him what time it is. Startled, the intruder stops and she continues to make conversation. As they talk they become no longer strangers, and she feels safe to ask him to leave. When he says he has nowhere to go, she gives him a clean set of sheets and has him make his own bed downstairs. She shares, "He went downstairs and I sat up in bed, wide awake and shaking for the rest of the night. The next morning we ate breakfast together and he left."[8]

How best is this story understood? The woman exhibited a surprising creativity in the face of violence. Instead of reacting to the violence the intruder intended, she treated him with a presumption of civility or even friendship, engaging him as fellow struggler.

> I realized with a certain clarity that either he and I made it through this situation safely — together — or we would both be damaged. Our safety was connected. If he raped me, I would be hurt both physically and emotionally. If he raped me he would be hurt as well. If he went to prison, the damage would be greater. That thought disarmed me. It freed me from my own desire to lash out and at the same time from my own paralysis. It did not free me from feelings of fear but from fear's control over my ability to respond. I found myself acting out of a concern for both our safety which caused me to react with a certain firmness but with surprisingly little hostility in my voice.[9]

From the standpoint of a transfigured ethic, the woman sought the opportunity to be faithful to this stranger even in the face of great harm. While there is a danger of presumptuousness, this is the kind of situation in which God can come, working toward the divine end of Creation.

Should this woman's response to her intruder be a general rule for all women being attacked? Being radically contextual, a transfigured ethic would say no. Her story serves as an example and inspiration that courage, creativity, and compassion are powerful forces in our world and that ultimately our willingness to trust God — the power that brought us into being — to fulfill the end of our lives can change the course of an attack or, when necessary, heal the wounds of violence.[10]

Conclusion

An ethic transfigured by the eschatological vision of the Scriptures is not only descriptively illuminating but also prescriptively imaginative. Created in the image of God, who creates time and space, people are empowered with the ability to create time and space. Every day people create specific times and particular spaces for appointments, errands, recreation, meditation, and more. People also have the opportunity to create time and space for God to work more fully and freely in their lives and world. While God is always faithful, God's self-limitation in love compels God to wait for people to prepare the way for God to accomplish more fully the ends for which all that is has been created.

In an eschatological ethic, only God accomplishes the divine end of Creation. As beings created in the image of God, people have the privilege of participating with God in the divine drama of new creation. People are never puppets, for God has so limited the divine sovereignty as to bestow upon humanity the dignity of free choice. While people's choices may squeeze God out of their lives, these choices cannot squeeze God out of the world. The resurrection of Jesus demonstrates this fact very clearly. But when people choose to invite God to come and fulfill the end of their lives, relationships, and endeavors, their experience on this side of God's new heaven and earth is not simply provisional, but proleptic of God's end for Creation in this time and space.

There are moments in life when the ordinary concerns of daily living recede before the need to reclaim God's faithfulness for all time. The Psalms are full of such laments that cry for God's faithfulness to become an active reality in the deepest night people experience.[11] A transfigured ethic challenges us to not wait for the deepest night, but to see every day, every relationship, and every endeavor as an opportunity to invoke God's coming in power and in love. The transfiguration of the moral life occurs as we realize that the God who acts definitively at the end of history also acts decisively within history and Creation. A transfigured understanding of the moral life arises from the discovery within history of a promising God whose gracious power is ever active creating, sustaining, and fulfilling. Moral action opens the door for this God to work more fully and freely in our lives and world.

PART TWO

ETERNAL LIFE

CHAPTER IV

Theology-Science Dialogue

Introduction

As freely acknowledged in the Introduction to John Polkinghorne and Michael Welker's collection *The End of the World and the Ends of God*, the Center's choice of "eschatology" as a parallel theme in its Research Consultation/Pastor-Theologian Program represents a conscious decision to give the dialogue between theology and science a genuinely *theological* focus. Earlier interdisciplinary teams repeatedly found that though both theology and science made truth and reality claims in the public sector, it was far too simplistic to caricature their mutual relation with such cultural clichés as (1) theology deals with realities unseen, science with visible reality; (2) theology deals with feelings, science deals with facts; and (3) theology deals with personal certainty, science with objective truths.

The lines of contrast simply cannot always be drawn so sharply: what is opposition here is complementarity there; mystery abounds everywhere, whether in the Eucharist or in quarks. Certainly in terms of biblical and creedal Christianity, one cannot exclusively correlate all theology with theism and all science with atheism. Many theologies are scientific and some sciences are at least metaphysical if not theological. Rather, careful research or eschatology discloses several shared concerns among persons of faith and those of no faith. Moreover, many religious persons are not theologically orthodox Christians, while many at work in the scientific professions are. It is likely the common search for truth about final and ultimate reality that drives this interdisciplinary dialogue in all its fascinating dimensions.

The thesis of Paul Wee's excerpt "Breaking the Cycle of Conflict" is that "the primary tension between science and religion, both historically and in the context of contemporary debate, has come about when these symbols and myths have lost their representational character and have instead come to be viewed as literal descriptions of reality itself." In brief, "fundamentalists" on both sides of the dialogue must become more modest in "their claims to know and describe what is really real." A historical reflection sketches some major philosophical struggles between science and religion (including those involving Copernicus, Bacon, Newton, Kant, Darwin, and Einstein). Hume and Mach have helped to de-absolutize the alleged "eternal truths" of both disciplines. All language provides "symbolic representations rather than literal descriptions of reality." A test case on the teaching of creationism and/or evolution in the Kansas public schools provides a current illustration of an unnecessary dilemma in a pluralistic society.

Richard Coleman affirms that the God of the big picture is also the same God of the small future, cosmically and personally, in the excerpt of his article on "The Beginning and the End." The church must still proclaim "a God of purpose, design, and providence in an age where science, as the dominant epistemology, projects a picture of cosmic futility and doom." The author depicts science and theology as "sibling rivals" in the quest for ultimate truth (rather than as consonant partners). Galileo and Newton changed the way we perceive the cosmos, and theology accommodated itself to a new view of the world. However, their new method of coming to know (epistemology) brought with it a new, anthropocentric worldview. In the face of human sin and evil, however, there is always a need to contrast the qualitative and teleological difference between a scientific outlook and Christian hope: "Jesus' resurrection surely bears cosmic significance because it protests the law that entropy is the last word."

In "Christian Eschatology: Prescription for Life," Byron Bangert claims that at its best, Christian eschatology "serves to help us live in the face of the knowledge that we and all things created will die." Eternal life therefore enables us to view death "as a form of blessing." Not forever will the wicked prosper. All that is within the providence of God will be transformed. Nevertheless, "the beginning and the ending of the universe is unfathomable." Even astrophysics reverts to mythological symbolism ("Big Bang" and "Big Crunch") in begging the question of the Absolute Beginning and the Absolute End. Whether in theology or in science, "imaginable possibilities boggle the mind." It is solely in the joy of existence that we are offered "tokens and foretastes" of what we may believe about "the Source and End of all existence."

Charles Valenti-Hein illustrates in "God's Time and Our Time in a Time of Science" how the scientific way of marking and measuring time is normatively misleading for other disciplines, notably theology. Insecure humans become obsessed by time and its quantitative gain or loss. In our preoccupation with chronologically identifiable and limited beginnings and endings *(chronos)*, we lose any real sense of the measuring of the whole *(kairos)*. The author suggests that different understandings of temporality complicate the relations between theology and science. While they are formally incommensurate, they are not necessarily incompatible or irreconcilable. This is illustrated in the function of memory within both disciplines, whether or not as a fundamental bearer of eschatological promise.

Deborah Clemens affirms the governing christological norm for all Christian hope in her essay on "Incarnation and Eschatology." Her comprehensive claim: "Christ is the key to the Christian understanding of Creation, and Christ is the key to our understanding of covenant and salvation. Christ is also the essential key in interpreting the Apocalypse. The assurance of the coming glory at the end of time is staked in the doctrine of the Incarnation. It is Christ who was the agent of Creation. It is Christ who holds the universe in organic connection. It is Christ who guarantees rapture in his Second Coming."

The author's paean of praise is developed in compiling such selective biblical terms as Apocalypse (Rev. 1:7-8), Second Coming (Matt. 25:31-32a), Consummation (Luke 1:34-35a), and Rapture (1 Thess. 4:17-18). The conclusion (Rom. 8:38-39) reiterates the conviction that only a comprehensive theology of the Incarnation can properly interpret the Eschaton for Christians. Through God's *kenosis* and Christ's resurrection, a new creation came into existence that will gloriously consummate all Christian hope in the Eschaton.

15. Breaking the Cycle of Conflict

PAUL A. WEE

Church Consultant
Alexandria, Virginia

Introduction

The apologetic task of the church concerns itself with the defense of faith from the attacks made against it. It seeks to respond to existential questions posed by people who ask, "Why doesn't God intervene and help me?" or "What does my life mean?" or "Is there a purpose to our history?" It seeks also to respond to questions raised by the disciplines, such as, "Is God not merely a projection?" (psychology) or "How can the idea of God find compatibility with the laws of nature?" (natural science).

It can be said that every sermon preached and every course in Christian education taught in the congregation is apologetic in the sense that it seeks to give an answer to questions implied in the human condition or in the present historical situation. Apologetic theology presupposes that there is point of contact *(Anknüpfungspunkt)* between the Word and the world, between the eternal message of God's grace and the questions that arise out of the ever-changing cultural milieu. It asks about the integrity of knowledge, how the claims of the Christian faith "integrate" with other claims to knowledge, whether of the humanities or the social or natural sciences. At base the question is this: do these claims contradict or do they complement each other?

This is not a new question. Yet in recent times it has been framed most starkly in the public debates on the relative merits of creationism's claim that God's creation of the world contradicts natural science's explanation of human evolution over a long period of time through a process of natural selection. This debate found one focus in the decision of the Kansas Board of Education (August 1999) to eradicate references to evolutionary theory from the science curriculum in the public schools in that state. The assumption behind this action was that there is a contradiction between the claims of evolutionary theory and the confession of faith that "in the beginning God created the heavens and the earth."

These claims, according to the board, are not complementary or otherwise reconcilable, but contradictory and irreconcilable. For the sake of integrity one must opt for either one or the other, but not both.

Behind the debate between so-called creationists and those espousing a form of evolutionary theory rest sometimes unexamined assumptions about how we know or believe something to be true. There are also assumptions about the nature of language, especially its ability to represent the way God relates to the world. Often the issue of language takes the form of a question: are the creation accounts to be understood literally or symbolically? Yet the action of the Board of Education also raises a question about the meaning of faith. Does faith entail the acceptance of a proposition as being a true description of factual reality, implying an accurate correspondence between a descriptive statement and what really is? Or is faith something different, something more subjective?

Both religion and science make claims about the origin and end of the world, about how things began and how they will end. Such claims have been made by both primitive and advanced civilizations. Given the fact that no simple and direct verification of such claims is possible (no one observed the creation of the world, and the end of the world has not yet occurred), both science and religion have resorted to theories, including models, metaphors, symbols, and myths, to convey that which is clearly beyond empirical verification. In science these include the Big Bang and the Big Crunch; in religion, they include *Creatio ex Nihilo*, the Eschaton, the Second Coming, and the resurrection of the body.

It is the thesis of this paper that the primary tension between science and religion, both historically and in the context of contemporary debate, has come about when these symbols and myths have lost their representational character and have instead come to be viewed as literal descriptions of reality itself. The only way to move beyond the irreconcilable conflict that results when symbols are robbed of their symbolic character — what might be termed "fundamentalism," whether of religion or science — is for both science and religion to be more modest in their claims to know and describe what is really real. This is to insist, with St. Paul, that "now we see through a mirror dimly," and with Gotthold Lessing, that "the pure truth is for God alone."[1] It will also be necessary for both science and religion to draw a sharper distinction between explaining or describing truth, on the one hand, and understanding truth on the other.

PAUL A. WEE

The Dilemma: A Historical Reflection

A brief overview of the historical tension between science and religion reveals a trend that has been both fascinating and fatal.[2] This trend might be characterized as follows: (1) a new scientific theory is introduced; (2) it is met with skepticism and hostility by theologians and philosophers because it is seen to be at variance with the way they understand the world; (3) in time, however, the theory becomes accepted and the disagreement is, at least momentarily, overcome; (4) but then the philosophers and theologians rush in to absolutize the new theory, that is, to declare its eternal veracity; (5) this absolutizing in turn makes it more difficult for a new scientific theory to be introduced; (6) when a new theory is introduced, it is treated with skepticism by theologians and philosophers because it does not conform to the old principles.

The tendency to ascribe an absolute or eternal status to theories about the physical universe has been detrimental to both science and religion throughout Western history. In the mid-sixteenth century, Copernicus introduced his understanding of the heliocentric universe, a theory that stood in stark contradiction to the commonly accepted geocentric view of Ptolemy. The Copernican theory was met with immediate hostility, not because it appeared to be at variance with observed phenomena or because its mathematical calculations were demonstrated to be false, but rather because it contradicted the existing biblical worldview and the accepted principles of Aristotelian physics and philosophy. Scholastic theologians had made the distinction between scientific truth and philosophical truth, the former being subject to experimentation, the latter subject to compatibility with established principles. Since pieces of the earth fall downward along a straight line, it was argued, the earth cannot itself have a circular motion. In the mid-seventeenth century, the Inquisition condemned the theories of Copernicus as being philosophically false. Similarly, Francis Bacon, considered to be the father of empirical science, accused Copernicus of not caring "what fictions he introduced into nature" because his theories contradicted the "one type of matter — one type of motion" principle of Aristotle.

With the advent of Newtonian physics the cycle repeats itself. Both the law of inertia and the law of gravitation were considered "philosophically absurd" by seventeenth-century philosopher and physicist Gottfried von Leibnitz when they were introduced, simply because they contradicted the general principles established by Aristotle and Democritus and confirmed by Descartes. Even though Newton's theories were based on extensive experimentation and observation and were subject to artic-ulation through precise mathematical models, the leading philosophers and theologians of the day considered them fallacious. It was only when Newtonian principles were confirmed over time through a wide range of experiments that the attitude gradually changed.

But no sooner had they gained credence in intellectual circles than the philosophers and theologians rushed in to baptize them as eternally valid principles. Immanuel Kant claimed that the law of inertia was easily demonstrable from pure reason. Even though the physical theories could theoretically be altered when new facts were introduced that were not compatible with the accepted theory, it was very difficult to do so be-cause the philosophical principles on which the theory rested were con-sidered part of the eternal forms of the human understanding. The petri-fying or absolutizing of philosophical principles has inhibited the ability of new experiential observations to call older physical theories into ques-tion.

By the mid-nineteenth century, the laws of inertia and gravity had be-come firmly established physical and philosophical principles. All new the-ories had to be demonstrated to be in harmony with them. And since ac-cepted principles were demonstrable through pure reason, it became very difficult for any future discovery to call them in question. A physical theory had become absolutized as an eternally valid philosophical principle.

The cycle repeated itself yet again with the advent of relativity and quantum theory in the early twentieth century. Advances in physics, based on innovation in technology and experimental method, began to erode a number of assumptions behind Newtonian physics. Yet once again the task of gaining acceptance for the new theories was made diffi-cult by the fact that the Newtonian laws of physics had become sanctified as eternally valid philosophical principles.

The disagreement between religion and science has stemmed in large measure from the tendency of theologians and philosophers to absolutize the physical theories of the scientists. Again, it is this absolutizing, that is, petrifying by presuming to be part of an "eternal philosophy," that has made it difficult for new theories to be advanced that call the old theories, theories that are no longer capable of account-ing for physical experiences, into question.

This brings us back to the decision of the Kansas Board of Education to disallow all teaching that supports the theory of the evolutionary development of humankind. Those who advocate creationism as the sole acceptable "scientific" description of the beginning of the world rest their case on a type of worldview that has been petrified and absolutized by fundamentalist theologians. Once this type of understanding of God's creating has become endowed with eternal and absolute validity, it becomes difficult if not impossible to introduce new evidence that might call such an understanding into question. Where new evidence is discovered it is frequently bludgeoned into the pre-established system of truth that has been made absolute and unchanging by the theologians.

Preserving the Integrity of Religion and Science

With the advance of relativity and quantum theory there emerged a new approach to science and its philosophy that sought to break in principle the need to endow scientific theory with absolute or eternal meaning. In essence this new approach, which built upon the empiricism of David Hume and his rejection of any "necessary" connections between ideas and matters of fact, said that the very language of "eternal truth" or "absolute reality" was inappropriate to the scientific enterprise. This new approach was also built on a rejection of the Kantian notion that the human mind imposed certain unchangeable forms or patterns of experience onto the physical world. Where Kant claimed, for example, that the mind organized our experiences according to eternally valid principles of Euclidean geometry, Henri Poincaré and others were beginning to reject the existence of eternally valid principles altogether.

Where Newton, following philosophers and scientists since the time of Lucretius, believed that atoms constituted the basic element of the reality of the entire material universe as God created it, physicists such as Ernst Mach (1838-1916) were unwilling to make any claim that purported to speak of "reality" itself. According to Mach, "atoms cannot be perceived by the senses; like all substances, they are things of thought."[3] Where Newton, in his "Rules of Reasoning in Philosophy," claimed that "the qualities of bodies, which admit neither intensification or remission of degrees, and which are found to belong to all bodies within the reach of our experiments, are to be esteemed the universal qualities of all bodies whatever,"[4] Mach disagreed. Since "atoms cannot be perceived by the senses," it is both absurd and unnecessary to claim that they comprise the actual constituency of bodies. Rather, "they are things of thought," a "mental artifice . . . especially devised for the purpose in view." In other words, atomic theory is a convenient fiction that helps to explain the way the physical world functions.

To assume that such a model is an accurate description of reality as such, and that it is absolute truth, however, is to make an unwarranted — and quite unnecessary — leap. The moment a given model for the atom becomes absolutized, that is, considered a valid description of the structure of all matter, the more difficult it will be for new theories to be advanced that call into question such an understanding.

For Mach and the positivists who followed, the test for whether or not a particular scientific theory is valid is whether, on the basis of the theory, certain empirically verifiable conclusions can be drawn. Rejected in this approach is the need for any reference to absolutes, eternally valid principles, or even reality itself. The use of one particular reference system over another to explain the functioning of natural phenomena is governed, one might say, by its symbolic value. Even the geocentric system of Ptolemy might in principle be acceptable to explain the motion of the universe, if from it certain conclusions could be deduced that could be verified through empirical means. The Copernican system proved to be more helpful, or "economical" as Mach would say, only because its implications — the conclusions that follow from it — were able to survive the scrutiny of empirical observation and experimentation.

What conclusions can be drawn from this brief analysis of a dilemma that has led to so much dissension and even suffering in the stormy history of the interaction between religion and science? The major conclusion is this: science and religion are able to coexist with integrity to the extent to which their respective assertions are considered to be symbolic representations rather than literal descriptions of reality.

For science this means that its theories on, for example, the origin of the universe will be understood as offering models that explain the functioning of physical phenomena. If from such models (e.g. kinetic theory based on billiard ball analogy, liquid drop picture of the nucleus of the atom) conclusions can be deduced that can be tested by empirical means, such models will be considered useful. If such models, on the other hand, are understood to be descriptions of reality as such, with an implied absolute validity, they will only serve to be a stumbling block to the introduction of new theories that might be capable of revealing a new understanding of the way the world functions. Of such models Ian Barbour rightly maintains that they are "to be taken seriously but not literally." Furthermore, the claim of such models to be literal descriptions of reality itself is bound to lead to collision and contradiction with the claims of religion.

But what can be said about the claims of religion? Here the conclusion is in principle precisely the same: the claims of religious symbols to express reality itself will only lead to collision with the claims of science. The language employed to express the most profound claims about God and the world must also be understood to be symbolic, by nature unable to capture or contain the fullness of the reality itself. The creation accounts of Genesis 1 and 2 are to be understood as historically conditioned symbolic and mythological expressions of the *meaning* of God's creating activity. Even the expression "God" is to be considered a symbolic expression of an ultimate reality that the term "God" can point to but not contain.

The decision of the Kansas Board of Education was based on misconceptions about the nature and role of both science and religion. Once these respective roles are clarified, it might be possible for students in Kansas schools to pursue with integrity the discipline of science, including theories of evolution, and also to confess with St. Paul that "in [Christ] all things *(ta panta)* in heaven and earth were created, things visible and invisible, whether thrones or dominions or rulers or powers — all things have been created through him and for him" (Colossians 1:16).

16. *The Beginning and the End*

RICHARD J. COLEMAN

First Congregational Church
Plympton, Massachuestts

"I am the Alpha and the Omega, the beginning and the end."

Rev. 21:6

"If for this life only we have hoped in Christ, we are of all people most to be pitied."

I Cor. 15:19

The popular impression is that when science speaks of ultimate things (eschatology), the picture is one of cosmic futility leading to despair. But how grim is it when such ultimate catastrophes are extremely remote? We are burdened with so many immediate concerns that what might happen 50 million years from now is of little or no significance. Nevertheless, beginnings and endings have a profound effect upon how one views the mid-range of time and space (the lifetime of three generations). We can express this connection by affirming that the God of the big picture is the God of the small picture. The creator of the universe is, after all, my creator; the God present at the beginning of time and space is the same God present at my birth. The way the universe began and the way the universe ends do affect the hope I have, or do not have, to live the next day. This paper, then, is an inquiry into how we proclaim a God of purpose, design, and providence in an age in which science, as the dominant cultural epistemology, projects a picture of cosmic futility and doom.

Theology and Science as Sibling Rivals

Beginnings and endings received a good deal of attention in the three-year consultation on eschatology sponsored by the Center of Theological

Inquiry. Many of the resulting twenty-three essays, published as John Polkinghorne and Michael Welker's *The End of the World and the Ends of God,* probed the relationship between theology and science.[1] I would like to do some further probing for two reasons: (1) we underestimate the extent to which science shapes the fundamental stories we tell (our view of the world) and (2) the standard models for conversation between theology and science are questionable.

In her essay "Eschatology with a Future?" Kathryn Tanner mentions and rejects an approach that would incorporate the facts of science by arguing, "God might indeed use the old world's destruction, as the scientists describe it, as a purgative means to a new heaven and earth."[2] Tanner then successfully repositions Christian eschatology so that it is not primarily about end-time predictions. No longer is there a preoccupation with how or when the universe will end (cold or hot, soon or unknown). Eschatology, she argues, deserves a more comprehensive framework than simply the future, because its central tenet is "an ongoing redemptive relationship to God that holds for the world of the past, present and future." The important question is not when the world will end but "absent of a vision of this world to come, what motivates and helps sustain action in history for a better world over the long haul?"[3]

But I wonder if we can so easily decouple the Christian view of the world from the scientific picture. What Tanner has not addressed is the much more powerful and subtle linkage between a dominant scientific rationality and the way we view the world. In his essay "Propositional and Attitudinal Aspects of Eschatology", Fraser Watts remarks:

> Bringing scientific predictions about the future of the universe into dialogue with eschatology can lead to a misrepresentation of eschatology as being more concerned with the scientific future than it really is. However, to say that eschatology has nothing whatsoever to say about the scientific future may misrepresent it in a different direction.[4]

Watts also remarks that it is "clear that Christian eschatology operates in a very different world from scientific predictions about the future of the universe."[5] The point of conflict between theology and science — if we dare to go that far — is about a prediction mentality and how it is inextricably linked with empiricism and optimism. Tanner fully recognizes that Christian eschatology is foremost about hope, and it is this hope that stays the Christian in the effort "to alleviate despair in the face of present injustice and suffering." If scientific optimism and Christian hope are not exactly on the same page, I would caution against moves that reposition one or the other in order to soften their disparities.

In his essay "Hope and Creation," Hans Weder represents another common conversational model. He begins by giving the reason why theology and science cannot ignore one another. "Theology is the methodological and hermeneutical reflection of what faith gives us to think."[6] He continues by saying that knowledge of God does not exist without knowledge of the world and knowledge of the self; "That is why theology, trying to grasp the knowledge of God that faith has given, has an indispensable relationship to natural science, describing the function and the structures of the world."[7] Weder is right to insist that the nature and explanation of the universe are a legitimate place for theology to test her understanding of God's nature.

A theme in Weder's essay is that theology does not contradict a natural scientific description, but enhances it. For instance, theology would enrich a metabolic description of life (excreting, breathing, reproducing, eating, etc.) with its understanding of a bodily existence as primarily constituted by relationship to others, to the world, and to God. In this way theology provides a deeper interpretation and prevents science from sinking too far into reductionism. Science, on the other hand, keeps theology honest by not allowing her to escape into speculation or to become dogmatic. Weder concludes, "It is the task of natural science to prevent theology from compulsive strategies, and it is the task of theology to remind science of the freedom to deeper interpretations and to prevent it in this way from the temptation of reductionism." I wonder, though, if reminding will do much to change the way scientists think or function. Weder writes, "the hope of eternal life implies a qualitative difference from natural life" because it embodies "traces of the eternal that can be perceived in the realm of natural life," but will science acknowledge a transcendent dimension to life?[8]

My depiction of science and theology as sibling rivals is a departure from the standard model of rapprochement. Nancey Murphy has pushed the discussion of how science and theology could interact to a new level in *Theology in the Age of Scientific Reasoning* (Ithaca: Cornell University Press, 1990). She argues that theology is potentially methodologically indistinguishable from the sciences. This is a significant step beyond the comparative-contrast approach represented so well by Ian Barbour, because it makes methodology the focal point. It is not an entirely new move, however. Since the triumph of empiricism as the "episteme" that defines modernity, theology has been trying to incorporate a similar model of empiricism in order to regain her lost status.

Murphy's model of Imre Lakotos's scientific research programs, then, is the culmination of the drive toward a shared methodology. Since then the momentum toward consonance has solidified and has become the preferred model.[9] The problem with consonance is its inherent tendency to dull cutting edges. I propose the conversation that will bear the greatest fruit will be one in which theology and science challenge each other in such a way as to expose the limitations, incoherencies, and poverty of resources that can be identified only from outside each tradition, since Alasdair MacIntyre has clearly shown that every knowledge tradition is self-authenticating on the basis of its own standards of what constitutes truth.[10]

John Polkinghorne and Michael Welker suggest "the sciences and theology share a cousinly relationship in the common search for truth and reality."[11] I would go further. Within this familial context, theology would be the first born, the former queen of the sciences. Science is the upstart younger sibling who has caught up and surpassed the eldest. Philosophy is the middle child, brokering disputes, clarifying and demanding further clarification on the part of the younger and older siblings. During science's ascendancy to the throne of intellectual queen there were skirmishes, but for the most part they were rivals contesting various paradigms: the metaphysics of perfection vs. principles of mathematics; special creation vs. natural selection; providence vs. progress.

In the nineteenth century there came a point when the conversation between science and theology virtually ceased. The primary reason was the simple fact that science had dethroned theology as queen because it demonstrated a superior methodology: empiricism. Theology was not silenced, but she no longer had an authoritative word to speak when it came to the nature of what is real. What happened can be described by making the distinction between a view of the world and a worldview. Galileo and Newton changed the way we picture the cosmos, and theology learned to accommodate a new view of the world. Galileo and Newton also introduced a new method of coming to know, which eventually became a new worldview. Michel Foucault's explanation of an *episteme* is very helpful here. An episteme is a communal definition of what is knowable. It is a historical a priori definition that in a given period "defines the conditions of possibility of all knowledge, whether expressed in a theory or silently invested in a practice." An episteme, then, is both conscious and unconscious and defines the "conditions of possibility" concerning what is true. While paradigms govern a specific field of science or theology, an episteme involves the idea of science or theology itself. Paradigms guide research; *epistemes* provide them the epistemology, logic, and assumptions that make research possible.[12]

I began this essay with the question: Why is it that the same science that expounds a cosmic futility seems to be immune from cosmic despair? Richard Dawkins exhibits the same optimism characteristic of most scientists. It seems there are very few pessimistic scientists. The reason for this is not hard to find: science is driven by a methodology that is confident it will succeed — if not today then tomorrow. In quite a few essays in *The End of the World and the Ends of God,* Christian hope is set apart and contrasted with scientific optimism and profane hopes. It is a worthy endeavor and one that I would like to extend.

Science is inherently optimistic, while the Christian faith is inherently hopeful. We can press this comparison still further by examining the ultimate hope of each. Idealistically, scientists hope to work toward world peace, the end of hunger and disease, a more complete understanding of the universe. These are all worthy endeavors shared by most everyone. What makes them part of the domain of science is the optimism that by human endeavor they can be realized. They become "futures" we can predict and hope for, because they are predictions based upon a confidence that with the proper application of scientific discoveries the world, and human beings, can be made new.

The contrast between Christian hope and scientific optimism is the difference between a transient emotion and a state of readiness.[13] It would be unfair to say that science does not inspire hope. It is, though, a hope on a short tether. Science inspires optimism because it has no doubt that it will take us to the next frontier (the very warning of Crichton's *Jurassic Park*). And so we "advance" by grasping one rope after another, but each rope is suspended in midair.

Janet Soskice speaks to the core characteristic of Christian hope when she writes that hope, like faith and love, *abides,* and it endures "even in the midst of profound evil, and without ignoring that profound evil."[14] Likewise, Fraser Watts comments, "Indeed, hope characteristically occurs in situations of darkness and uncertainty in which optimism would be impossible or out of place."[15] Hope abides because it is not tethered to a visible or predictable future. Its teleological end is not the Rapture or the transformation of the earth. Jesus' resurrection surely bears cosmic significance because it protests the law that entropy is the last word. The decay of matter is not the "sting" that throws us into the darkness of cosmic futility. God's ultimate purpose is not dependent upon humankind or planet Earth; that would render God small and human beings gigantic. Christian hope abides because of the particular faith that nothing can separate us from the love of God, including things present, things to come, life, death, powers, principalities, or anything else in all creation (Romans 8:38-39).

Science can also afford to rebuff beginnings and endings as inconsequential because it is teleologically bankrupt, and consequentially it can only enjoin local or short narratives.[16] Once you eliminate teleological purpose, not much of any story can be told. The narrative that science does manage to tell is one of evolution blindly groping (natural selection) punctuated by emergent probabilities such as the beginning of life. Beginnings and endings, as well as the in-between, become important only when there are connections to be made and emergent events disclose information about the larger narrative. Science provides important raw material (facts) for the story about the universe and our place in it. But science has a particular epistemological-ontological fit that excludes many of the perennial questions necessary for a full understanding. Because God is God of both the big and the small, the beginning and the end, the Christian tradition, as Donald Juel eloquently states, "has everything invested . . . in the character of the one who makes promises."[17]

It is no trifle that sin and evil do not show up on science's radar; nor are they topics at scientific symposiums. As the new queen of the intellectual world, science has no rival. Its reign of technological progress is rooted in the triumph of empiricism as the dominant epistemology of the modern era. The fruit or content of empiricism is progress. What constitutes its progress is unambiguous. For many its hope is material gain. For others it is accruing technological knowledge. For everyone it is the hope of a better tomorrow. What will we become if that hope is wrapped in an optimism that denies sin and discounts evil? It matters greatly how our story begins and how we think it will end, and we should not dare believe science and theology tell the same story.

17. Christian Eschatology: Prescription for Life

BYRON C. BANGERT

Presbytery of Ohio Valley
Bloomington, Indiana

I would suggest that Christian eschatology at its best serves to help us live in the face of the knowledge that we and all creatures will die. It does so in ways that may appear somewhat paradoxical. For one thing, the meaningfulness of life, its vitality and purpose, are related in a very important sense to the fact that one's own life will have an end. This end signifies a point of closure, beyond which one is not called to plan or labor. The various parts of the story of one's life will ultimately converge, or at least cease to undergo development and change. Each of us can hope to come to the point where we can say, "It is finished!" We have fulfilled our calling. We have done what was set before us, fought the good fight, and kept the faith.

Granted, many lives do not end on such a note of affirmation. The point is that knowing we will die does give meaning to our years in terms of an envisioned closure and completion. We do not have to go on forever, knowing that our labors are never to be completed, that like Sisyphus, the stone we have rolled up the hill will need to be rolled up again and again and ever again. People who have had near-death experiences often speak of how precious and joyous each day becomes, now that they know in a more vivid and compelling way that their lives will not last forever. And for those whose lives are filled with suffering, the envisioned end of this life may be seen as a blessing. They do not have to keep faith, or maintain integrity (as did Job), forever.

Moreover, the personal aspects of traditional Christian eschatology demand that we embrace human finitude. As Hans Weder observes in his essay "Hope and Creation,"

> The Christian concept of resurrection, which has risen in the context of early Jewish eschatological insights, cannot think of an eternal life that has not undergone death. Thus, finitude (death) is at least a necessary presupposition of eternal life, if not an important element of it in

113

the sense that a pure eternal life can only come after death as the end of any human fight against truth and purity. . . . The life of the risen Christ had . . . a quality that differs in a qualitative way from any earthly life. The most predominant difference is the character of eternity, that is of not being subjected to finitude any more. . . . As a consequence of Christology the Christian eschatological concept of life after death had an extremely positive relationship to finitude. The qualitative newness of eternal life cannot do without the radical end of temporal life. This implies a specific and positive understanding of finitude.[1]

One need not share every theological commitment that seems implied in this statement in order to recognize the general force of Weder's argument. Whatever else may be understood by Christian resurrection, it surely implies a qualitative newness of life that also requires us to view death in larger perspective as a form of blessing.

The knowledge that there will be an end also has a moral significance that helps sustain our existence. Not forever will the wicked prosper. Not forever will the righteous suffer and endure misfortune. At the very least, we are thus assured that the ultimate dispensation of things does not include an ultimate, absolute, or enduring acceptance of the moral injustices, inequalities, and disparities of earthly existence that mark our temporal condition. This is so whether or not we also believe that beyond the grave lies another dispensation of rewards and punishments that will reverse and rectify the injustices of this life. The last word on wickedness may be death, or it may be worse than death, but it assuredly is not life.

But what is the last word on righteousness, or goodness, or faith? What is the last word on life itself? It is difficult enough to imagine one's own non-existence. It is even more difficult to imagine the non-existence of all that one cherishes and loves. What ultimately happens to the goodness that we know, experience, see, taste, touch, feel, enjoy? Christian eschatology, at its best, does not envision the destruction of all that is within the providence of God, but rather its transformation. Nonetheless, it acknowledges the reality of radical destruction of temporal expressions of goodness: people suffer horribly and often die without fulfillment, nature is ravaged, species are decimated, the beauty of the world is scarred beyond recognition. Simply imagine what it must have been like, and what it would be like again, for an asteroid to strike this planet as may have happened 65 million years ago, when so much was destroyed. Some

Christians would say that God would never let that sort of thing happen again. Or they would say that if it should happen, God would re-populate the world. In short, life will go on, and the wonders of creation as we know them will not cease.

The biblical view, however, is that "heaven and earth will pass away."[2] It is in any case much too glib to suppose that life as we know it will never cease. Even if it were in God's power to preserve humanity indefinitely, God would hardly be obliged to keep us on retainer forever. This is not to say that we necessarily need a Christian eschatology that envisions radical destruction as a part of God's plan and purpose. It is at least as problematic to maintain that the Creator may intend the destruction of the creation as it is to assert that God will never countenance our destruction.[3] But should the end of life as we know it come to pass, Christian eschatology affirms that God would be able from whatever remains "to raise up children to Abraham."[4] Not that these children would ever know Abraham, or even resemble Abraham in any recognizable way; only that the possibility for conscious, intelligent life coming into existence in some future place and time must be considered to be within the realm of divine providence. Indeed, once this is understood, it must be considered to be within the realm of divine possibility that there already have existed or now exist such forms of life elsewhere within the universe.

What can be said from this perspective is that all of the endings we can envision for ourselves and all that we cherish receive their ultimate meaning and significance from God, who "lays to heart" all that is precious in creation.[5] Nothing good is lost on God. So long as we believe in the continuing presence and work of God as creator of the universe, we can make this affirmation in the context of all eschatological visions regarding the world as we know it. The Apostle Paul affirmed that "from God and through God and to God are all things. To God be the glory forever!"[6] All things find their source and end in God, the Alpha and Omega. All life, indeed all existence, is "in God."

This brings us to the threshold of what is historically unique about the intellectual challenge to Christian eschatology, and Christian faith, in our times. The thought of our own individual beginnings and endings is difficult. The thought of the beginning and ending of life and the world as we know it is thoroughly bracing. But the thought of the beginning and ending of the universe is unfathomable — at least I cannot fathom it. For many scientists, the great mystery is that there is something and not nothing. It seems no less a mystery to think that, there having been something, there could ever be nothing. The Big Bang theory of the universe may provide a believable account of the origins of our universe, but in many respects it begs the larger question of the *absolute* beginning. After all, if our universe got started with such a bang 12-15 billion years ago, what was happening before then? What existed before then? And if this universe will ultimately some day burn up and die out, or collapse back in upon itself, then what? Surely that does not answer the question of an *absolute* end.

There are certain kinds of questions that our ways of thinking make impossible to answer. For example — assuming an evolutionary account of the origins of life on earth — when did humankind first become humankind? That is, when, precisely, did we cease to be apes or whatever else we were and become human? And, assuming our continued evolution, when might we cease to be human and become an even higher — or at least different — form of life? This is not just a question of taxonomy of the sort familiar to students of natural history, though it may be that. It is also a question regarding the fundamental meaning of being human. We do not fret about what it means to be a cat, or a bear, or even an ape. We assume that the focal point of God's creation is humankind, and that the central theological questions all have to do with humankind's existence. Within this ultimately inescapably anthropocentric framework of thinking, however, we are probably prevented from recognizing the profound inadequacy of many of our assumptions, theological and cosmological, about the way things must be.

What if there is no beginning, and no ending? What if space has no boundaries, time no starting or ending point? What if there are multiple universes, perhaps even an infinite number? What if, to borrow Freeman Dyson's phrase, everything is "infinite in all directions"? I am not suggesting the classical distinction between the temporal condition of things created and the eternal being of God; I am not suggesting a realm of "timelessness" in which all things and all time are eternally co-present with God. Instead I wonder whether it makes any sense anymore to speak of beginnings and endings in any but a highly relative and contingent sense. I am wondering whether there might *not* be a beginning or ending of this universe, and even if there was and will be, whether that has any theological significance as such. We have come to the point where we no longer think of God only as the God of Israel, or the God of the Church of

116

Jesus Christ, or even as the God of heaven and earth. We now think of God as God of the universe. Why not God of a multiplicity of universes? Was the Big Bang God's first and only experience of creating a universe? Are we a prototype, or one of the more highly advanced models? The imaginable possibilities boggle the mind.

The caveat remains: there is no theology of beginnings or endings that is completely intellectually satisfying. Thus theological belief or conviction about first and last things requires confirmation in the joy of existence itself. Apart from the experience of life as good, one can hardly be persuaded that God is good. In the discernment, discovery, and experience of value in existence we are offered tokens and foretastes of what we may believe to be true of all existence, and thus of the Source and End of all existence. This is more an existential realization born out of our joyous participation in the community of living beings with all creation than it is an intellectual achievement. It is a faith that is given to us as a gift of grace by the Author within whose providence we have been granted supporting roles to play in the unfolding drama that extends much further than we can know beyond the story of our lives.

18. God's Time and Our Time in a Time of Science

CHARLES VALENTI-HEIN

*Memorial Presbyterian Church
Appleton, Wisconsin*

For a thousand years in your sight are like yesterday when it is past, or like a watch in the night. . . . So teach us to count our days that we may gain a wise heart.

Psalm 90

One of the most troubling side effects of the scientific revolution may well be that its peculiar way of marking and measuring time has become normative for most other disciplines, and for human interaction in general. Our ability to place temporality on a single plane and then dissect it into longer and shorter bits of string proves most useful for all manner of scientific investigations, from understanding the chemical processes and interactions that make what we eat either nutrition or poison to complex calculations regarding the size, shape, and age of the known physical universe.

While there is nothing, to be sure, particularly modern about noting the passage of days, months, and years, "clock speed" has the intriguing capacity of robbing humanity of precisely that quantity it measures. Though the movement of the earth around the sun has not changed perceptibly throughout the course of human history, it seems a uniquely modern phenomenon that we are virtually obsessed with saving and marking time, often to the fraction of a second, all the while feeling that time is, in a very important way, running out, or at least escaping from us. The irony of scientific time is that the delimitations that make the measurement of meaningful effect possible leave as their aftereffect disjointed blocks of time in a heap. "Meaning," in its broadest sense, is the victim of effect.

In contrast, the temporality implicit in religious thought seems too often to find itself, within the contemporary milieu, skirting effects in order to maintain the fabrics of meaning that have sustained it for centuries. Too much of biblical scholarship through the first part of the twentieth century revolved around reasoned attempts to explain miracles, and to treat the causal anomalies contained within the biblical narrative as one might the data of a laboratory experiment. From creation to the flood to the miracles of Jesus and the claim of resurrection, biblical scholarship seemed content to seek explanation above meaning. It is only in the last decades of the twentieth century that these broader questions of meaning have been vaulted back into the center of discussions of Scripture, responding in part to the very effect noted above: once the stories had been thoroughly historicized, and reduced to understandable beginnings and endings, what was lost in the explication of effects was any real sense of the meaning of the whole.

A fundamental problem must be addressed as we enter a new millennium, one that centers on the diverse but not necessarily exclusive understandings of temporality that dominate the discrete investigations of science and theology. The distinctions may best be understood by seeking to understand clearly the function of memory within each of the disciplines. Simply put, I will argue that within the Christian theological imagination, memory is a fundamental bearer of eschatological promise. This is in marked contrast to the scientific imagination, in which memory may provide the starting point for proper investigation, but its proper objective lies, in the words of Edmund Husserl, "in the thing itself."

Memory and Eschatology
in the Theological Imagination

To get a sense of the role of memory in the theological imagination, one need only think of the sacramental acts of the community of faith and their liturgical expression. The church of my youth was not exceptional in its architecture or appointments, but the center of its focus, immediately beneath the pulpit, was an ornately carved communion table, edged with the words, "This Do In Remembrance Of Me." The first act of imagination in the Christian faith is reconstructive, identifying and claiming those places in which God's presence has historically been affirmed by the community of faith.

But while Christian imagination begins in memory, it clearly does not reside there. The theological impulse, at its best, is not an attempt to re-create an ideal past, but rather, to "remember" the future hope that gives meaning and direction to our present. A unique feature of the biblical narrative, as seen for example in the Davidic narratives, is that the past re-presented in the narrative is decidedly *not* idealized. David, though the idealized King of Israel, is presented with all manner of human weakness such that his real life contains a cipher for the promise of God manifest in him. The past, in this theological imagining, bears but does not contain the promise of the future.

The same dynamic can be seen in the use of the passion narratives in early Christianity. The "scandal" of the cross is presented without apology and becomes one of the most sacred moments in Christian history and memory not because it constitutes the ideal human destiny, but because in this past a future is disclosed that transforms and fulfills all human destinies. We "survey the wondrous cross" not because it is in itself particularly edifying, but because it constitutes the moment in our human past when the divine future is disclosed. In sum, memory, as a theological act, is essential not because it provides us with the necessary data

119

for construing our present or because, like the pirate's map, it leads us to where our buried treasure was hidden long ago, but because in the act of remembrance we are able to imaginatively reconstruct the future that is in one sense already but in another not yet disclosed in our communal past.

This leads to one final aspect of the function of memory within the theological imagination, and that is that, strictly speaking, no theological memory is purely personal, but is always mediated through, and comprehended by the community of faith. In an individualistic culture in which the final arbiter of truth seems to be "it makes sense to me," it at least bears reflection that the nature of the Christian story is carried in its telling and liturgical expression. We baptize not ourselves but each other, while insisting that together we "remember our own baptism." Our Eucharistic celebration makes no sense except that it is a *communion* — a communal act of both remembrance and defiance in which we claim a history for ourselves that transforms our present and projects a future that is neither contained nor hidden in our past.

Memory and Eschatology in the Scientific Imagination

Before we go any further, a caveat is necessary: I write as a pastor and theologian who has, for some time, been engaged as a conversation partner with scientists. My knowledge of the scientific imagination, therefore, is necessarily limited by my own vocational choices. It is thus obvious that at this point I step well outside my sphere of knowledge and expertise. Any observations that follow are subject to the correction that might properly emerge through the very course of the conversation giving rise to these reflections.

My first observation is that within the scientific imagination, what happens "between times" matters far more than what happens before or after. Modern science is predicated on measurable and replicable results, so if "before" and "after" have any particular meaning, both terms are in a sense acts of memory which are replicable in the present by any competent observer. The two modalities of time exist as *precedent* and *prediction,* the past providing the data upon which theoretical assumptions of future action might be based, while the modality of future is always limited by the skeptical edge of the scientific method, which insists that truth is a function of demonstrability. So, for example, the scientific mind understands that water will boil if heat is applied long enough for the liquid temperature to reach 100 degrees Celsius. In fact, the measurement itself (the Celsius scale) is predicated on the predictability and replicability of this little experiment. If different effects were observed during the application of heat, we would conclude with certainty that the substance was not, indeed, water.

Historical questions, then, bear some interest in the scientific imagination, but unlike the theological imagination, the disclosive power of the past is limited to the actions and interactions of recorded events. While the theological mind might speak of a future disclosed in past events, from a scientific perspective the content of the past is archival, perhaps containing incongruities or conundrums that can be fertile ground for scientific speculation and even hypothesis in the present, but that do not properly "disclose" the future.

The obvious virtue of this scientific approach is that it can predict with some certainty what will become of water if heated to the boiling point, but the scientist's prediction will always be couched in conditional statements: *if* the clear substance is water, *if* the surrounding air pressure is maintained at a certain point. The future (or at the least prediction of the future) is thus from a scientific viewpoint conditional upon the past and present. To put it another way, the future (or prediction of the future) is contingent upon past observation and present action. It is in the ability to control variables in the future, based on past observation and present action, that the efficacy of science is born.

The concomitant danger of the scientific approach is that if *meaning* is addressed at all, it is collapsed into claims of *truth:* it is *true* that water will boil at 100 degrees on a Celsius scale. But if the scientist is pressed to consider what it *means* that water will so react to heat, the proper scientific response will either be reductionistic or tautological. It would be possible to describe the molecular processes that occur when heat is applied to the bonded hydrogen and oxygen atoms, but such explanations would ultimately reduce to the idea that the *meaning* and the *truth* of the statement are identical, and both the meaning and truth statements assume a stable universe of replicable experiment.

The import of this distinction between theological and scientific imagination may be negligible in reference to claims such as the boiling point of water, but it becomes more problematic when applied especially to aspects of religious narrative. For example, in the second chapter of John's Gospel, the claim is made that through Jesus' intercession, water is turned to wine. The observations open to the scientist *qua* scientist are necessarily limited, especially since the archived physical data are not open to present manipulation. The scientist might be able to offer the opinion that such an event, were its veracity discernable through controlled tests on the substance in the jars before and after Jesus' intercession, is still an anomaly in the physical world. A curious scientist might even be tempted to investigate the molecular structures involved to develop a hypothesis as to *how* Jesus might have accomplished this feat *if* indeed it occurred. Working within the confines of the scientific imagination and construal of time, the scientist would simply not be authorized to determine when the transformation *truly* occurred (insofar as the historical remnants are not available) nor to speculate on what such a transubstantiation might *mean,* except to offer the observation that such an event would stand as an anomaly within the normal confines of the physical world.

On the other hand, a theologian might be competent to make judgments as to the *meaning* of this scene in relation to the larger narrative of the Christian story. In such reflection, emphasis would be placed on the disclosive power of the past event. As to the question of whether the events so narrated *really happened,* the theologian would not be authorized to make such judgment any more than the scientist would be authorized to ascertain its meaning. While for the scientist truth and meaning are collapsed, for the theologian truth might best be seen as a function of meaning. The story of water changing to wine, from the perspective of the theological imagination, is true because it is meaningful — the inverse of the scientist's evaluation of the boiling water, that it is meaningful because it is true.

The point to bear in mind for the purposes of this paper is that the reason for these at least seemingly disparate observations regarding a single event is rooted in conceptualizations of time. Insofar as in science the future is a realm of prediction based on precedent, the past serves a limit function on the construal of future. Continuity constitutes good science. But for the theological imagination the past does not limit but rather discloses future possibility. What remains to be discerned is whether there is any commensurability between these two imaginations.

I would argue that while the models of science and theology are formally incommensurate, that does not necessarily mean that they are incompatible or irreconcilable. Rather, the problem rests in disparate understandings of the functionality of time. Put simply, in the theological imagination time is the arena within which events are played out; in the scientific imagination time is an agent by which the arena of events is constructed.

These functionalities are discrete but complementary. The academic discipline of historians has essentially proven that a theological construal of time can function without scientific paradigms, and that the effectiveness of the scientific imagination is not hindered by lack of reference to God. Instrumentally, each sense of time offers insights that benefit human existence without necessary reference to the other. But I would suggest that in the creative dialogue between science and theology a deeper understanding of the meaning and power of each discipline will emerge, and that such a dialogue is vital, especially in a world in which the questions of science and theology find themselves sharing the same stage, if acting in different dramas.

19. Incarnation and Eschatology

DEBORAH RAHN CLEMENS

Frieden's United Church of Christ
Sumneytown, Pennsylvania

As Christ is the key to the Christian understanding of Creation, and Christ is the key to our understanding of covenant and salvation, Christ is also the essential key in interpreting the Apocalypse. The assurance of the coming glory at the end of time is staked in the doctrine of the Incarnation. It is Christ who was the agent of Creation. It is Christ who holds the universe in organic connection. It is Christ who guarantees rapture in his Second Coming.

Four words describe the end times in classic Christian culture. They are Apocalypse, Second Coming (Parousia), Consummation, and Rapture. These words in themselves give us a clue as to the nature of the end in light of the Incarnation. None of these words convey any sense of termination, annihilation, extinction, or damnation. Instead they imply that there will be a return of the Christ, that there will be a completion of a process, and that the result will be glorious.

Apocalypse

Look! He is coming with the clouds; every eye will see him, even those who pierced him; and on his account all the tribes of the earth will wail. So it is to be. Amen. "I am the Alpha and the Omega," says the Lord God, who is and was and who is to come, the Almighty. (Rev. 1:7-8)

The word apocalypse simply means revelation. Obviously, then, what is not understood or comprehended now will be made clear in the end. The faithful will no longer need to resort to mythological language. Scientists will have no need for experiments. The truth and the meaning of everything will be available to the whole of creation. We can trust that as the early Christians were able to look back into the prophetic writings of their Jewish ancestors and see the Messiah in the ancient prophecies, when the Apocalypse occurs it will be in accordance with the New Testament witness.

This can be summarized to mean that the full revelation of what is already given to us in faith in Jesus will be seen. We will see that the true Word of God is the word of Love, that the love of God is the first and last thing through which we and the world were created. This love will be manifest without concealment by the world and God "will be all in all." This is the meaning of the gospel.[1]

Second Coming

When the Son of Man comes in his glory, and all the angels with him, then he will sit on the throne of his glory. All the nations will be gathered before him. (Matt. 25:31)

Despite any myths to the contrary, Christians know that the return of Christ will be the ultimate blessing. Any suggestion that Christ's return might be a curse is utter blasphemy. The one who revealed himself as a loving, gentle, sacrificial Savior will not, cannot deny his own being. Christ's return therefore must be first and foremost incarnational. Is this to say that there will be yet another incarnation at that time, that God will change the world again and also be changed? I believe it does mean precisely that, although details of how that might be manifested remain an utter mystery.

As Jesus came to preach about the Kingdom of God, we can be sure that the kingdom will be the new reality that the world will experience fully.[2] The Nicene Creed reaffirms the fact that his kingdom shall have no end. What has been accomplished in Christ in time has timeless dimensions.[3] This may suggest that the Kingdom of God will be the new incarnation, incarnate into the universe so that the whole universe will be a compound substance in union with God. The Kingdom of God will be one of perfect humanity where justice, mercy, and compassion define society.[4]

The difference between the first and second comings, according to St. Athanasius, is that "He shall come no longer in lowliness but in glory, no longer in humiliation, but in majesty, no longer to suffer but to bestow on us the fruits of the cross — the resurrection and incorruptibility."[5] Biblically speaking, at the end of time the Son will turn everything over to the Father, and the Father will be all in all. Perhaps this means that mediation between God and Creation will no longer be necessary.[6] We will see God face to face, actually able to apprehend the Spirit of our God.

Consummation

> Mary said to the angel, "How can this be, since I am a virgin?" Then the angel said to her, "The Holy Spirit will come upon you, and the power of the Most High will overshadow you." (Luke 1:34-35a)

Consummation is completion. The word itself also has biological implications. To consume means to absorb, to digest. I do not think that connotation is irrelevant; in some unexplainable way, the universe will be digested into the Godhead. Without the organic union of God and creation, the life of the world, no matter how long or how fruitful, would essentially and ultimately be futile.[7] This consumption, however, is not a physical occurrence but a sacramental one. Georges Florovsky helps clarify the vision and avoid the obvious dangers: "It does appear as though the goal of the creation is the divinization of the world. The danger is corrected when recognizing that there is not a transubstantiation of nature (the world is not of the same substance with God) but a mystical union of the universe with the Maker."[8]

The Incarnate Word somehow calls space and time into the embrace of the eternal and infinite God, who preceded both time and the universe. The universe will not revert to a timeless and chaotic void. Instead, chaos will be absorbed into the Prince of Peace. There will be a time when there is no more time. Change will cease. Time will no longer be measured by days and nights; instead there will be day without evening, light without darkness, creation without decay.[9] Time and Creation are two distinct things, even though Creation happened in time and the Consummation will happen in time. Creation happened by the Word of God. God's Word proceeds but does not recede, and that Word endures forever.

Now the universe is infused with endless possibilities because it is linked with the inexhaustible possibilities of God.[10] Faith in Christ means faith in these godly possibilities. God's will is to reconcile the whole world to himself. The plan will be completed once and for all in the Consummation. This is the gospel. There is no alternative way for Christians to interpret it.

Rapture

> Then we who are alive, we who are left, will be caught up in the clouds together with them to meet the Lord in the air; and so we will be with the Lord forever. Therefore encourage one another with these words. (I Thess. 4:17-18)

This is a frightening concept to many faithful Christians. It has been distorted into a vision of escape for the "righteous" and damnation for the rest. In light of the Incarnation, however, the false separation of Christ from the world he came to redeem is intolerable. Nevertheless, the concept of rapture still can be helpful for defining Christian expectations if it is understood as a taking up in a spiritual sense. To be enraptured is to be in love. It is to relish in the glory of another's being. The end time is God's ultimate glorification.

God's glorifying of himself, which is identical with his self-communication in love, reaches its goal only by dissolving this form of the world and transforming the world into the form of glory.[11] What is at stake is primarily the glorifying of God and not human happiness and salvation. Individual salvation is not primary, but secondary. Persons will not be deified, and neither will creation. There is no room for boasting even in the rapture of the Christian theanthropic system. Neither humans nor the universal elements have value in themselves outside of Christ. There is no life at all without him.[12]

As much as our divinization is a result of the Incarnation, so is our humanization. We will never lose our humanness. In Biblical terms, we will see God "face to face," which illustrates the intimacy of the future bond between us. At the same time, the vision preserves God's exclusivity;[13] the divinity is in the principle of the consummation of the universe and not in the substance of the universe itself.[14]

Ironically, or perhaps miraculously, the final *kenosis* of God is not God's limitation but God's ultimate glorification. It increases rather than detracts from God's majesty. It means that hell is finally and forever vanquished.[15]

Conclusion

I am convinced that neither death, nor life, nor angels, nor rulers, nor things present, nor things to come, nor powers, nor height, nor depth, nor anything else in all creation, will be able to separate us from the love of God in Christ Jesus our Lord. (Romans 8:38-39)

A theology of the Incarnation is to be the first and controlling theology for Christians to use in interpreting the Eschaton. The Incarnation is the God particle loaned from above to all creation. It endows the universe with weight and meaning. It is so basic and so ubiquitous that it would be impossible for Christians to conceive of life without this doctrine. Once Incarnational theology is in place, all other revelations concerning God's relationship to the universe and to the future assist in defining the overwhelming hope Christians demonstrate when they anticipate the culmination of history.

Christians understand the whole world to be oriented toward Christ.

This orientation is not for the sake of humans alone, but so that the whole universe might be redeemed in him.[16] Incarnational theology corrects secular perspectives concerning the meaning of humanity: it neither accepts the idea of humans as merely particles among millions of other natural particles and therefore without moral value or essential meaning, nor does it assume the universe revolves around them. Understanding the Incarnation this way helps us see the unique role we humans have in cooperating in universal destiny. It encompasses far more than our own existence, yet it does not lessen our importance.[17]

In God's *kenosis,* the universe was created for so much more than making the possibility of hell a reality. In the Incarnation God humbled himself, taking on the form of a servant for the sake of community. Through the Cross, a union was consummated. In the Resurrection a substantial New Creation has come into existence. In the Eschaton the completion of the *kenotic* principle will be accomplished. God will encompass all in the New Creation beyond time, corruption, and decay.[18]

If we live in the body of Christ, nothing can ever separate us from the love that restores and redeems. If the Christian faith is not about this, it is about nothing. Faith is just an illusion if it does not culminate in the consummation of God's glory.[19]

CHAPTER V

Cultural Intimations

Introduction

While many in this year's Pastor-Theologian Program wrote eloquent testimonies about the unique revelation of God's saving knowledge in the person and work of Jesus Christ, there were also some other papers from members who did not want to neglect intimations of eschatological fulfillment and hope to be found in such ennobling cultural expressions of God's general revelation as scientific medicine, poetic imaginations, music, and the arts. Especially the Psalms of David and the miracles of Christ have shaped a realistic piety throughout the Judeo-Christian tradition in which hopes are embodied, visions are covenanted, the hungry are fed, the suffering are healed, and God's inbreaking reign takes on proleptic, tangible, earthy expressions of inaugurated realization. The precise relation of these gifts of the Spirit to the lordship of Christ does raise all kinds of theological, and not least eschatological issues for the Christian church, but there has never been an age without some impressive claims of God's "sacred" power universally at work in some totally unexpected "secular" sources.

Barry Downing's excerpt on "Medical Technology and Eschatological Hope" is predicated on the conviction that "there are many clues in the New Testament that the church does not control or own the Spirit." If the Spirit has been poured out "on *all* flesh" in our Pentecostal age (Acts 2:17; Joel 2:28), "then why shouldn't we also see scientific technology as the work of the Spirit?" This is especially pertinent to modern medical technology, which functions "in a very similar way to the ministry of Jesus" (cf. Lazarus, Jairus's daughter). Did the "signs of the coming kingdom" end with the healing miracles of Jesus? Modern medical technology has expanded both our knowledge of, and our power over, the universe. It should be viewed "in some kind of penultimate relation to eschatology, another sign of the first fruits of the Spirit." If Michael Welker can include the charismatic movement and the spread of liberation and feminist theologies "as examples of the outpouring of the Holy Spirit in our time," then why not also modern medical technology?

Pamela Fickenscher similarly analyzes "Health in This Life and the Life of the World to Come," but goes on to define a distinctive Christian voice in the world of alternative healthcare. She first analyzes a theology of the afterlife with a postmodern twist. She endorses Nancey Murphy's move to affirm "the bodiliness of human existence and every human religious experience," even in connection with the resurrection of the dead. This "physicalist" view of human life supports the relationality that is already embodied to be glorified by those incorporated by baptism into the body of Christ. Anticipating such bodily glorification by hope, Christians should now ennoble the body, nurture it as relational, affirm its life value, respect its finite limits, and relate it to the wellness of the whole creation.

Kenneth Carter likewise analyzes "The Human Genome Project" as an unprecedented scientific achievement in "mapping the genetic instructions that shape a human being" to assist in the future prevention and treatment of illness and suffering as well as to assist in the prolongation and quality of finite human life. "Could it be," the author asks, "that scientists, as stewards of considerable gifts, will be used by God in ways that bring fulfillment to biblical passages such as Isaiah 65?" The prophetic books of the Old Testament included both lament and hope, all grounded in the vision of the preferred future *(shalom)* that God has revealed. On the frontiers of human genetics, "an inadequate hope could deny the power and providence of God, for whom we have been created and in whose image we are being restored."

Poetic expression joins medical technology as another intimation of God's transcendent reign in Brenda Pelc-Faszcza's essay excerpt on "Science, Religion and the Language of Faith." She sees science's service to faith by helping us with critical analysis to move beyond our "first naiveté" in accepting the literal meaning of ancient Judeo-Christian texts in order to achieve a higher stage of a "second naiveté" that appropriates a far more complex, rich, and nuanced embrace of sacred traditions and their fullest meanings (Paul Ricoeur, *The Symbolism of Evil*). Advocates of "fundamentalism" remain at the first level, those of "scientism" at the intermediate, neither reaching the second. Walter Brueggemann recommends that the total movement is best achieved in the postmodern world through the use of religious language (Word) and acts (sacraments) that are poetic rather than pedantic, that disclose rather than explain, that evoke rather than provoke, "whose function it is to cherish the truth, to open the truth from its pervasive reductionism in our society, to break the fearful rationality that keeps the news from being news." In short, the current loss of certainty is a time of opportunity "to reclaim our role as poets."

Finally, Douglas Vaughan proposes "A (Natural?) Theology of Music" to witness to God's general revelation in human culture "in exploring that realm of human personality in which the aesthetic experience occurs and through which we gain certain knowledge of our eschatological hope." Many scriptural texts reinforce an understanding of music serving as a vehicle of God's activity in ways that other human activities cannot (cf. in Psalms, hymns and liturgies). Barth and Küng have especially praised the liberating music of Mozart: "traces of transcendence." Steiner talks of music as communicating "from a spiritual realm beyond, where the real presence cannot be analytically shown or paraphrased." Testimonies are further cited from Ralph Vaughan Williams, Deems Taylor, Elder Olson, et al. While not acceptable in our day as an "argument from beauty" for a natural theology of God, music does move persons to "another realm of which we already have some experience and toward which we long to go."

20. Medical Technology and Eschatological Hope

BARRY H. DOWNING

Northminster Presbyterian Church
Endwell, New York

The Christian church has always ministered to the sick and the dying. The healing ministry of Jesus was central not only to who he was, but also to our understanding of a God who has made an eschatological promise to make all things new. The death and resurrection of Lazarus (John 11), Jairus's daughter (Luke 8:40-42, 49-56), and Jesus himself make it clear that a central part of our faith is that both death and resurrection are our destiny. And death can come anytime — to a child, an aged adult, or anyone in between.

But when should death occur? The story of Lazarus seems to indicate that he became ill and died a natural death, as did the only daughter of Jairus. But Jesus intervened and raised both from the dead, leaving them both, we suppose, to face a natural death again later.

Modern medical technology functions in a way very similar to the ministry of Jesus in relation to Lazarus and Jairus's daughter — it intervenes and frequently delays natural death. But at the same time, eventually natural death wins out over the best medical technology. As the healing miracles of Jesus were a "sign" of the coming kingdom, should we also see modern technology as a further "sign" of the coming kingdom?

A New Heaven, a New Earth, a New Technology

Technology dominates Western human life, and the rest of the world is catching up. We pastors are doing our work in a highly technical world, and the technology that impacts our ministry most directly is medical technology.

The larger world may be concerned about the negative side of technology — we built a big bomb and are going to blow ourselves up, or we are polluting our earth and poisoning our life. Liberal Protestant theology has landed here with joy, playing Jeremiah, moaning of apocalyptic doom. Mainline pastors wring their proverbial hands on the Internet about the evils of technology and talk on their cell phones while they watch C-Span before going out to pray for a church member going through heart bypass surgery. Maybe our mainline anti-technology stance is prophetic, and Walter Miller's *A Canticle for Leibowitz*[1] is an imaginative expression of technology as a source of doom, perhaps an instrument of the Antichrist. Indeed, technology seems to have replaced Christ as the one who brings us bread, heals our diseases, and at least tries to wipe away every tear and create a world where death is no more. Is this the Antichrist, is technology the molten calf worshiped by a godless secular culture, or is technology the unseen work of the Holy Spirit

— "greater works than these will he do, because I go to the Father" (John 14:12)?

Most members of our congregations look to technology to enrich their lives. They look to easy travel, easy electronic communication, and the world of medical technology to save their lives, or at least lessen the pain, in a crisis. Most pastors rejoice in this world. I wonder if liberal Protestantism celebrates Leibowitz not because he is truly prophetic, but because he is a voice from before Galileo, when the church, not Christ, was all in all. And all Christian clergy miss those days, for we clergy are not heroes now.

Technology has set the agenda for theology in our century, although the problem began when Galileo asked the church to look through his telescope and the church refused. Technology has done two things. It has expanded our knowledge of the universe through better and better instrumentation. We know beyond doubt that the earth is not the center of a domed universe.[2] And technology has expanded our power over our environment, for better or worse. No biblical author could comprehend, for example, that some of the stars in the sky are actually galaxies. Thus, in our Protestant tradition, a tradition of *sola scriptura,* how do we preach the truth of God's cosmology from a document of clearly limited truth?

At the beginning of "New Heaven — New Earth," Jürgen Moltmann says,

> In the scientific and technological civilization of modern times, the programme of a cosmic eschatology runs up against considerable difficulties, for the cosmos, both as a whole and in all its different sectors, has become the object of the natural sciences. Since these are bound to proceed agnostically in their methods, they permit no theological statements to be made within their own sphere, either about the beginning of the cosmos or about its end. It was therefore understandable that modern theology should have withdrawn from the sector "nature" and should have concentrated on the sector "history" and, within the sector history, should have concentrated on its innermost side, human existence. In this process nothing split apart more widely than cosmology and eschatology. But without cosmology, eschatology must inevitably turn into a gnostic myth of redemption, as modern existentialism shows.[3]

Modern sciences "are bound to proceed agnostically in their methods." In giving his theoretical house tour, Moltmann takes us into the living room, points to the agnostic elephant science, and then points out that theology lives in the attic, where we are stuck with a personalized existential eschatology that is basically a gnostic myth. Modern science, agnostic though it is, now occupies the living room. It is not clear that Moltmann wants to in any way displace technology from the living room, which may be neither possible nor desirable, but we do need to see technology in some kind of penultimate relation to eschatology, as another sign of the first fruits of the Spirit.

If the New Heaven is going to be as fully inclusive, as universally redemptive as Moltmann argues throughout *The Coming of God,* then how will human technology be redeemed in the New Heaven and New Earth? If technology is part of human work, then "each man's work will become manifest: for the Day will disclose it, because it will be revealed with fire, and the fire will test what sort of work each one has done" (1 Cor. 3:13). Do we not have the right to suppose that not only humanity and Creation will share in the New Heaven and the New Earth, but that human technology will also share this renewal? This then leads us to wonder: is the heavenly kingdom of the angels already something of a technological world? The Christian doctrine of the resurrection suggests that the new earth will be embodied. Why wouldn't technology be part of an eternal embodied world?

This question has yet to be addressed by theology, although it is being asked by secular writers such as Erich Von Daniken in *Chariots of the Gods?*[4] Von Daniken wonders if the wheels of Ezekiel might have been a spaceship, and if the angels might have been ancient astronauts. But the response of the religious community to these types of questions has been, who let that Gentile into our theological house?[5]

If God's redemption is total, of humanity and Creation, how can technology be left out of the salvation process, unless all of it is condemned as stubble? But technology can be used for good or for ill; it is like the field that is planted with both wheat and weeds.[6] We cannot make a blanket condemnation of technology. The best technologists were chosen to build the Tabernacle and Solomon's Temple. Jesus grew up in the home of a carpenter.

Michael Welker, in his book *God the Spirit,* lists the charismatic movement and the spread of liberation and feminist theologies as examples of the outpouring of the Holy Spirit in our time.[7] He does not, however, list the explosion of modern scientific technology as such. In one sense, this is not surprising, because modern theology does not see technology this way. If anything, liberation theologies have seen a strong connection between technology and oppressive capitalist economies and therefore condemned technology as an enemy of humanity and the environment. There is justified fear that if modern nuclear weapons do not destroy us, environmental pollution will. Genetic manipulation may change humanity beyond biological recognition, and mind-altering drugs may change our psychology beyond recognition. We fear that technology is dehumanizing us. But at the same time, technology is one of the things that make humanity distinctly human.

Welker asks, "How are we to connect the observation that God's Spirit is in *everything* and effects *everything*, with the recognition that the Spirit is *creatively* effective?"[8] If Welker were to answer his own question, he might admit that if the Spirit is in everything, then the Spirit has to be somehow "in" technological discovery, and that if the Spirit is the driving force of human creativity — because Jesus has gone to the Father — then technological creativity must be seen as one work of the Holy Spirit.

Welker understands that the relation between the Holy Spirit and technology is already seminally present in the biblical account of building first the Tabernacle and then the Temple.[9] Welker comments on the biblical view that technical skills are a gift of the Spirit of God:

> At issue here are not only highly developed technical skills. At issue are not only a gift for invention and an understanding of art, although these and many additional endowments are regarded as characteristic of the person filled with God's Spirit (cf. Exod. 31:3; 34:34). At issue rather is an artistry that plans the coherent interconnection of the extensively described and very different artistic and technical labor processes.[10]

Having seen this biblical foundation for describing modern technology as an outpouring of the Spirit, Welker nevertheless does not explore this possibility in his book. It is beyond the scope of this paper to give a detailed analysis of the way in which modern technology should be seen as a work of the Spirit, but some of the issues to be considered would seem to be as follows.

Theology has perhaps been blind to technology as the creative work of the Spirit because of the way the Spirit is seen in the New Testament. There was a tendency in the early church to see baptism and the Holy Spirit as gifts to the church, not to the world as a whole. When the scientific explosion began in the sixteenth century, with the church unwilling to look through the telescope of Galileo, a pattern was established that has continued to this day. Science is what the "world" does, Spirit is what the church does.

But there are many clues in the New Testament that the church does not control or own the Spirit. The interpretation of Pentecost is taken from the prophet Joel, who said, "And in the last days it shall be, God declares, that I will pour out my Spirit upon all flesh" (Acts 2:17; Joel 2:28). Because the Spirit was given to the church at Pentecost, there has been a tendency to interpret the Joel passage as saying, "I will pour out my Spirit upon all Christian flesh." This interpretation has especially been true of charismatic Christians, and to some extent in a Roman Catholic doctrine of authority that focuses the power of the Spirit in the pope, as well as Protestants channeling the Spirit through Scripture alone. But if the Spirit has been poured out on *all flesh* in our age, then why shouldn't we see scientific technology as the work of the Spirit?

21. Health in This Life and the Life of the World to Come

PAMELA FICKENSCHER

The Spirit Garage
Minneapolis, Minnesota

Between Immortality and Resurrection

Nancey Murphy, in *Beyond Liberalism and Fundamentalism,* argues that one way forward from the loggerheads of twentieth-century theological anthropology is to consider a wholly new metaphysic. Murphy calls this point of view "physicalist," wholly affirming the bodiliness of human existence and even human religious experience, yet also "nonreductive," acknowledging that the great complexity of the human mind and spirit cannot be reduced to their smallest chemical or physical parts. Her colleague Warren Brown writes that

> although the emergent properties traditionally identified with the human soul or mind or both are dependent on the cognitive capacities from which they emerge (and indeed cannot exist without them), they cannot be fully understood by, or reduced to neurobiology. And these emergent properties in turn exercise a causative influence — "top-down causation" — on the neurophysiological systems that instantiate them.[1]

This "monist" view of the human person is of course highly controversial, especially among evangelicals who have spent the better part of the century defending God's intervention in natural laws. But Murphy and others may in fact be offering a way of thinking that makes sense of some of Paul's more puzzling statements about the resurrection.

The doctrine of the resurrection of the body acts as a brake in the move toward any version of the human soul that minimizes its connection to the human body. In the popular mind, Paul's references to "the flesh" and its weaknesses seem to confirm a dualist view of mind and matter, suggesting that the body is not a necessary part of our relation to God but instead a hindrance. And in spite of the gospel's repeated references to Jesus' wounds, hunger, and other signs of his physical presence following the resurrection, many Christians continue to believe in a life after death in which the body is irrelevant. M. Scott Peck argues that it is merely "lack of imagination" that makes us want to posit an afterlife in which we retain bodily existence.[2] But for Brown, Murphy, Moltmann and others, the doctrine of the resurrection of the dead requires us to think imaginatively about what happens to personhood immediately following death. It is our self-centered concept of time, rather than the wholeness of the person, that is challenged.

None of the theologians writing today about eternity engage in fully fleshed out visions of what eternal life will "look like." When challenged to imagine what heaven will be, only lay theologians with a propensity toward metaphor, such as C. S. Lewis or, more recently, M. Scott Peck, are willing to put spatial qualities on eternal life, usually in the form of fiction or allegory. However, the scriptures speak very clearly of a resurrected *body*, both for Christ in the gospels and, according to Paul, for those who are "in Christ." Michael Welker points out that Jesus' resurrection body is not entirely continuous with the pre-resurrection Jesus — not simply a re-suscitated corpse. This body nevertheless has corporal qualities, such as hunger and physical wounds. At the same time, Jesus' body does not con-form to all the laws of a normal mortal body, having what Michael Welker classifies as "appearances" rather than continuous life with the disciples.[3]

Paul's use of the term "body" in his description of the resurrected life in 1 Corinthians 15 is particularly worthy of note, given his tendency elsewhere to contrast the way of the "flesh" with the way of the "spirit." Hans Weder has made the helpful suggestion that the "body" signifies for Paul human relatedness.[4] When we are gathered "into Christ" we will not be absorbed into an undifferentiated All. Instead we retain our essential selves, a relatedness, what Moltmann calls "all we are" and the world that has become part of us.

While these interpretations of the resurrection may make more sense to a "physicalist" understanding of human life, affirming both the resurrec-tion of the body and the biological necessity of physical death in this world, such an interpretation does not completely alleviate the epistemological difficulties of belief in the resurrection. The resurrection of the dead re-mains, as Moltmann says, "a hope"; while the logic of the monist view is palatable for many people in the scientific community, the hope for a resur-rected person rests firmly in the realm of Christian faith and cannot be af-firmed as a matter of logic.[5] This leaves Christians in a peculiar place re-garding apologetics and conversation with the secular culture that is so desperately seeking a "spiritual" view of the world free from the constraints of institutional religion. Murphy delineates this kind of thinking as "nonfoundational theology," which as articulated by Ronald Thiemann and others is "located squarely within the Christian community and tradition and seeks to describe the internal logic of the Christian faith."[6] We can, to some degree, make that internal logic resonate more clearly with what we know about neuroscience and human psychology, but the resurrection re-mains a matter that cannot be "logically" approached. We are not likely to see a Christian version of Deepak Chopra arguing that a physical resurrec-tion can be deduced from modern brain science.

Perhaps the voice Christians must adopt in this secular conversation is not, as Peck argues, a "non-materialist" voice, but one in which relationality is a primary factor in defining human life. Christians argue for neither the elimination of individuality nor an egocentric existence after death. Instead, our identity is transformed in the resurrection, being "in Christ" in a new way, a way that nevertheless is continuous with the life that begins at our baptisms. This life "in God" is qualitatively different from an afterlife in which the singular soul maintains its individuality, having sloughed off its bodily core. Thus, the role of community relationships is not optional or secondary to our "personal spirituality" in this life. From a Christian perspective, the relationality of our being constitutes who we are now in a way that is at least partly continuous with the life that will be.

A Distinctively Christian Voice in the Quest for Personal Healing

1. A View of the Human Person That Acknowledges Both the Reality of the Body and Its Limits

Christian faith, in spite of frequent detours into gnosticism or extreme asceticism, has always maintained the importance and reality of our physical bodies. Religious practice can never be reduced merely to mystical prayer or intellectual reasoning, but instead demands that we, with our Jewish brothers and sisters, love God "with heart, mind, and strength." Moreover, we maintain the importance of God's incarnation among us, the full physical presence of the divine in a body like ours, mortal and vulnerable. The finite bears the infinite, and therefore deserves care and dignity, even when its finitude is particularly apparent. This "ennobling" of the human body does not, however, immortalize it. Jesus died, and so will we. Only in God is there hope of a new life beyond natural death.

2. A View of the Person That Is Intensely Relational

The Christian community can bear witness to the role of the whole creation and the communion of saints as active participants in our relationship to God. Because the human soul is not immutable but integral to our personhood and in need of redemption by God, we cannot excuse any abuse of others or of the earth for spiritual reasons. Human commitments such as marriage, parenthood, and care for community cannot be sloughed off easily in the name of "spiritual growth." Enlightenment is not a prize to be gained at the cost of relationships, although discipleship may at times cause conflict in community. Christians acknowledge that while these relationships can be a source of sustenance and joy, they may also cause us pain and sacrifice; the individual is not given complete freedom to reject the claims of the community, but instead must discern God's calling within those commitments. The transcendence we seek is to be found only in God and not in achieving a higher state of wellness or by minimizing any emotional or physical pain we may experience.

The Christian insistence on the presence of God in the visible, embodied, and gathered people of God also serves as a mitigating force against an increasingly individualized, atomized search for spirituality. As the Internet discovers religion and the profits spirituality can bring, the local Christian community can stand in opposition to a view of relationship based only on exchange of ideas and "products." While many local communities may make use of the Internet for communication and even prayer, the practice of gathering together in body and spirit continues to bear witness to our wholeness as human beings who rely on all of the senses to learn and grow. The sacramental presence of the church is a needed antidote to the commodification of spirituality.

3. Affirming the Value of Life without Denying Death

John Updike has written that "America is hindered not so much by limits, but by its dreams."[7] While much pop spirituality serves to gloss over mortality, to promote the illusion that one's ego will not face the harsh limit of death, Christians stand in the unique position of acknowledging death while at the same time affirming the sacredness of human life. Christians can affirm the need for redemption without in any way relativizing the importance of this life, this individual story and memory. It is the totality of our beings, hearts, minds, and wills that is redeemed by God; there is therefore no part of this life that can be dismissed as mere illusion. We can unabashedly remind people at Ash Wednesday that they are dust, and to dust they shall return; yet the cross with which they are marked reminds them of their baptisms, when they truly died to this life and began the life that will be continuous with this one. With a "non-reductive physicalist" view of the human person, the dialectic between the harsh reality of death and the hope of the new creation takes on "meat" that challenges the vague notions of immortality so prevalent in pop spirituality.

4. Relief from the Relentlessly Progressive Attitude of Middle-class America towards Well-being and Achievement

Health and spirituality for the Christian consist in "right relation" to God, not in achievement of mystical experience, constant boundless energy, or any other "higher state" to be commodified, seminarized, published, or propagated by a market culture. This approach to bodily life says a clear "no" to the self-centered pursuit of self-actualization, while at the same time giving a clear "yes" to the hope of reconciliation with God and others, for the "peace which passes all understanding." Miroslav Volf points out the difficulty in imagining a state of wholeness or salvation that does not entail some sense of "progress" or change, but he rejects the Kantian notion of change as necessarily linear. It is the sense of lack, the pain of discontentment with the present, that plagues our current longing for progress. Volf suggests that the eternal contentment that is our salvation is not incompatible with temporality. Quoting Gregory of Nyssa, he suggests instead that "'by enjoying what is more worthy, the memory of inferior things is blotted out,' since at each stage the greater and superior good holds the attention of those who enjoy it and does not allow them to look at the past."[8]

This is not a super-consumer vision of heaven; we cannot have it all, since it all belongs to God, in whom we live and move and have our being. Instead we are offered a vision of life, of change and progress that is in harmony with time and with all of Creation. This life is surely a gift, but such an approach requires surrender, a relinquishing of the control that many self-help authors urge us to regain. Volf provides the helpful qualification that because this reconciliation is relational in its nature, it still requires a self with agency, one who can "accept all others" as they have been accepted.[9] The gift of God's grace offers healing that cannot be quantified or sold, freeing us to pursue in this life the healing of the world, not merely our own soul.

5. A Calling from God to Honor the Wholeness of Others and to Seek the Wellness of the Whole Creation, Not Merely Our Own

Our belief that our bodies are not inconsequential to our spiritual beings also gives Christians a distinctive voice when it comes to ethical decisions regarding personal health and ecological health. If relationality is essential, then how does the rest of Creation play a part? Is harvesting the prairie for virgin echniacea, useful in fighting off the common cold, a justifiable use of earthly resources for human well-being? If relationality is essential to the human person, then larger systems of family, community, and justice must play a part in the story of salvation. Christian salvation is relational in such a way that we cannot talk about spiritual healing without addressing justice.

If healing is for the nations, if reconciliation is essentially a communal effort, Christians have good reason to be suspicious of the "mining" of traditional healing methods by best-selling American authors. Indeed, the "evolutionary" nature of the spirituality espoused by Carolyn Myss and others is often baldly parochial. Myss summarizes recent history thus: "Today our Tribal elders are far more focused on maintaining peace than on sending our young men to fight a war. . . . Yet other nations around the world are still divided internally in Tribal warfare and brutal suppressions of individual civil rights and religious freedom, as Piscean energy ignites its democratizing effect."[10] Myss does not consider whether U.S. leaders' interest in protecting American lives has a distinctly imperial effect on less wealthy nations. Moreover, she does not consider why the astrological account of history she offers seems to play out most powerfully and primarily in the northern hemisphere.

Some popular healers are aware that the healing of the wealthy may be bound up with justice for the poor. Andrew Weil's *Spontaneous Healing* has a glimmer of awareness in his foreword, in which he describes a visit to a South American shaman in 1972. He is surprised, even indignant, when his friend announces that he is giving up healing work in order to fight the effects of Texaco drilling in his native forests. Weil concludes that in twenty-five years "the destruction of the rain forest caused by the removal of oil has reached levels that Pedro and his people could never have imagined. . . . Simply put, the Kofan people have been put out of business. They are finished, terminated, and any knowledge held by their wise elders and traditional healers is soon to be lost forever."[11] The rest of the book, however, has no call to action, no suggestion that patients consider the source of their treatments or the impact of their "optimal" health on that of others.

For Christians who are simultaneously saints and sinners, there is no point at which we are exempt from loving as we have been loved, pardoning as we were pardoned. There is no "excuse" for the personal search for well-being to the exclusion of all others. The end of this world does not destroy the reality of the joys and pains of this life; because God redeems our lives, rather than simply obliterating them, there is no room in the Christian story for the notion that this life is mere illusion. Evil and death are conquered at the resurrection, but their concrete effects on human life are not therefore to be ignored. Steadfast devotion to the reality of our lives and relationships is a needed antidote to any attempt to obscure or overlook human pain. Indeed, the "search" for wellness may paradoxically find its rest in seeking the wholeness of others.

22. The Human Genome Project

KENNETH H. CARTER, JR.

Mount Tabor United Methodist Church
Winston-Salem, North Carolina

Introduction

The goal of the Human Genome Project (HGP) is to map, in comprehensive detail, "the genetic instructions that shape a human being."[1] It has been called the most important biology project ever, biology's "Holy Grail," and "more important than the moon race." The project itself aims to map the identity of roughly 100,000 genes, and, coupled with additional information about structure of proteins encoded within the genes, to gain new insights into the origins of and susceptibility to diseases. HGP Director Francis Collins and colleagues write, "An understanding of the variation between genetic risk promises to change significantly the future prevention and treatment of illness."[2]

In summary, the maps produced by the HGP have the potential to enhance diagnosis of pathology, prevent the onset of disease, reconfigure molecular defects, and prolong the human life span. The HGP, a fifteen-year, $3 billion international research effort, successfully completed all of its major goals in the period of 1993-98, and current progress is two years ahead of schedule.

The purpose of this discussion is to reflect on the Human Genome Project in light of three Christian concepts: creation, justice, and hope. In a sense, I hope to create a dialogue between the aims of the HGP and the broader work being done in the discipline of genetics and these three concepts. While one cannot understand creation, justice, and hope apart from each other, I will concentrate here on hope.

Hope: Eugenics or Glorification?

This perishable body must put on imperishability and the mortal body must put on immortality. (1 Corinthians 15:53)

I will rejoice in Jerusalem, and delight in my people; no more shall the sound of weeping be heard in it, or the cry of distress. No more shall there be in it an infant that lives but a few days, or an old person who does not live out a lifetime; for one who dies at a hundred years will be considered a youth, and one who falls short of a hundred will be considered accursed. (Isaiah 65:19-20)

For what do I hope? Short term goal: that man can survive himself long enough to explore the infinite potential of himself and the world around him. . . . Personal goal: to survive my own bad habits.[3] (Walker Percy)

Genetic therapy is emerging as a form of secular hope. Indeed, scientists must sometimes restrain themselves as they envision the possibilities of the near and distant future. Religious language is employed by scientists who speak of, in Francis Collins's words, the "powerful revelations of human genetics." "The average life span will reach 90-95 years, and a detailed understanding of human aging genes will spur efforts to expand the maximum length of human life," Collins and Karin Jegalian insist.[4] Of course these can be understood as inadequate sources of hope — especially the latter, which might simply be the denial of death. John Polkinghorne likens the "eventual futility of the universe, over a timescale of tens of billions of years, [to] the eventual futility of ourselves, over a timescale of tens of years."[5]

We can either respond to the theological problem — about the faithfulness or providence of God — or engage in denial. Conflict is inherent within our human predicament, as Sondra Wheeler has noted: "On the one hand, to accept our status as embodied and contingent creatures is to accept the bodily limit of death. . . . On the other hand, our tradition gives more than a suggestion that death, at least in its power to isolate and alienate us from one another, is a kind of affront: a sign that something in God's good creation has gone awry. . . . Death is rightfully seen as an enemy of sorts."[6]

A Christian understanding of hope will help us to be truthful to one another, even amidst the necessary conflict presented by our human contingency and finitude on the one hand, and God's power and providence on the other. An inadequate hope bypasses the conflict. Richard Hays notes:

> The New Testament's vision of a final resurrection of the dead enables us to tell the truth about the present, including its tragedies and injustices, without sentimental sugar-coating, without cynicism or despair. It allows us to name suffering and death as real and evil, but not final. Too often, Christians use pious language about how those who have died have "gone to heaven" or "have gone to a better place" in order to deny the reality of death. . . . Against all of this, the New Testament's apocalyptic eschatology offers a sturdy realism that acknowledges the reality of death, while looking to God ultimately to restore life and set all things right.[7]

We avoid the denial of death by entering into the drama of human suffering as lived within the context of the cross and the resurrection. Donald

Juel has correctly noted that "At the center of Christian eschatology is the cross of Christ. While it is the promise of resurrection and the final triumph of God and the Lord Jesus that will furnish the content of Christian hope, a real barrier to Christian hope is not the idea of resurrection — an idea not unique to early Christianity — but the denial of death."[8] Our hopes for the life to come, which are fully inclusive of the reality of bodily death, shape our hopes in this life.

Of course, efforts such as the Human Genome Project may well offer hope to persons in this life through the completion of research. For example, Francis Collins and David Galas reported in 1993 that "genes that confer a predisposition to common diseases such as breast cancer, colon cancer, hypertension, diabetes and Alzheimer's disease have been localized to specific chromosomal regions."[9] Certainly we give thanks for those whose vocational lives serve to alleviate human suffering.

Many persons who serve in scientific and medical professions clearly do so from a motivation of hope. And in so doing they seek the kind of concrete and material outcome envisioned by the prophecy of Isaiah. Religious people are commonly stereotyped as spiritualizing matters in ways that exclude human reality. Scientists, on the other hand, are said to deny spiritual reality in ways that are reductionistic. Christians within the mainline churches often go a third route, collapsing hope into a "realized eschatology" (read most closely from John's Gospel) and thus minimizing its effect. However, Carl Braaten is correct in noting that "not only are hopes the genes of biblical faith, but hope is essential to meaningful existence."[10] Could it be that scientists, as stewards of considerable gifts, will be used by God in ways that bring fulfillment to biblical passages such as Isaiah 65? If so, surely this could help us to enlarge the basis for our hope, in this life and in the life to come.

If one listens to the dialogue between theologians and scientists in the context of genetic therapy and engineering, there is of course an initial need for rhetorical evaluation. When the question "Should scientists play God?" is asked, what occurs is the cessation of argument. When scientists rely upon inadequate religious resources and then ignore them for their inadequacy, a religious vacuum is created. When the church silences the voices of justice and thereby loses its connection with the prophets, it is unprepared for participation in a matter that demands its support of human life in the fullness of its creation in the image of God.

There is a starkness that borders on the apocalyptic in the mapping of the human genome and its subsequent effects upon human life, for good and ill. According to novelist Walker Percy, himself a scientist and also a man of faith, "If the first great intellectual discovery of my life was the beauty of the scientific method, surely the second was the discovery of the single predicament of humanity in the very world which has been transformed by science." He continues, "You don't have to be a sage or a prophet to point out the fact the 20th Century, which should have been the greatest triumph of civilization of all time — the triumph of science, technology, consumership — has been the most murderous century in all of history."[11]

Will the Human Genome Project issue in a triumph of science and technology? Without seeking to halt scientific progress, we should nevertheless listen to voices speaking a cautionary word. Walker Percy speaks of science, technology, and consumership. There is in these words an echo of cautions voiced by others: the limitations of science, the allocation and misallocation of technological advances, and the temptation to reduce human life to a commodity. The potential triumph lies in the human hope for the alleviation of unnecessary suffering. The potential curse is evident in our capacity for self-deception, and in the sin that leads to a distorted vision.

Within the Christian tradition, renewed attention to the concepts of creation, justice, and hope will help us to contribute to the present and future dialogue about the wonderful possibilities and the tremendous challenges arising from the Human Genome Project. We will also benefit from humility on each side of the science/religion debate, and accountability to one another. Christians are called to be neither silent nor careless in our rhetoric.[12]

Creation, justice, and hope are at the core of what we as Christians can contribute to the discussion about human genetics. An inadequate understanding of creation, grounded in an explicit or implicit gnosticism,[13] might lead to a disregard for the body. An inadequate account of justice might lead to an egocentrism or anthropocentrism. An inadequate hope would deny the power and providence of God, for whom we have been created and in whose image we are being restored.[14]

Ultimately, God chooses to operate within the contingency of our creation in ways that are mysterious to us; God challenges us to live justly and mercifully with one another; God plants within us a hope for a life that transcends our present human experience or imagination (Ephesians 3:20-21). A famous hymn text of Charles Wesley beautifully expresses this hope and confidence in God's continual creation *(creatio continua):*

> Finish then thy new creation,
> pure and spotless let us be.
> Let us see thy great salvation,
> perfectly restored in thee;
> changed from glory into glory,
> till in heaven we take our place,
> till we cast our crowns before thee,
> lost in wonder, love and praise.[15]

23. *Science, Religion and the Language of Faith*

BRENDA M. PELC-FASZCZA

First Church of Christ, Congregational
Suffield, Connecticut

Passional Glances toward the Universe

In the United Church of Christ, we affirm in our Statement of Faith the "cost and joy of discipleship." It is one of the best things we say, if not the best understood. In an ordinary, everyday sense, we are fairly sure we know what a "cost" is — mainly time, energy, or money given up for the sake of a ministry. However, these days we also perceive, though perhaps with less clarity, that this definition is not quite the whole truth. Less easy to articulate but important to our lives is another kind of cost related to faith, a psychic one that makes itself regularly felt. It is the burden of the compartmentalized world in which so many of us seem to live, in which we seek to grant authority simultaneously to both theology and science, to rationality and faith, while being relatively clueless about where the common ground between them might be or how either of them might speak in the presence of the other. So far as we have been taught, they are two different languages, like French and Chinese.

What's more, they seem to claim to be talking about different things altogether, with different sets of experts and different certainties to offer, and thus it is hard to be engaged by both of them at the same time. We can in fact still find, at the beginning of the twenty-first century, a lively battle in our culture between creationism (religion) and evolution (science) where the premise is that they are mutually exclusive realms of knowing, and we must choose between them.

Many of us have been raised on the idea that the historical relationship between religion and science is sequential. That is, first came religion, among the primitives and ancients, who did not "know" the world as we do, but only "believed" things about the world, in superstitious ways. Another word for this is *naiveté*. We suppose it lasted until it was superseded by true knowledge, science, which by this way of thinking has displaced naive religiosity with the much more direct certainties of modern empirical science.

Several assumptions are taken for granted within this view. One is that religion and its related expressions are for the central purpose of *explanation;* as we progressively close the gaps in our knowledge of how the world works, we less and less need the notion of God, where the word "God" stands for that which we humans cannot yet explain. Another is that science is perfectly capable of providing absolute truth, and that it does not itself hinge upon any of the "naivetés" of religion. Yet another is that religious truth, being of a different variety from scientific truth, does not offer anything worth keeping once we have the preferable scientific truth available. The ambiguity, roominess, and passion of religious truth — especially religious metaphor — are seen as flawed beside the black-and-white analysis of science, so that, to paraphrase Pauline scripture, when the perfect comes, the imperfect is tossed aside.

Each of these assumptions is inadequate for our present historical moment, and is challenged by a larger view. Most importantly, science in our time is becoming understood as itself an enterprise where values, assumptions, and passions come into play; where no purely objective or dispassionate knowing of the world is possible; where previously held certainties come undone with new discovery; where the universe seems no longer a static "given," waiting inertly to be discovered, but a dynamic, unfolding whole that in amazing and mysterious ways is disclosing itself to us, even while we are ourselves a part of the very unfolding. Science, once thought to be the enemy of faith in its role of eliminating mystery, now seems in a position to be something of a partner, as it throws open our inherited cosmology and renders the whole thing mysterious again. Even some scientists are speaking of the necessarily poetic quality to our speech about ultimate reality. We are beginning to understand anew how much we do not understand. In spite of, or perhaps because of, how much we have learned through science in the last century alone, we are becoming naive again in the face of the vast mysteries of the huge universe.

For Christian faith, this is a good thing. Naiveté, as the term is used here, might be thought of along the lines of humility: the simple admission that we do not know everything, the basic capacity to sustain a sense of the sacred that is larger than we are, the stance of awe and reverence before the majestic complexity of the universe. How and where the sacred stories of our religious traditions, bearing their own claims and truths, can be appropriated in this world is the question.

Are we in a time when the old dualism between science and religion is dissolving such that religious language — sacred story — can have a new, fresh hearing in communities of faith, not in spite of scientific claims but because of them? Is there a way in which our developing empirical knowledge of the universe can contribute to rather than undermine our religious understandings of ourselves in relation to God and God's creation? What is at stake in Christian tradition in order to allow such a dialogue with science and its ways of knowing? What are the "costs and joys" of such a dialogue?

John Shea, a teller of Christian sacred stories, sees it this way:

> Scientific advance does not render the world opaque, but from a certain mindset increases its sacramentality. . . . The future relationship of science and religious consciousness may be one of those reversals which historians love to point out. The very endeavor — science and technology — which at one stage of history obscured the religious dimension of human existence, at another stage will discover it on its own terms and with its own nuances. Science does not threaten to exhaust transcendence, but reaffirms it at every advance.[1]

For the sake of the increase of the sacramentality of the world, and of a "passional glance" toward it, all this is worth exploring.

The Second Naiveté

One voice needing to be heard in our new conversation is that of philosopher Paul Ricoeur, who in *The Symbolism of Evil* (1967) offered the notion of the "second naiveté" as a way of appropriating in the modern world the truth of ancient religious symbols and narratives. Ricoeur addresses the epistemological problem we encounter in the post-Enlightenment age when we attempt to bear the truth claims of sacred texts as literal and historical. Expressly rejecting a dualism that would make scientific or historical thought and religious thought mutually exclusive, he sees them rather as related and necessary stages in a continuum of knowing, each giving us something we cannot do without.

There is, he posits, a first naiveté, or an initial stance, before sacred texts that is immediate: we take them initially at their face value, at their literal, surface meaning. Our experience, however, as citizens of the modern world invites us to bring critical thought to bear upon the texts and their apparent claims, such that we suspend for a time a decision about their "truth" so that we can ask questions of them in light of other realms of knowledge — scientific, historical , anthropological, literary. This may leave us, if we stop there, with dismembered texts, with stories whose value is questionable when read from a historical or scientific point of view. This may leave us, in other words, with "mythology" in the pejorative sense: stories that we decide are not true when held against materialist ways of knowing.

But we must not, in Ricoeur's view, stop with this second stage of critical interpretation. What we need the most is then to go on to reappropriate the sacred texts, making full use of whatever light our critical thought has shed on them for meaning, but ultimately reclaiming them as mythology in the higher sense: stories, symbols, and metaphors that bear to us the highest and deepest truths, because they are the only language that can do so. We stand before them again as texts that tell us the truth — only now our understanding of the "truth" has been deepened:

> [Could we] go back to a primitive naiveté? Not at all. In every way, something has been lost, irremediably lost: immediacy of belief. But if we can no longer live the great symbolisms of the sacred in accordance with the original belief in them, we can, we modern men, aim at a sec-

151

ond naiveté in and through criticism. In short, it is by interpreting that we can hear again. Thus it is in hermeneutics that the symbol's gift of meaning and the endeavor to understand by deciphering are knotted together.[2]

The fascinating thing here is that science is considered to be essential in the service of faith: it is only because we bring scientific thought to bear upon sacred texts and symbols that we can be pushed past a simplistic "first naiveté" on to a more complex, rich, nuanced embrace of sacred traditions and their fullest meanings. Without the role of scientific and historical thought — necessary but not sufficient — we would remain ignorant of the true purposes of the stories we tell; this is my reading of Ricoeur's ultimate point.

Sara Maitland concurs and adds to this when she writes about the dangers of glorifying and remaining at the second stage, which we might call "scientism":

Scientism is a myth too, a myth as pernicious as any other sort of fundamentalism. Any stance towards the world which holds that it can be read off and lived at one level only, and that God must be forced to perform according to the requirements of that level, is dangerous to our wholeness. It is a denial that God is — of necessity, of divine ontology — beyond the boundaries of our categorization. Biblical fundamentalists may be attacked for wishing to confine God's activities to those laid down in the Bible; but rationalist fundamentalists are attempting to do the same thing. They want to limit God to what we know how to articulate within the structures of a distinctly restrictive epistemological code. In fact our ability to think, to imagine, to create mythologically is becoming severely restricted, and this is worrying. . . .

. . . The naiveté of childhood is the naiveté of ignorance; the second naiveté is to become innocent, knowing that while ignorance is an unfortunate fact of life, innocence is a demanding virtue: open-minded, simple-minded without loss of knowledge or integrity, becoming as a little child again without the security blanket of lack of data; with a determination to find the world beautiful, magical, wild beyond dreams, dancing its complex patterns of truth, weaving its multi-coloured threads of discourse so that all things can be true and we can more be ravished by the beauty of God. . . .[3]

"Innocence is a demanding virtue" indeed. And truths that we do not already suspect do have a hard time making themselves felt. How do we, in the community of faith, cultivate this kind of innocence and receptivity, awakening to the ways of God that we may not yet have suspected and that we therefore are not prepared to see or participate in? What kind of language can open us, inspire us, and help us hear again, bringing us to wisdom and something like innocence in God's universe?

Finally Comes the Poet

A second voice to be heard in this conversation is that of Walter Brueggemann, Christian scholar of Hebrew Biblical texts, who insists that we are at a critical juncture in the relationship between Christian faith and culture, or more specifically, between the epistemology and language of the faith and the epistemology and language of the culture. Granting that the postmodern era in which we now find ourselves is requiring of us a major shift in consciousness, Brueggemann says:

> It is my thesis that our context for ministry is the failure of the imagination of modernity, in both its moral-theological and its economic-political aspects. We are at a moment when the imagination of modernity is being replaced by the post-modern imagination, which is less sure and less ambitious and which more modestly makes a local claim . . . our culture is one in which the old imagined world is lost, but still powerfully cherished, and in which there is bewilderment and fear, because there is no clear way on how to order our shared imagination differently or better. . . .
>
> It is not, in my judgment, the work of the church (or of the preacher) to construct a full alternative world, for that would be to act as preemptively and imperialistically as all those old construals and impositions. Rather, the task is to fund — to provide the pieces, materials and resources out of which a new world can be imagined. Our responsibility, then, is not a grand scheme or a coherent system, but the voicing of a lot of little pieces out of which people can put life together in fresh configurations.[4]

What kind of language can provide this "funding"? Brueggemann's answer is the poetic, whose function is to "cherish the truth, to open the truth from its pervasive reductionism in our society, to break the fearful rationality that keeps the news from being new."[5]

> Because of the very character of sacrament, textual speech about sacrament cannot be direct, frontal speech. Sacrament requires speech that concerns elusive, symbolic gestures in which the participants discern more than is visible to an outsider. The act of sacrament requires the speech of poetry to keep hidden what must not be profaned by description. . . .[6]

And of preaching:

> The moment of speech is a poetic rendering in a community that has come all too often to expect nothing but prose. It is a prose world for all those who must meet payrolls and grade papers and pump gas and fly planes. When the text too has been reduced to prose, life becomes so prosaic that only poetic articulation has a chance to let us live.[7]

Like Ricoeur, Brueggemann argues that the purpose of religious language, and of sacred text, is not to explain, but to disclose; not to encase reality within determined and certain boundaries, but to evoke in the human heart and world a response to a Reality that is utterly unbounded and never altogether certain, that has the capacity to surprise us with genuine newness. What is possible for us to enact — ethically, socially, culturally, aesthetically — derives from what we have first been able to imagine, such that the language in which we imagine alternatives must be as trusting as possible of freedom.

But Brueggemann is also saying more. His advocacy of a faith language that concerns itself with the providing of "a lot of little pieces" out of which we can construe a new world is a direct challenge to any point of view that claims to be able to say everything because it knows everything. The classic identifier of the postmodern perspective is "incredulity toward metanarrative." We need to be telling smaller stories now, in other words, willing to take reality and discern its meaning one experience, one text, at a time. The great pastoral fact among us, Brueggemann claims, is the failure of the white, Western, male hegemony that has dominated our whole view of the world for centuries now.

... the practice of modernity, of which we are all the children, since the seventeenth century has given us a world imagined through the privilege of white, male, Western, colonial hegemony, with all its pluses and minuses. It is a world that we have come to trust and take for granted as a given. It is a world that has wrought great good, but that has also accomplished enormous mischief against some for the sake of others. The simple truth is that this construed world can no longer be sustained, is no longer persuasive or viable, and we are able to discern no large image to put in its place.[8]

Thus, Christian theology is now *theologies*, as feminist, womanist, and liberationist movements of various kinds have challenged the assumption that there could be one rendering of truth from one cultural point of view that could viably include and address the experience of everyone everywhere.

This may be seen as a gain or a loss, depending upon one's starting premises for doing theology. For those willing to entertain it as potential gain, as possible new life for Christian faith itself in the postmodern world, what is the upshot for the language and proclamation of faith? Finally this from Brueggemann:

The formal premise I urge is that our knowing is essentially imaginative, that is, an act of organizing social reality around dominant, authoritative images. This means that the assumptions that have long had unexamined privilege among us are now seen to be sturdy, powerful acts of imagination, reinforced, imposed and legitimated by power.[9]

If new knowing, then, requires the authorizing of new images, can science and religion be partners in this enterprise, for the sake of the whole world? Do we now perceive that even scientific knowledge is itself imaginative in a certain sense, presuming and being organized around certain dominant images, authorized within interests of a political kind, at least some of which may now need to be outgrown? For those of us who care about speech in the community of faith, what new naiveté might be possible for us in our proclamation, what new sense of innocence and humility, what poetry might redeem us from the overreaching claims to the truth that we have made in the past?

24. A (Natural?) Theology of Music

DOUGLAS VAUGHAN

First Presbyterian Church
Wilmington, North Carolina

The author of 2 Chronicles 20 tells a fascinating story of God's faithfulness to Judah, a story in which music plays an unusual role. When King Jehoshaphat learns of a conspiracy against Judah, he prays to God. Soon, God's spirit falls on Jahaziel, a descendant of Asaph, the musician whom David put in charge of music in worship (1 Chronicles 6:39) and who sang at the dedication of Solomon's Temple (2 Chronicles 5:12). Jahaziel foresees that God will give victory to Judah. He even tells Jehoshaphat where to find the enemy's advancing armies.

The next morning finds the king and his army in the wilderness of Tekoa preparing for battle. Jehoshaphat gives a brief pep talk to his troops and then does a surprising thing. He first forms a choir and then puts this musical ensemble at the front of the battle line so that Judah marches into battle behind a group of men who sing "Give thanks to the Lord, for his love endures forever." And the story tells us that the sound of that choir wrought confusion among the enemy who proceeded to decimate each other. By the time Judah reached a vantage point all they could see was a battlefield strewn with dead bodies.

What's more, the author seems at pains to tell us that while Judah's victory is God's doing, there is nevertheless a causal link between the sound of the singing and the enemy's demise. "And when they began to sing and praise, the Lord set an ambush against the men of Ammon, Moab, and Mount Seir, who had come against Judah, so that they were routed" (2 Chr. 20:22). God was active in and through the music.

Other Old Testament texts reinforce an understanding of music as a vehicle of God's activity. Indeed, music in Scripture is never just an aesthetic embellishment in worship or background sound for domestic activity. Saul, Israel's first king, for example, is subject to attacks by "an evil spirit from God." His servants seem to know that the cure for such an attack is the sound of the lyre, hence their arrangement with the boy David (cf. 1 Sam. 16:14-23). Contemporary interpretations of Saul's problems usually invoke modern psychiatry to explain his mood disorder. Yet the Scriptures are careful to tell us that God was behind Saul's problem ("an evil spirit from God") and that the music communicated with that spirit, hence with God, in ways that other human activities could not.

The Psalms are songs to be sung to God. Many of them have "superscriptions" that preachers usually skip and to which scholars make only passing reference; but in these we are told that a particular psalm is to be accompanied by stringed instruments, or that it is a *miktam,* or that it is to be sung to the tune "The Lily of Testimony." The Psalms are replete with musical indications. In addition, the texts of some of the Psalms themselves call for the use of musical instruments, or for singing God's praises. Furthermore, the Psalms are not just our human hymns to God. They are a part of Scripture, formed by an act of inspiration. In some sense, then, the Psalms are God's words and music given to us with which to communicate with God. All of this suggests that sometimes God prefers communication from and with us that takes a musical form.

Such an understanding sheds light on the role of music in the sacrificial liturgies of the Temple, where music played as long as the ritual continued (2 Chr. 29:20-30). Light is also shed on the strange exhortation of Ephesians 5:19 (cf. Col. 3:16) where the faithful are instructed to "speak to one another in psalms, hymns, and spiritual songs. . . ." At the very least, that instruction encourages us to raise the level of conversation within the Christian community to a God-like one. But even more than that, the exhortation is encouragement for the faithful here and now to foreshadow in their manner of life the singing of the saints in heaven as depicted in Revelation.

Closer to our own time, both Karl Barth and Hans Küng have written about their own experiences with the music of Mozart. Barth, of course, was quite fond of Mozart's music and insisted, probably tongue-in-cheek, that when the angels in heaven are at work officially praising God, they play only the music of Bach; but when these same angels are off duty and playing for their own good pleasure, they play Mozart and God listens with great joy. Barth also insisted that "if I ever get to heaven, I would first of all seek out Mozart and only then inquire after Augustine, St. Thomas, Luther, Calvin, and Schleiermacher."[1]

In his little book *Wolfgang Amadeus Mozart,* Barth tells us that when he listens to the music of Mozart he hears the message of freedom. He doesn't actually say that listening to Mozart is like listening to the Christian gospel, but he comes very close. "Mozart never lamented, never quarreled, though he certainly was entitled to. Instead, he always achieved this consoling turn, which for everyone who hears it is priceless. And that seems to me, insofar as one can say it at all, to be the secret of his *freedom* and with it the essence of Mozart's special *quality* which engaged our attention at the beginning."[2] It is the unique quality of Mozart's music, according to Barth, that the light always triumphs over the dark without extinguishing it, with the result that Mozart's music always sounds "unburdened, effortless, and light. That is why it unburdens, releases, and liberates us."[3]

What Barth implies, Küng asserts. In his book, *Mozart: Traces of Transcendence,* Küng tells us that

> there are countless men and women who can confirm that in certain moments of attunement a gift may be given to those sensitive people who are ready to hear, alone yet not alone, and to open themselves in that rational yet supra-rational trust of which I have spoken. With keen ears they may also perceive in the pure, utterly internalized sound, for example of the *adagio* of the Clarinet Concerto, which embraces us without using any words, something wholly other: the sound of the beautiful in its infinity, indeed the sound of an infinite which transcends us and for which "beauty" is no description. So here are ciphers, traces of transcendence. . . . If I allow myself to be open, then precisely in this event of music which speaks without words I can be touched by an inexpressible, unspeakable mystery. In this overwhelming, liberating experience of music, which brings such bliss, I can myself trace, feel and experience the presence of a deepest depth or a highest height. Pure presence, silent joy, happiness.[4]

I take Küng to be saying that at least some people, upon hearing some music, do hear "the sound of an infinite" that "speaks without words." Indeed, in another place, Küng says that this is precisely the experience that he has listening to Mozart and that when it happens, he says, the "statement comes to mind: 'In it we live and move and have our being.'"[5]

Starting at a different point but arriving at a similar conclusion,

A (Natural?) Theology of Music

George Steiner in *Real Presences* talks of music as communication from a realm beyond:

> Music makes utterly substantive what I have sought to suggest of the real presence in meaning where that presence cannot be analytically shown or paraphrased. Music brings to our daily lives an immediate encounter with a logic of sense other than that of reason. It is, precisely, the truest name we have for the logic at work in the springs of being that generate vital forms. Music has celebrated the mystery of intuitions of transcendence from the songs of Orpheus, counter-creative to death, to the *Missa Solemnis,* from Schubert's late piano sonatas to Schoenberg's *Moses und Aron* and Messiaen's *Quatuor pour la fin du temps.* Countless times, this celebration has had manifest relations to religion. But the core-relation far exceeds any specific religious motive or occasion. In ways so obvious as to make any statement a tired cliché, yet of an indefinable and tremendous nature, music puts our being as men and women in touch with that which transcends the sayable, which outstrips the analyzable.[6]

Music history is replete with statements from musicians that echo and expand our understanding of music as a way in which the numinous reaches out to us. Ralph Vaughan Williams, for example, defined music as "a reaching out to the ultimate realities by means of ordered sound . . . music transports us from the particular to the universal."[7] He goes even further to state that "those great patterns in sound, designed by Beethoven or Bach . . . open the magic casements and enable us to understand what is beyond the appearances of life."[8]

Quoting a fellow music critic, Deems Taylor writes: "'Tchaikovsky's music awakens in the breast the haunting, unanswerable questions of life and death that concern us directly and personally.'" Taylor's comment on that statement: "That is quite true. It is also quite true of any great music, whether it be Beethoven's Ninth Symphony, Mozart's G Minor, Brahms' First, the *Liebestod,* or *The Afternoon of the Faun*."[9]

Elder Olson captured the essence of music's capacity to communicate from a realm beyond in his poem "A Recital By Rudolf Serkin."

Music, oldest of the arts,
Unlike all others

159

Moves immediately upon the mind,
Presents no Lear for pity,
No awakening Adam for wonder;
We exult or grieve, unable to say why;

Nor can we say how it was
That suffering, thought, toil
Became the fleeting touch of a fingertip,
How the insensate instrument
Shook the insensate air
To make passion into sound, sound into passion.

How a man became music,
We became that music,
All the many listeners became one,
Differences like discords
Resolved in concord.[10]

We could cite the example of Scriabin, who claimed that when play-ing certain of his own pieces on the piano he heard the beating of angels' wings above his head. We could also cite the often repeated story of Han-del, who is alleged to have stated that while writing *Messiah* "the very gates of heaven seemed to open above me and as the music went onto the paper, choirs of angels with glad eyes sang the Hallelujah Chorus."[11]

Of course, references to such names as Handel, Bach, Mozart, and Beethoven raise the question of whether the experience of which we write is a culturally conditioned one available only to persons condi-tioned by Western culture and its music. While I am not competent to generalize about the music of other cultures and the ways in which per-sons in those cultures experience their music, I did raise the question ca-sually with a family member who is very knowledgeable about the music of the Indian subcontinent. He went immediately to his CD collection and read to me from the liner notes of a tamboura recording: "The sound of the Tamboura resonates with the primordial sound of 'Om.' . . ." Else-where on the same CD cover was this quote from the *Vijnana Bhairava:* "If a yogi listens with undivided attention to the sounds of stringed in-struments where resonance is prolonged, he will finally be absorbed in the space of Consciousness and will attain the state of the Self."[12] I would

160

speculate, on the basis of this evidence from Indian music, that the experience of which we write is known in other cultures, perhaps even in all other cultures. Suffice it to say, at any rate, that some music, for some persons, under some circumstances, behaves like a communication from a realm beyond.

But how is this experience different from an emotional response to music? After all, it is entirely possible that Barth, Küng, and Steiner, like so many persons who not only listen to great music but absorb themselves in it, could be having an emotional reaction to the music, a reaction they have confused with a "trace of transcendence." The power of music to affect a person's mood is widely acknowledged. Indeed, "mood music" is a recognizable genre — not to mention a highly lucrative enterprise! Furthermore, an aesthetic experience involves the emotions; indeed, the etymology of "aesthetic" points us to the emotions. So it is possible that, rather than music's being a vehicle for awakening an awareness of a realm beyond, a wordless message from the numinous, it could be merely a stimulus for an emotional response.

But what is emotion? Building on the work of John Dewey, Leonard B. Meyer, in *Emotion and Meaning in Music*,[13] espouses a "conflict theory of emotions." It is his belief that emotion or affect is aroused in us when a tendency to respond is arrested or inhibited. Meyer is not talking, in this context, of mood, which is temporary and passing, but rather of emotion, a longer-lasting state. According to this understanding, then, for example, wanting to punch an offensive person in the nose but being constrained from doing so by good manners is going to make us emotional.

If that is the case, what is it that is arrested or inhibited when we listen to music? To be sure, we are not talking about all music, nor are we talking about an experience that happens each time we listen, and we are certainly not talking about all people. Barth and Küng write about their own experience in listening to the music of one composer and, one suspects, that experience is not guaranteed every time Mozart comes on the radio. But in those instances when we listen to certain music and perceive it as a form of communication from the numinous, what is going on with our emotions? What impulse to respond is being blocked or arrested?

Lewis Thomas, medical researcher and essayist, has written two pieces that help us make the connection between an emotional response to music and a perception of music as a vehicle for those traces of transcendence. In *The Lives of a Cell,* Thomas includes the essay "Music of *This* Sphere," in which he notes how every animal seems to have a purposeful and patterned way of making sounds. He hypothesizes that if we could hear all of those sounds at once, from the smallest termite to the largest of the whales, those sounds would fit together into something like a symphony composed and performed by nature itself. Delving further into the field of "bioacoustics," Thomas believes that there is something about our very biology that predisposes in us the urge to make music. That something is "an earliest memory, a score for the transformation of inanimate, random matter in chaos into the improbable, ordered dance of living forms."[14]

In a more recent work, *Et Cetera, Et Cetera: Notes of a Word-Watcher,* Thomas includes an essay in which he notes that our English word for music comes from the Indo-European root *men,* from which we get all those words having to do with our minds. He believes that when we listen to music, we are listening to the "sounds of thought."[15] He comments further:

> The individual human brain is an immense living creature made of interacting, interconnected thoughts, moving about in a nonlinear, dynamical system at something near the speed of light, always vulnerable to huge rearrangements and changes in patterns in the order of any part of any thought. It might be like the metaphor in the mathematicians' "butterfly effect": the slight disturbance of the air over Shanghai by a butterfly will cause, months later, sustained storms in New York. Music has the power to introduce any number of such disturbances, unpredictably and sequentially, and the result is something like chaos, but a chaos with its own, unpredicted form and order. The pleasure of music is, in part anyway, the unexpected, sustained sense of surprise that it induces in the mind. It is hard to imagine utter surprise as more than a momentary sensation, *on* then *off,* but what profound music does in the receptive, attentive mind is to produce a steady, unwavering high plateau of surprise, lasting as long as the music lasts.[16]

He concludes by confessing that "we possess no vocabulary to account, even lamely, for the sensation of music."[17] He even wonders if those who trace the etymology of our word *music* to the root *mu,* from which we also get the word *mystery,* might be on to something.[18]

Unwittingly, perhaps, Thomas has pointed us in the direction of a so-lution to the question of the relation of our emotional response to music and our perceiving in music some traces of transcendence. Following Dewey, I would suggest we become emotional in listening to profound music because some urge is being blocked, the urge to respond in some way to what we are hearing. What is blocked is the urge to join the music — but not just to hum along or whistle the tune. No, profound music trig-gers that "recapitulation of something else" within us, that "earliest mem-ory, a score for the transformation of inanimate, random matter in chaos into the improbable, ordered dance of living forms."[19] Sometimes when we listen to music, it happens that at some archetypal level, we remember being a part of the music of creation, of which God speaks to Job (Job 38:6, 7). And, no, that memory is not a rational one; it occurs much deeper in the psyche. And Thomas is right — it cannot be expressed in words. But even as that memory is triggered by the sounds that stir us, our status as fallen creatures in a fallen world blocks us from making those sounds in which we once participated and for which we were cre-ated.

And even as we move deeper into the realm of metaphor, let us be clear that the feelings that are stirred by great music and the intuition we have about what is going on in that experience are quite real and con-crete. Nevertheless, words cannot capture, even partially, the profundity of that reality. Mendelssohn was surely right when he insisted that the meaning of music is too precise for words.

Coda

In *The Faith of a Physicist*, John Polkinghorne writes in passing of "a nat-ural theology of the arts."[20] He seems impressed with George Steiner's as-sertion that "the matter of music [is] central to that of the meanings of man, of man's access to or abstention from metaphysical experience."[21] In this connection, Polkinghorne himself observes, "That a temporal suc-cession of vibrations in the air can speak to us of eternity is a fact that must be accommodated in any adequate account of reality."[22] He goes on to remark, "I want to say to my friends who have difficulty with religious belief, 'Can you deny music? If not, then you acknowledge a dimension of reality transcending the material, which may prove for you the intimation of what Steiner calls a real presence.'"[23] It will be clear to the reader that I agree with Polkinghorne at this point. Music, as it turns out, has significant theological importance.

But is this a *natural* theology of music? A working definition of "natural theology," reaching back to Aristotle and Aquinas, would be the attempt to derive truths about God by examining God's works in nature apart from any special revelation. The "argument from beauty," for example, one of the classic "proofs" for the existence of God, recognized all the beauty and symmetry in nature and thus posited a God who loved beauty and order. Such a God was, of course, more believable in an earlier age, especially in the Romantic era, than in the modern one so shaped by the devastations of world wars and environmental disasters. Nevertheless, natural theology was an important theological concept in its day.

In this paper, we have looked at the testimonies of persons who have been moved by music to an awareness of a reality beyond this one, an experience that put them in touch with a sublime hope and peace. On the evidence, this experience is not reasoned after the fact as a reflection on the nature of the combination of melody, rhythm, and harmony that constitutes music. It is not something that is consonant with a "natural theology." Rather, the evidence points us to a reality that looks and feels like revelation itself. In some way, God uses the vehicle of music to communicate to us that there is another realm of which we already have some experience and toward which we long to go. In the end, music and faith both operate at a level that is, at the same time, deeper and higher than cognition and reason. A theology of music, therefore, needs to be open to exploring that realm of human personality in which the aesthetic experience occurs and through which we gain certain knowledge of our eschatological hope.

CHAPTER VI

Transformation in Congregations

Introduction

In an ironic reversal of roles at the outset of the American twenty-first century, optimistic mainline religion is reverting to this-worldly management and entertainment, while pessimistic mainline science is capitulating to otherworldly fire and brimstone. In agreement with neither and in response to both, a strong minority movement within the churches is calling for a critical partnership of Scriptures and telescopes in a realistic eschatology that gives God the glory as both Creator and Redeemer in the power of the Spirit. In this movement, the church is viewed not merely as a social but primarily as a cosmic change agent, in which pastor-theologians are faithfully proclaiming in word and deeds, sermons and sacraments, that the crucified and risen Lord has promised to "make all things new." Christ centers that transforming activity in a counter-cultural, indeed trans-cultural, communion of believers, who are being radically forgiven and renewed in daily worship and service. The body of Christ, emulating its divine head, is not essentially an earthly institution with heavenly visions of "pie in the sky by and by"; it is, rather, a divine reality that assumes human forms and structures within human history in order to regenerate the present with the future power and purpose of God: "May the God of hope fill you with all joy and peace, so that you may abound in hope by the power of the Holy Spirit" (Rom. 15:13).

The opening excerpt from David Henderson's "The Eschatological and Doxological Character of the Church in the World" develops the church as an eschatological reality. Like Christ its living Lord, the church exists in but not of this world. It is a resurrection people, empowered by the Holy Spirit, set apart as the communion of saints, both "bearing witness to and participating in the divine action in the world." It hopefully occupies the historical space between the "already" of Christ's cross and the "not yet" of the fulfillment of God's new creation. Consonant with this eschatological character is its doxological praise and prayer. If sin is the world's faithless talking about God as if he were not present ("secondary discourse"), then it is the church's faithful calling to address God in prayer and thanksgiving directly in his real presence ("primary discourse"). While being restored to the loving life in community primevally enjoyed with God and others in the Garden, Christians now begin to construe all of reality sacramentally. Our discipleship consists of our offering of the world to the glory of God through our baptismal participation in Christ's self-sacrifice for the world, now viewed as an icon "pointing beyond itself to its Creator and Redeemer."

"Worship as Sign of the End" by Erik Strand avers that authentic Christian worship is itself an eschatological expression of God's inbreaking reign among us. Deploring those gatherings "where, in their pandering to culture and class, eschatology has been covered over," the author champions the historical *ordo* of the church catholic (word and sacrament) where the community of the faithful (1) witnesses to the end of things, (2) welcomes scientific insights into the cosmos that is God's creation, (3) worships in eschatological depth, (4) points to a different understanding of time and history, and (5) proclaims memory and meaning to the world from the perspective of the promise of God in Christ to "make all things new."

Among the church's unique sources of hopeful renewal, Paul Matheny highlights "Christian Proclamation in Eschatological Perspective." The hope that we receive from the Spirit is normed by the church's Christocentric message of reconciliation. "God's Spirit invites us to participate in the service of God's future." Developed are distinctive eschatological affirmations of faith that insure the Christian character of proclamation: (1) hope lies in a future with God; (2) this world dies; (3) the boundaries of death and finitude have been sprung; (4) God is present when the kingdom is proclaimed; (5) the end of time has begun with Christ's incarnation and resurrection; (6) the presence of the Spirit brings the future into the conditions of the present. Proclamation is the ministry of reconciliation. His urgent conclusion: "Silence concerning the eschatological themes of Scripture needs to be broken."

166

The homiletical employment of eschatological insights is demonstrated in Jonathan Jenkins' excerpt, "The Future Belongs to Jesus!" This slogan is proposed as "a summary for the 'theological content of the christological story in its eschatological significance.'" Whatever the future may be, it will be a creature of the Creator God and of Jesus Christ, through whom all things were made by the Father. What is unique in Christian proclamation is the promise Jesus made to the future: he preached the message of the immediate coming of the kingdom of God, bringing the future "age to come" into the present. Proclaiming an unconditional blessing to all, his mission was to gather Israel to himself in order that Israel might share in his own unique relationship to the Lord God of Israel — "my Father." The author illustrates by numerous quotes from former sermons his essay's trinitarian conclusion: "In the end, creation will find her shape ever anew within the history of the Son, the originality of the Father, and the interpretive liberty of the Holy Spirit."

Our volume's final excerpt explores "Hopeful Feasting: Eucharist and Eschatology." This section develops the characteristic way in which Geoffrey Wainwright connects the church's Eucharist with eschatological hope. Doctrinal conflicts over Christ's presence or the church's sacrifice have frequently marginalized the significance of the Eucharist as "the common meal of the whole churchly people of God in the last days, and its relation to the Messiah's banquet in the kingdom and the abundant feeding that the Bible looked for in the days of the new heavens and the new earth." The Hebrew Scriptures offer a rich background for Jesus and the church's understanding of eating and drinking in the kingdom of God in both the present and the future (e.g. Ex. 24:11; Ps. 23; Is. 25:6-9). Later this messianic banquet imagery became linked to the Jewish Passover, and still later to the Eucharist and to the risen Christ's return in glory. Theologically, it is of importance to the author that the Eucharist (1) expresses both continuity and discontinuity in the relation between the present and future reign of God; (2) takes ordinary gifts of food and drink for divine self-disclosure; and (3) transcends any dualistic categories between the material and spiritual in our notions of God's reign. Especially in the liturgies of the Orthodox East, there is also a stronger stress on the second coming of Christ, judgment, and heavenly blessings.

25. The Eschatological and Doxological Character of the Church in the World

DAVID HENDERSON

St. Paul's Episcopal Church
Steamboat Springs, Colorado

"ut legem credendi lex statuat supplicandi" — *The law of worship establishes the law of belief.*

Prosper of Aquitaine

"The Word became flesh, and lived among us, and we have seen his glory. . . ."

John 1:14

The church is an eschatological reality. This is to say that the church, as the gathered community of the faithful, bears witness to God's saving activity in the world in the past, the present, and the future. The people of God, historically constituted as Israel and the church, live with the knowledge and experience of God working in and through them to accomplish his purposes with the hope that God will carry out his plan of redemption to fulfillment in the future. The church exists as an eschatological reality insofar as it recognizes that it lives within a creation, not merely a cosmos, and that this creation itself is shot through with the active presence of the One who creates, redeems, and sustains it. The church is the eschatological community, bearing witness to and participating in the divine action in the world.

This means that ecclesiology cannot be separated from eschatology. It is the church, enlivened and empowered by the Spirit, that proclaims the fulfillment of the promises of God in the person and work of Jesus Christ and bears witness to the world that he is making all things new. The church occupies that space between the "already" of the cross and resurrection of Christ and the "not yet" of the fulfillment of God's new creation, and as such, is a provisional institution. As Ben Witherington points out, the church is not equivalent to the dominion of God but bears witness to that dominion, which has been inaugurated in Jesus Christ and moves towards final consummation.[1] This should warn us away from an overly realized eschatology. The church does not initiate the dominion of God on earth; neither does it passively await the consummation. Rather, the church in its proclamation and witness to Christ *participates* in that which God is bringing about for his creation. The church, the people of God, exists to be God's agent of reconciliation, a transforming presence in the world until all things are subjected to Christ.

In this regard, the church lives in both *chronos* and *kairos;* that is, temporality as well as God-filled time — eschatological time. The church does not look toward the end of time so much as it looks for time's redemption. The church does not so much hope for heaven as it hopes and looks forward to a new heaven *and a new earth,* when the City of Man is transformed into the City of God — when the world is re-created, when chaos gives way to new creation. As Walter Brueggemann puts it, the resurrection of Jesus from the dead is the "quintessential case in Christian parlance" of this eschatological hope.[2] Christ's resurrection is the foundation for the church's eschatological hope that all things are being made new in him through whom all things were made. The eschatological hope, therefore, is rooted in the historical saving event of Christ's death and resurrection, while at the same time living within the perspective of a not-yet-realized future. This tension is what shapes how the church lives in the present and defines its message and mission. The church's hope, therefore, is profoundly worldly in its focus. The world, the creation, is the realm of God's saving activity. Far from an eschatology that hopes for flight from this world in decay or an apocalypticism that views the end as a divine wiping-clean of the slate, the church engages the world as an active participant in and witness to the transforming power of God, who brings the exiles home and who causes rivers to spring forth in the desert.

As Christ's resurrection was not an escape from death but an overcoming of the power of death, so is the church's relation to the world one of transformation through the power of the Spirit working in and through the church. (The miracles of healing and exorcism as signs of the inbreaking of the kingdom of God, and the disciples' commission to carry on this work, speak to the world-transforming character of the church's mission.) An ecclesiology, so construed eschatologically, therefore requires an ethic that takes the world seriously as the focus of God's redeeming work. This world is the world for which Christ died. It is the object of God's redemption and re-creation through Christ. Christ's resurrection from the dead is the first fruits of the resurrection of a world bound in death and decay. The tension of the "already/not yet" experience of the church is focused in the experience of the believer who, by faith and baptism, *already* shares in the death and resurrection life of Christ, and faithfully works for and *awaits* the coming of the Lord.

A second observation concerns the essential character of the church that defines and shapes its existence in the world. This is a critical point, as it bears on the very issue at the core of the relationship between science and theology. What follows I hope serves to describe the disjunction between theology and ministry that we have been seeking to address in the Pastor-Theologian Program itself.

Bonhoeffer, in his work *Creation and Fall*, describes what he calls the first "religious question."[3] The serpent asks Eve, "Did God say, 'You shall not eat from any tree in the garden'?" Not only does the question distort the command of God (as he had prohibited the eating of only the Tree of the Knowledge of Good and Evil); it also invites Eve into a conversation *about* God, as if he were not even present. The narrative represents the disjunction between what might be termed "primary discourse" and "secondary discourse" regarding both God and creation. Primary discourse is language with God as its subject, addressing God in praise and thanksgiving *(theologia prima)*. Secondary discourse is language about God, making God the object of our conversation *(theologia secunda)*. If not firmly rooted in primary discourse, secondary discourse about God lapses into idolatry. The same is true with regard to how we construe the world around us. Primary discourse regarding the world is language that views the world as a creation, sustained by the continual creative power of the Creator, the sphere in which we transact reality in cooperation with the creative purposes of God (Psalm 104). Adam names the animals and eats of the fruit of the trees of the Garden and in so doing acts as one created in the image of God, naming and eating to God's glory. Secondary discourse, divorced from this primary relationship, lapses into engagement with the world as an object *for us* rather than as the workshop of the Creator in whose employ we live and move and have our being.[4]

The sin of the Garden consisted not in eating, but in not eating to God's glory and in accordance with God's purpose. In essence, the sin of Adam and Eve in eating incorrectly amounted to a lapse into secondary discourse about the world and God, cut off from the primary discourse of relationship with the Creator, which is doxology. Such a disjunction of secondary discourse from primary is thus idolatrous, and leaves a person alienated from God, the world, and others. Cut off from relationship with God, one experiences death. The creation, no longer the "workshop" in which we participate in God's creative purposes by engaging the world for God's sake, becomes subject to futility and decay: "Claiming to be wise, they became fools; and they exchanged the glory of the immortal God for images resembling a mortal human being or birds or four-footed animals or reptiles" (Rom. 1:22, 23).

God in Christ enters into the midst of his creation and, as the Second Adam, engages the world for God's glory. In offering his life for the life of the world, he restores the doxological order of creature-Creator. And God, in raising Jesus from the dead, goes beyond mere restoration and inaugurates a new humanity that is exalted beyond the category of creature to the status of adopted sons and daughters. It is of some note that Paul recognizes the relationship between human beings and creation in that as Adam's trespass subjected the creation to futility, so also our glorification as children of God is the event that sets the creation itself free from its bondage to decay to "obtain the freedom of the glory of the children of God" (Rom. 8:21). (Jesus' own relation to creation, observed for example in the multiplication of the loaves and fishes and in the calming of the storm, may well be understood as eschatological signs of the relationship of the new humanity to the new creation.)

The primary work of the church (to arrive at my second point of observation) is therefore doxological, and its primary language is the language of worship. Another way of stating this is that the church construes all of reality sacramentally, as an offering of the world to the glory of God, for God's purposes and ends. But the church's offering is not its own but ultimately Christ's, in whose self-offering the faithful participate by means of baptism into his death. The self-offering of Christ, therefore, is the content of the church's primary discourse of praise and thanksgiving. This means that from the church's doxological perspective, the world is no longer an object to be used by us and for us, which is idolatry; but the world is understood as icon, pointing beyond itself to its Creator and Redeemer. Living between the times, the church bears witness to God's saving action in Christ in which a person's relationship to the creation is transformed in Christ from magic (manipulation of the creation/Creator for one's own ends) and idol (worship of the creation instead of the Creator) to sacrament (an outward and visible sign of God's gracious activity) and icon (pointing not to the "thing in itself" but to the Creator and source).

The church lives very much in the world, speaking a new language of sacrament and icon until that day when Christ shall be all in all. In its Eucharistic vocabulary, in "proclaiming the Lord's death until he comes," the church describes reality as it is and ever shall be. It celebrates the memory of the past event of Christ's death in the present from a future perspective of what will ultimately be fulfilled. It is an offering of praise and thanksgiving for what was and is and ever shall be in Jesus Christ. (This is why in Orthodox liturgical theology, the divine liturgy is understood in strikingly literal terms as the gathered community participating in the eternal heavenly worship of the Banquet of the Lamb — a sense of true communion with all the company of heaven, past, present, and future.)

How does the eschatological character of the church's life and mission, expressed in the primary discourse of doxology, inform how the church construes and engages the world? It is this primary discourse, I believe, that provides the key to understanding how the biblical vision is to inform and engage the natural and social sciences of our culture.

The issue is not merely one of different "language games" addressing very different realities, of science dealing with what is observable and theology with what is transcendent and not available to scientific scrutiny.[5] In light of the worldliness of the biblical eschatological vision, this move seems to me to have the air of Gnosticism about it, as it relegates the church and its proclamation to the fringes of what is "spiritual" and otherworldly. Again, the biblical eschatological vision is precisely not an escape from but a re-creation of the world, presumably in observable glory. This is not to say that there is not a degree of discontinuity involved, but I believe the discontinuity consists in the spiritual transfiguration of our bodies and all of creation, not in so radical a break that the future bears no relation to the past so as to be utterly incomprehensible. (The resurrection accounts are instructive insofar as they describe the resurrected Jesus in terms of continuity *and* discontinuity.)

If the church is to develop an eschatology that is both biblical and realistic, it must maintain the proper relationship between its primary and secondary discourse. Second-level discourse, which is theological reflection and engagement with the sciences, must never be divorced from primary discourse, which is worship and prayer borne of relationship to

172

God through the Spirit. Secondary discourse is necessary, of course, as reflection upon the subject of discourse yields greater understanding and disciplined life. But if such reflection is offered as if God is not present, if such secondary discourse is not the handmaiden of doxological language addressed to God in worship, then we find that once again the serpent has entered the conversation. This is true whether we are speaking of the natural sciences or of theology.

26. *Worship as Sign of the End*

ERIK STRAND

Edina Community Lutheran Church
Edina, Minnesota

Almighty Father, in your Son
You loved us, when not yet begun
Was this old earth's foundation!
Your Son has ransomed us in love
To live in him here and above:
This is your great salvation.
Alleluia!
Christ the living,
To us giving
Life forever,
Keeps us yours and fails us never!

What joy to know, when life is past,
The Lord we love is first and last,
The end and the beginning!
He will one day, oh, glorious grace,
Transport us to that happy place
Beyond all tears and sinning!
Amen! Amen!

Come, Lord Jesus!
Crown of gladness!
We are yearning
For the day of your returning.[1]

Philipp Nicolai (1556-1608)

Despite the importance of the conversation in the academy between academic theologians and academic scientists, the church itself will need to
anchor and secure its contributions to the conversation from the patterns
and witness that arise in worship. It will be the engagement of the worshiping community that will determine finally whether this dialogue of
science and theology "works" from the perspective of the church.

Christian worship[2] is one[3] occasion in our society and culture where
every week[4] witness is given to the end of things. Witness is given to a
view of time *(kairos)* that is at odds with the *chronos* of the world. In worship, the end of this world is proclaimed, confessed, sung, and prayed for.
In such a gathering, in such a community, the insights of the community
of scientists concerning the end of the cosmos can find a place and be
welcomed[5] as the community seeks orientation and integration for life in
the world and for the new life to come.[6]

Worship can be both receptive and welcoming of scientific language
and assertions of fecundity and limit and ending.[7] Correlative promises
of the abundance of creation, the reality of limits, and God's eternal embrace are spoken and symbolized and enacted in the weekly gathering of
the baptized. The gathered community in worship gives witness to the
limits of creature life, including limits in the universe itself, and a witness
to the abundant overflowing of life hosted in the universe by God. Experienced in such utterance and listening, the gathered community of faith
should welcome the insights of science as providing more insight into the
richness of the cosmos that is God's creation.

Worship[8] is a sign of the End.[9] The nature of Christian worship witnesses to the end of all things. Eschatology and even apocalypse are woven into the gathering of Christians for praise and prayer. Scripture,
hymns, prayers, sacraments, and proclamation are full of the signs and
promises of the end (as well, of course, of the new creation). When the
baptized community gathers, it is a sign that there is another future and
another end than the one imagined by the world. As a poetic event, an
occasion for metaphor and song, worship can be enriched in its use of the

scientific reflections upon the cosmos. Metaphors and words can be given more density and evocative power as scientific constructs of end, limit, fecundity, and beginning are appropriated[10] for the work of prayer, praise, and thanksgiving.[11]

Scientific theories such as complexity theory and the notion of pattern can strengthen and thicken metaphors used to speak of the "walk in newness of life." Complexity theory gives a sturdy grounding to scriptural and doctrinal insights concerning the essential relationality inherent in the universe — between Creator and creatures, among creatures, between creatures and matter, and within the Triune Godhead itself. Creative use of the insights of science might well enrich our religious language. The discernment of pattern in the creation, for example, can be a conversation partner with Christology and the notion of pattern reflected in the thinking of Hans Frei (particularly in his book *The Identity of Jesus Christ*) or with theological anthropology in the work by John Polkinghorne on the nature of the soul.[12]

Worship also points to a different understanding of time[13] and history than the one by which the world operates. In its witness to the one who is alpha and omega, it asserts an alpha and omega in the journey of creation. At the same time it has the capacity to hold and offer textured understandings of time. Worship has the capacity to allow for divergent and paradoxical notions of time to be present at the same event.

A community shaped by the witness of scripture and tradition has the resources available to consider other notions of time besides that of *chronos.* While participants arrive and sometimes even depart at set times, it is often the case that notions of past, present, and future are intertwined and even blurred (as is the case during Holy Week and Easter when we "enter in" to the events of passion and resurrection as they are made present). This capacity of worship to host even paradoxical notions of time is of particular importance during this period of the depreciation of cultural memory.[14] Worship is the "time" of the telling and retelling and the enacting of the metanarrative of faith. We experience this on the Third Sunday of Easter (year B in the lectionary) when Jesus instructs his disciples by opening their minds to the torah, prophets, and psalms.[15] What we encounter in worship is a narrative that encompasses time and offers meaning to the passing of time and the coming of time.

In the evocative work of the anthropologist Victor Turner,[16] worship is shown to be a liminal[17] event in which memory and meaning are "worked out" in a society. It is an in-between space that images *communitas*[18] in the face of hierarchy, divisions of class and status, and power differentials. One might posit a liminal sense of time in worship, time that is in between time, where one enters in the "orthodox" sense into the eternal throne room of God, where time-bound, gravity-borne conditions of hierarchy are set aside for a gathering around the table where all are welcome and all receive the same treatment. It would be interesting to compare Moltmann's notion of aeonic time and aeonic eternity[19] (descriptions of the "time" of the world to come) with Turner's description of the state of the liminal in worship. Could liminal time be a foretaste of aeonic time "whose contents are the gathered moments of meaningfully lived time"?[20]

Worship gathers a people with the story, metanarrative, moral cosmology, and metaphors that trust that time is not empty but rather filled with meaning. Worship gives witness that the "future is not something people strive for and fill with meaning" but rather that "it comes to the present, and interrupts the course of life."[21] Alexander Schmemann writes that we can worship only in time, yet it is worship that ultimately not only reveals the meaning of time but truly "renews" time itself and gives it meaning. As an example, Schmemann sees Easter as the "sacrament of time" after which time begins again, but it is now filled from "inside" with that unique and truly "eschatological" experience of joy. As we leave worship we are sent into time as the church to serve and to give witness not to a God who saves us from time but a God who has fulfilled and redeemed it. This Christian understanding of time is one which we can offer to science as a different understanding of time that can complement, inform, and enrich an understanding of time as measurement.

In the current cultural social environment of the depreciation of cultural memory, worship is a space, an event that still offers "hot memory"[22] and a "hot future." As Schmemann writes, "worship is an expression of an all-encompassing world-view."[23] Similarly, Christoph Schwöbel views worship as an event that offers a place to integrate into a field of meaning issues of cosmic, historical, and eschatological import.[24] In worship we act out our moral cosmology as a people of God. It reveals our "beliefs and valuations . . . about how human beings are to orient themselves rightly and meaningfully in the texture of the physical cosmos."[25] Worship is one of the forms of discourse needed to give a thick, multilayered account of reality. Worship offers its capacity for poetry, metaphor, and symbol to attend to the "profoundly relational character of reality."[26] Worship is an event in which the scientific description of our physical cosmos can be received as one of the many accounts of reality — one that we need to engage seriously in an imaginative effort of integration and accountability.

Schmemann, an Eastern Orthodox theologian, offers powerful insights concerning worship as that moment in which we see the world in its true nature. In his book *For the Life of the World* he writes,

> We need water and oil, bread and wine in order to be in communion with God and to know Him. Yet conversely — and such is the teaching, if not of our modern theological manuals, at least of the liturgy itself — it is this communion with God by means of "matter" that reveals the true meaning of "matter," i.e., of the world itself. There is no worship without the participation of the body, without words and silence, light and darkness, movement and stillness — yet it is in and through worship that all these essential expressions of man in his relation to the world are given their ultimate "term" of reference, revealed in their highest and deepest meaning.[27]

Schmemann also makes a wonderful argument concerning the true meaning of secular and sacred. He argues that by denying the world its natural "sacramentality" and radically opposing the natural to the supernatural, we make the world "grace-proof," and ultimately are led to secularism (a state of denying that we are essentially worshiping beings). With this perspective, then, a worshiping community would need to take seriously scientific descriptions of matter and its relationships. It will need to take seriously the degradation of matter by the human creature and our distortion of our relatedness to the creation. It will also need to celebrate the continuity of the eschaton with the created world by the God who promises to make all things new and not simply make new things.

Worship is also where those gathered encounter proclamation, story, and metaphor that is counterintuitive. In worship the witness of God's people is received and spoken that what seems to be the case is *not*. The community that gathers for word and sacrament gathers on Good Friday and sings with St. Gregory of Nyssa at the vigil of Easter of the night that becomes "brighter than the day." It is the community that hears, "He has been raised; he is not here. Look, there is the place they laid him. But go, tell his disciples and Peter that he is going ahead of you to Galilee; there you will see him, just as he told you."

Worship itself disturbs and disrupts secure worldviews by rendering them penultimate. Worship includes proclamation of a Word that creates dissonance with common sense and the ways of the world. As such, worship can also challenge old ways of living and give rise to new ones. These new ways of living involve awareness of our relation not only to our fellow humans but to all creatures and all matter. They also include following Jesus in a way that is mindful not only of what he did but also of a creative extrapolation from Scripture and tradition to understand how we are now to function.

Christoph Schwöbel, in his article "The Church as a Cultural Space," offers us a way to consider the church a public, open space for the consideration of a "comprehensive interpretation of reality that takes the challenge of scientific prognoses of cosmic futility seriously and tries to respond to them in such a way that it neither ignores them nor simply adopts them as the ultimate truth for all spheres of reality."[28] He makes clear that while the tendency in the church and its worship life has been too often to close off the conversation with science, this is neither necessary nor in our best interest. He reminds us that we are concerned about the same world, and that it is the very nature of the eschatological character of the gospel that prevents the closing off of the conversation with science or the necessity of some total fideism. I would argue that a Christian worshiping community has both the capacity and experience to engage the conversation, as well as the need for the conversation to inform and give the Christian community material for its work of proclamation and service in the world.

Worship also determines whether or not the conversation between theology and science will finally be validated. It is the moment in which the community of faith gathers, rehearses, hears, and is sent. Worship images meaning for the Christian community, shapes and forms our horizons of meaning, and shows whether or not new metaphors are adequate. Worship, then, is an event that lives in the promised new creation where all shall be gathered to the feast on the mountain, even as it is mindful of present realities. Worship delimits worldly principalities and powers and horizons of meanings and confesses an ending that is also a new beginning. It makes available information concerning matter and the creation to be tested and woven into an evangelical worldview. Worship then ought to welcome metaphors and constructs that cohere with its confession of faith and critique and shape and even undermine those constructs that are not helpful. It also needs to judge the adequacy of its own metaphors and speech in conversation with scientific understandings of the world.

27. Christian Proclamation in Eschatological Perspective

PAUL D. MATHENY

*First Christian Church
Conroe, Texas*

The beginning of the future, the end of historical time, takes place in us through the Spirit. It is the power of the Spirit that makes our hope rise and gives new life. It is the power of the Spirit that made it possible for Thomas to touch the wounds of Christ on that day with the disciples. Through the resurrection, the human situation has been totally changed: "Therefore, if any one is in Christ, he is a new creation; the old has passed away, behold, the new has come" (2 Cor. 5:17). The text continues, "All this is from God, who through Christ reconciled us to himself and gave us the ministry of reconciliation; that is, God was in Christ reconciling the world to himself, not counting their trespasses against them, and entrusting to us the message of reconciliation" (v. 18).

The hope we receive presses on to the ministry of proclamation. The presence of the Spirit leads to creative participation in the service of God's future. Christian hope leads to the reconciling ministry of proclamation.

1. Hope Lies in a Future with God

A theology of proclamation addresses the question, "What is it that we hope for?" This is a fundamental question for all theology. It cannot be ignored. When Christians confess that God is Father, Son, and Holy Spirit,

179

they confess their belief in the promise of God to be faithful to creation. Proclamation addresses from the beginning eschatological reality. What is proclaimed is the Word of God, the good news of life with God, of eternal life. When we hear this news, we receive the promise of salvation and eternal life and the call to repentance and to faith. The focal point is the faithfulness of God fulfilled in Jesus Christ. When we lose this focus, we no longer are proclaiming the gospel. If we give priority to a scientific or philosophical understanding of reality, we are not opening up the truth of eschatological reality.

2. This World Dies

The future lies with God. Proclamation is not futurology: it is not the attempt to foresee what the end of the world will be like or to interpret the signs of God's coming in political or ideological terms. It is based upon faith that we are able to discern the truth about God from the biblical story. This story reveals that God acts in history and acts with God's people to lead them to live as his community. It shows us how we may live by pointing to God's acts in Christ. Its point is not, however, ideological. It does not show us the ideal political way of existence.

This world dies. The future belongs to God and is given to those who are raised to eternal life. We are not to proclaim an apocalyptic vision of the future; we are to proclaim the good news of Christ. Our hope is not bound to the false security of historical prognoses. It is the vision of a future with God that brings life to our churches and renews our communities. This is the biblical vision of hope.

3. The Boundaries of Death and
Finitude Have Been Sprung

The biblical story is not a story of world renewal, but of new creation. Christian hope is hope that the limits of human existence and history will be totally destroyed. Human history will be taken up into God's history, and finitude will be taken up into eternity. Our responsibilities to live as Christians cannot be tested in ideological terms; they must be tested instead according to the eschatological framework of Christian hope. God is not calling us to renew the world according to our hopes and dreams, but rather to participate in the end of the world as we prepare to live in the kingdom as the people of God.

The Christian life is preparation for eternal life. It is witness in the world to the truth of God's presence in history and among God's people. It is, as such, a reconciling ministry for the world.

4. When the Kingdom Is Proclaimed, God Is Present

We do not understand completely the truth about God's love and grace in the story of the final moments of human and natural history. The community of believers is founded not on apocalyptic visions of the future but upon the unique action of God accomplished in Christ. It is founded upon the overflowing of God's grace. God is not just waiting for the last person to die in order to reveal the truth. The church's perspective on the truth is God's perspective, and this perspective is eschatological. The church is to proclaim God's will, and his will is that the kingdom come. We are to live according to God's will.

The biblical story communicates to us that eternity is possible. The history of God is the primary history encompassing all history. Eternity, the very dwelling place of God, is possible. Because God's time is prepared to receive our time, because we believe that the old creation will be taken up into the new creation, because we know that these boundaries have been sprung, we are assured of the inbreaking of God into human history. God has begun a history with his people and he continues this history with us. In Christ, God has taken on human nature and has put on sinful humanity. God is revealed through proclamation. God reveals his truth when we proclaim the truth. When the kingdom is proclaimed, we experience God's presence through the Spirit. It is God who makes the proclamation of truth possible.

5. With Christ's Incarnation and Resurrection, the End of Time Has Begun

As Martin Luther pointed out, the movement of redemption is from death to life. Because Christ came, died, and lives, we too may have life.

History and nature will end. All that happens is relative to what has happened or will happen. Only the incarnation and the resurrection are events in history that are *sui generis.* The life and work of Christ are completely unique in history. It is the life and work of Christ through the Spirit that are by definition new. It is this radical event of novelty that has begun the movement from death to life; it is Christ who has begun the end of time. With the resurrection, the truth about the end of time has been revealed. Proclamation is therefore to declare the resurrection, revealing the truth about God's relationship with humanity.

6. The Presence of the Spirit Brings the Future into the Conditions of the Present

We cannot understand the meaning of God's story from the standpoint of historical or natural investigation. Neither the historical-critical method nor scientific observation, for example, opens up for us the eschatological reality of God's participation in human history. The biblical story is God's story. It is irresponsible, on our part, to read this story as the revealer of truths about history or nature or of the future.

This does not mean that historical study and science are at odds with the Christian faith, or that their results are irrelevant. It does, however, mean that their results are inconclusive for Christian belief and hope. Their focus is different from that of Christianity, and we must not confuse them.

Scientific assessment of nature and history rules out the possibility of revelation; faith in the creative will of God rules out the limits of nature and history. Revelation happens because the God of the Bible springs the bounds and is present and active in our lives. Creation must be prepared to receive the eternal, and eternity must be capable of breaking into the limits of finitude. The presence of the Spirit brings to the community of the faithful a foretaste of the kingdom. It shares the divine with the human. The Eucharistic feast of our Lord is real. The Lord's presence at the table, for example, is an eschatological event.

7. Proclamation Is the Ministry of Reconciliation

It is only as a result of proclamation that the Christian community is renewed through the Spirit. This is true because it is proclamation that brings new life to the church and the world through God's life-giving Spirit. The fundamental task of proclamation is to speak of the kingdom. The biblical story leads us to proclaim the reality of God as creator of the new world. The communication of this story evokes response. The response of the community is decision, repentance, faith, and the strength to share the good news with the world. Through the Spirit we are initiated into a new and transforming life. We are guided constantly to choose the new way of living by grace over the old way of following the law. The hearing of the Word creates a community formed by faith, forgiveness, and reconciliation.

In the Scriptures, eschatology cannot be separated from the life of the church. It cannot be isolated from the evangelical, ecumenical task of the Christian church. Proclamation of Christian hope for the new creation gives the church unity and vision. Proclamation is the ministry of reconciliation of the people of God.

Silence concerning the eschatological themes of Scripture needs to be broken. When we read the strange apocalyptic stories of the Bible, they seem unreal and implausible to our modern minds. Their truth, however, is central to our faith. We can no longer be silent. If we believe in the God of the biblical story, we cannot ignore the inbreaking of God's presence into history and nature. If God acts, then God reveals the truth about not only divinity and eternity but also humanity and finitude. Only when we realize this can the community of faith become the witnessing and reconciling community. Only then can the people of God prepare for the life and future that God offers us.

Theology has an important critical role to play in proclamation. It asks, "Is the proclamation of the church truthful and faithful or not?" The theologian tests for truthfulness new insights into the story of the God whom the worshiping community proclaims. It is proclamation, not theology, that reforms the church by pointing us to Christ and reforming our beliefs, so that the eschatological reality of God continues to be proclaimed and confessed. The theology of proclamation has as its task the guiding of proclamation toward its focus on the reality of God. This is essential for the very life of the church, for without it the life-giving talk of the kingdom of God — of the new creation — would not happen.

28. *"The Future Belongs to Jesus!"*

JONATHAN L. JENKINS

*Holy Spirit Lutheran Church
Lancaster, Pennsylvania*

*The theological content of the christological story is the key to
its eschatological significance.*

Christoph Schwoebel

Let us consider a straightforward proposition: *"The future belongs to
Jesus!"*[1] The burden of this paper is to defend that claim and to demonstrate its role in preaching the gospel. Such a project would have been regarded as uncontroversial at other periods in the church's history. To St.
Paul, this is the good news: "At the name of Jesus every knee shall bend, in
heaven and on earth and under the earth, and every tongue confess that
Jesus Christ is Lord to the glory of God the Father!" (Philippians 2:10-11).
As Isaac Watts' hymn illustrates, it used to be foundational to Christian
thought and piety: "Jesus shall reign where'er the sun doth its successive
journeys run." Has Jesus been demoted from his leading role in
Protestant eschatology? If so, I hope to remind (or perhaps persuade) the
reader that "The future belongs to Jesus" — or some equivalent statement
— is an essential proposition for eschatology and preaching.

"The future belongs to Jesus!" We can characterize this as a slogan,
because it is a catchphrase for the point of the gospel. The greater part of
our task will be to justify the proposition as a reading of the
"christological story" and to illustrate the preaching of its "eschatological
significance," in Christoph Schwoebel's words. For these purposes, the
main sections of the paper employ excerpts from sermons I have
preached. "Can it be preached?" is the acid test for a pastor-theologian.
Our vocational concern is to know how to articulate what we need to say
from the pulpit. The sermon excerpts are intended to demonstrate one
way that eschatology functions in preaching.

"To Jesus"

The Gospel is and should be nothing else than a discourse or history about Christ . . . a story told in various ways. The chief article and foundation of the gospel is that before you take Christ as an example, you accept and recognize him as a gift, as a present that God has given you and that is your own. . . . For the preaching of the gospel is nothing else than Christ coming to us, or we being brought to him. (Martin Luther)[1]

The Promised Kingdom

The gospel is a story about Jesus. As Luther reminds us, it is by telling Jesus' story that we are able to recognize him as a "gift" from God to us, and more importantly, what sort of gift he is. What follows, if the future is his gift and not someone else's?

If Jesus is risen from the dead, you should not be too surprised to find yourself in community with your worst enemies. If, instead, the Ayatollah Khomeini is risen from the dead, it's a different story. Then we're all in trouble. Khomeini's kingdom is only for Iranian warriors, not their enemies. (Easter 7, Matthew 5:38-48)[2]

The first question of eschatology is: Who was Jesus, and what can we expect of him? Jesus was a wandering prophet and rabbi. He preached the message of the immediate coming of the kingdom of God.

A friend calls the life of Jesus the "Operation Headstart" for the kingdom. His life was a kind of "spear-heading" of the kingdom coming into this world. (Lent 2, Philippians 3:17-21)

Jesus did not have to explain the expression "kingdom of God," because it summed up the hopes of Israel's scriptures.

Like John the Baptist, Jesus was certainly a prophet — a messenger from God in line with the prophets of old. Like Amos and Micah, he warned the people of Israel of the judgment falling on those who ig-

185

nored the requirements of righteousness. Like Jeremiah and Ezekiel, he predicted the destruction of Jerusalem, if the people refused to heed his message.

Nevertheless, Jesus proclaimed the coming kingdom as good news.

The Lord was coming to rule and to judge. The Lord was coming to save and forgive. His was the message about the eyes of the blind being opened and the ears of the deaf able to hear. The long night was nearly over, and a new day was about to dawn. His was the message of Israel renewed. The message, in other words of our first reading, Isaiah 35: "The ransomed of the LORD shall return and come to Zion with song; everlasting joy shall be upon their heads; they shall obtain joy and gladness, and sorrow and sighing shall flee away." (Advent 3, Matthew 11:2-11)

His was the message that all would be well at last.

Jesus is remembered for the unlimited way in which he preached the kingdom of God. He brought the future "age to come" into the present.

Here's how to think about Jesus: as the kingdom of God, the End of time, suddenly appearing in the middle of time. For example, Jesus made the Last Judgment of God something happening now, because he forgave sins — he forgives sins *now* — ahead of the Last Judgment.

He preached the kingdom of God unconditionally.

Or another example: he called all sorts of people "blessed" or "happy" whom you wouldn't consider blessed. The hungry, the meek, people in mourning, people who want righteousness so much it's like hunger or thirst. Why call them blessed *now?* Only because they will be happy in the kind of community the coming kingdom will be, and it is already present somehow with Jesus. Jesus didn't make the future kingdom and its blessings something to be worked up to, a little bit at a time. (Christ the King, Matthew 5:1-11)

Jesus did not say that the people "should" work to inaugurate the kingdom.

"Blessed are the meek, for they shall inherit the earth." That's what Jesus says, but that's not what we usually hear, is it? People seem to hear him saying something else, something like: "You should be meek and mild." But Jesus is not teaching us rules. He is not saying, "Do this" or "Do that." Actually, he is doing something.

He was bringing a blessing — a blessing from his Father in heaven.

> In the same way that you say, "Good morning!" he says, "Blessings on you!" When I way "Good morning!" I'm not giving my opinion. I'm saying that I want it to be a good morning for you, and that I intend to help it become a good morning, or at least a better morning, by my being there with you. So it is when Jesus gives any of his "blessings." (Epiphany 4, Matthew 5:1-12)

His preaching was "unconditional" in the sense that Jesus took away time to get ready and gave it back as time to begin.

The immediacy of the message made entrance requirements irrelevant and, therefore, failure to live up to them, too. Jesus thus widened the audience to whom the kingdom was open.

> Jesus brought the outcasts into his life, not in terms of a plan to reform them, but in terms of the new persons they will be only by God's miracle. It wasn't that "there is a little bit of good in everyone." The only good they had or needed was the good in Jesus himself. It's the same way now, as it was then. Through the preaching of the gospel, the risen Jesus continues to establish the same kind of fellowship with the modern-day equivalent of tax collectors and sinners. I'm talking about crack dealers, pornographers, and loan sharks — hardened criminals, nasty people. (St. Matthew, Matthew 9:9-13)

His mission was to gather Israel to himself in order that Israel might share in his own unique relationship to the Lord God of Israel — "my Father."

> In the Lord's Prayer, Jesus invites us to pray *with* him — to call God "our" Father. We are welcome to join Jesus in calling God by the same name he used in the Garden of Gethsemane and later, on the cross:

"Father!" The way Jesus prays suggests that his Father's life is inseparable from his own. (Pentecost 10, Luke 11:1-13)

What was offensive about Jesus was the claim to a unique standing before the Lord, and therefore to a unique role in Israel's future.

"So everyone who acknowledges me before men, I also will acknowledge before my Father who is in heaven; but whoever denies me before men, I also will deny before my Father who is in heaven." When we stand before the judgment seat of God in heaven, we certainly don't want the fact that we belong to Jesus to be something he keeps to himself! How can we expect him to stand up for us then, if we are ashamed of him now? (Pentecost 5, Matthew 10:24-33)

The unconditional way in which Jesus preached the kingdom is as unsettling to us as it was to his first hearers. It also could be less dramatic than one might expect.

Can't you see the faces of these bachelors when they hear that if they want to deal with Jesus, they've got to deal with these kids? If they want to go ahead into the kingdom of heaven, they might have to change somebody's diapers? Heavenly greatness means wiping runny noses? "Whoever receives one such child in my name, receives me." (Pentecost 18, Mark 9:30-37)

He is the one to whom the future belongs!
The future belongs to Jesus because of the way he lived his life. Jesus was "full of the Holy Spirit" (Luke 4:1). He was free to speak and act for a future that cannot be projected from the present situation.

Jesus of Nazareth lived differently. His life was one long defiance of what everybody knows for sure. He preached of the surprises that God has in store for the despairing and the confident alike. He made his friends among those for whom normally there was little hope, the "losers" of his age. He bet his life and work on the unlikely idea that death would not be the conclusion. . . . To Christian faith there belongs a kind of naive optimism, an optimism that — not always, but sometimes — acts against the odds and bets on the long shot. That can say to a sick woman, "Be healed," or to a troubled marriage, "You can make it," or to an entrenched injustice, "Down with it!" or to a risky career, "Let's try it," for the sake of life itself. For the story of Jesus' resurrection is the message that the future is, after all, on the side of the risk-takers. (Epiphany 5, Mark 1:29-39)

Jesus did not confine himself to probable outcomes. Here is where miracles fit into his story.

> In the background of today's gospel (if we follow Luther) is a broken relationship between nature and sinful persons, yet in today's gospel, we witness Christ overcoming the rift and restoring peace. The Messiah's presence permits the water to support Peter. The Holy Spirit relieves the water of its role as an "executioner." The water need not threaten people with death, the wages of sin.

A miracle is an instance of Jesus' freedom in the Spirit of the Lord.

> Our Lord's miracle is a gift of the Spirit, just as any miracle is a glimpse of things still to come. Walking on water and calming the wind are promises, promises proclaiming the peace between nature and sinful humanity that God will restore in his new heaven and new earth. In the kingdom, water will not drown, nor will the wind frighten, because they will no longer need to serve God as messengers of wrath. (Pentecost 12, Matthew 14:22-33)

In the freedom of the Spirit, he was a true son of Israel and of his mother, Mary.

> We love Mary because we feel in her what St. Paul says about God's power being made perfect in weakness (2 Corinthians 12:9). She is the one who brought God himself into our earthly situation. This frail virgin who represents all Israel, with so much on her shoulders — defeating sin in her, defeating hell, defeating everything by the power of God. No wonder, at moments of trial and trouble, when indeed God's power is made manifest in weakness, Christians have always looked to Mary as an example of faith who can intercede for them: "Behold, I am the handmaid of the LORD; let it be to me ac-

cording to your word." This is the sum total of life in the Holy Spirit. (Annunciation, Luke 1:38)

By contrast:

> A funny thing happens when people hear that God is the free and sovereign Lord whose power shapes even the course of nature. People say to themselves: "Ah, if only I were God. Then I'd really be free. Nobody would tell *me* what to do!" When we imagine ourselves having God's free Spirit, often we would make ourselves unbearable, proud little tyrants, self-moved spirits who wouldn't listen to anybody. As different as day and night is God's freedom from our own. What happens when the Holy Spirit takes flesh and blood? What do our eyes behold when the freedom of God became a living human being? (Advent 4, Matthew 1:18-25)

The Gospel announces the end of the world! The birth of Jesus Christ means an end to the old world trapped in falsehood and death, but what does it imply about the cosmos?

> One day even the stars above will yield to him. Even the physical universe will give way to Christ Jesus. Even objects as old and substantial as the galaxies are going to move out of the way of his future. Not one thing is so permanent that it won't have to make room for his purposes. This is why the gospel pictures for us "signs in the sun, the moon, and the stars, and on earth, distress among nations confused by the roaring of the seas and waves.... For the powers of the heavens will be shaken." (Advent 1, Luke 21:25-36)

The "shaking up" will occur mainly in human society; but in some way, the cosmos will have to accommodate itself to whatever new conditions are required to fulfill Jesus' intentions.

> The promise of the kingdom is the promise of a society in God in which death has been put to death and our basic needs are met. Our needs are not just eliminated. Were our basic bodily needs merely to disappear, we would disappear. If God's kingdom or any other society could not provide a safe place to live and food to eat and freedom from

suffering, we would die. Such a place would be inhuman, a place where we could not exist. "He who sits upon the throne will shelter them with his presence. . . . They shall hunger no more, neither thirst any more, and God will wipe away every tear from their eyes." (Easter 4, Revelation 7:9-17)

How honored we are by God in the Holy Communion! How honored to be receiving the one who died and rose on high, and this only a foretaste, only a beginning, to what he will reveal in us. A great Lutheran teacher of the seventeenth century, Johann Gerhardt, writes, "This Holy Supper will transform our souls; this most divine sacrament will make us divine men, until finally we shall enter upon the fullness of the blessedness that is to come, filled with all the fullness of God and wholly like Him. What we have here only by faith and in a mystery, we shall enjoy in reality and openly. These bodies of ours which are now temples of the Holy Spirit, and are sanctified and quickened by the body and blood of Christ dwelling in us, shall be crowned with this glory, that in them we shall see God face to face" (Meditation XX). (Easter 3, 1 John 3:1-7)

The future belongs to Jesus, we believe, because of who Jesus was — and who he is. Nothing can defeat his promise of a "new heaven and a new earth," and we have described what we may anticipate in the kingdom that "will have no end." In the end, creation will find her shape ever anew within the history of the Son, the originality of the Father, and the interpretive liberty of the Holy Spirit.

29. Hopeful Feasting: Eucharist and Eschatology

REBECCA KUIKEN

Stone Presbyterian Church
San Jose, California

When the hour came, he took his place at the table, and the apostles with him. He said to them, "I have eagerly desired to eat this Passover with you before I suffer; for I tell you, I will not eat it until it is fulfilled in the kingdom of God." Then he took a cup, and after giving thanks he said, "Take this and divide it among yourselves; for I tell you that from now on I will not drink of the fruit of the vine until the kingdom of God comes."

Luke 22:14-18 (Matt. 26:20-30; Mark 14:17-26)

In *Eucharist and Eschatology,* Geoffrey Wainwright moves out from this key text to explore the language and links — from Old Testament to New Testament, from the words of Jesus to the liturgies of the primitive church and the early centuries of Eastern and Western Christianity — that describe the connections between Eucharist and eschatology.

He notes that theological treatises have concentrated attention on the ontological questions of Christ in the Eucharist in the bread and wine, or the sacrificial nature of the Eucharist. In the process, we have lost sight of the ways that Christ's advent or coming in judgment and salvation is revealed in this sacred meal. We have also lost the communal reference of the Eucharist as "the common meal of the whole churchly people of God in the last days, and its relation to the Messiah's banquet in the kingdom and the abundant feeding that the Bible looked for in the days of the new heavens and the new earth."[1]

While Wainwright focuses on three central images: (1) the messianic feast, (2) the advent of Christ, and (3) the first fruits of the kingdom, I will concentrate here only on the first.

The Messianic Banquet:
The Background in Hebrew Scriptures

The Eucharist is first of all a *meal.* The Hebrew Scriptures offer a rich background to Jesus' and the church's understanding of eating and drinking in the kingdom of God. Eating and drinking, particularly in a cultic setting, offer a means for encountering divine blessing.

Meal imagery has multiple references in Hebrew scripture. Meals are linked to critical moments in the life of the Hebrew people: the making of the covenant with Moses on Mount Sinai (Exod. 24:9-11), and the many instances where sacred meals were held in places of sacrifice. In the Eucharist language of "this cup is the new covenant in my blood" (1 Cor. 11:25; cf. Luke 22:20), we hear echoes of Exodus 24, where the covenant was made with Moses on Mount Sinai. Moses splashes the blood of sacrifice against the altar and on the people, and "they beheld God, and they ate and drank" (Exodus 24:11). In wisdom literature, meal imagery expresses the giving and receiving of divine blessing.[2] And of course there is Psalm 23, with its powerful portrait of God's unfailing care in the words, "You prepare a table before me in the presence of my enemies; you anoint my head with oil; my cup overflows."

While the above examples speak of feasting and feeding in the present, there are abundant passages that point to a *future time of feasting and feeding.* Out of the experience of the Babylonian exile come prophetic images of Ezekiel and Isaiah of a renewed journey through the desert (Isa. 49:9) and being fed in the wilderness (Isa. 48:21). Of greatest import is the passage of the Isaianic apocalypse in Isaiah 25:6-9, which offers extravagant language about a future feast for all peoples, where there is no death, on a day of salvation and rejoicing:

> On this mountain the Lord of hosts will make for all peoples a feast of rich food, a feast of well-aged wines, of rich food filled with marrow, of well-aged wines strained clear. And he will destroy on this mountain the shroud that is cast over all peoples, the sheet that is spread over all nations. He will swallow up death forever. Then the Lord God will wipe away the tears from all faces, and the disgrace of his people he will take away from all the earth; for the Lord has spoken. It will be said on that day, Lo, this is our God; we have waited for him that he might

save us. This is the Lord; we have waited for him; let us be glad and rejoice in his salvation.

In his article "Judgment and Joy," Patrick Miller describes the banquet as one of the two places in the Isaiah 24–27 apocalypse where "the divine choice of life over death is made, despite the choices that have been made by the inhabitants of the world."[3] The banquet imagery is part and parcel of God's ultimate wrapping up of history, where both divine judgment and divine creativity are displayed.

There is a universal thrust to this meal; it is not exclusive, but is a feast "for all peoples." It presents the end of death and sorrow. It is a feast of life and goodness, celebrated by the people as an act of salvation that has come to a hope-filled people.

In the inter-testamental period and up to the Judaism of Jesus' day, the messianic banquet imagery in the Old Testament, with its futurist and eschatological expectations, became linked to the Jewish Passover. Wainwright concludes,

> We may therefore confidently suppose that in the time of Jesus the Jews looked for the coming of the Messiah in the same night as that in which the great deliverance from Egypt had been wrought. This messianic expectation would then mark the meal during which, according to the synoptic gospels, Jesus instituted the Eucharist.[4]

The church held on to this notion of messianic expectation, transposing it from Passover to Eucharist, the notion of Christ's return. In the fourth century, Jerome believed that Christian expectation of Christ's coming during the Easter vigil dated from apostolic times:

> There is a Jewish tradition that the Messiah will come in the middle of the night in likeness of what happened in Egypt. . . . Whence I consider also the apostolic tradition to have been drawn, that it is not lawful to dismiss the people before midnight from the paschal vigil, for we expect the advent of Christ.

The Messianic Significance
of Meals during Jesus' Ministry

In parables and in the beatitudes, Jesus spoke of a future feast of the kingdom, even as the meals during his own ministry contained messianic significance. Jesus' table fellowship with prostitutes, tax collectors and other outcasts earned him notoriety and stands as a "sign and metaphor" in the tradition of Old Testament prophecy, in which the action performed by the prophet imitates the action of God.

How much theological weight do we place on the Eucharist as the fulfillment of the signs of Jesus? How much do we point in expectation and hope toward images of the perfect and completed communion with God? After citing several centuries of church theologians, Wainwright comes through with a "Goldilocks" solution (in other words, not *too* past or *too* future, but "just right"). First, the Eucharist expresses both continuity and discontinuity in the relationship between the present and future reign of God, between the earthly meal and the heavenly banquet. It is an earthly snack, not a full-course messianic meal. Second, the Eucharist takes ordinary gifts of food and drink, thus expressing both human dependence on the Creator and the Creator's choosing to use "the structure of reality": "Christ is food, table companion and host."[5] We acknowledge and enjoy God's presence and reign inasmuch as we express our thanksgiving and our dependence. Third, the Eucharistic meal transcends any dualistic categories between the material and spiritual in our notions of God's reign. On the one hand, it does point to the eternal purposes of God; "It is a sign of the new heaven and the new earth on which risen men and women will enjoy perfect fellowship with God in the consummated kingdom."[6] On the other, the meal expresses the fact that this world, this material creation, is afforded a positive value, because it is the medium through which God and humanity meet and commune. Finally, the Eucharist expresses the communal nature of God's reign — we cannot enter into the kingdom of God one by one, any more than one can become human alone. It is a communal table and a communal reign. It thus offers a corrective for Western individualism and sounds a loud refrain for justice.

An eastward orientation for Eucharistic prayer and even architecture offer other clues for the connection between eschatology and Eucharist in early Christian thought. Scriptural designations of Christ as the "Sun of righteousness" (Mal. 4:2, Luke 1:78) led to the practice of praying toward the east in expectation of Christ's return. For example, the *Syriac Teaching of the Apostles* says,

> Pray ye toward the east: because, "as the lightning which lighteneth from the east and is seen even to the west, so shall the coming of the Son of man be" — that by this we might know and understand that He will appear from the east suddenly.[7]

In Egyptian liturgies, the deacon summoned worshipers to look towards the east during the great Eucharistic prayer. Early church documents exist that call for the disposition of the church building to be turned east. In the Alexandrian *Canons of Basil* (circa 400), the deacon summons people to stand and turn east.

Moving from examples that orient the Eucharist towards an eschatological calendar and compass, Wainwright explores the more foreboding side of the Parousia. How does the Eucharist express or point to the "day of judgment"?

The Day of Judgment

The New Testament presents images of the close and consummation of time and history, when all people will be judged: "For all of us must appear before the judgment seat of Christ, so that each may receive recompense for what has been done in the body, whether good or evil" (2 Cor. 5:10). The intent of this imagery is to help us make sense of evil and injustice in human history, and to affirm that, in the end, good triumphs and God is God.

Judgment is already present, inasmuch as the believer responds to the encounter with the living Christ — in the past event of Christ's death and Resurrection. Our baptism marks us as having participated in this passage from death to Resurrection. Dipped into the baptismal waters, we land on the other shore and, in Christ, experience mercy.

Wainwright suggests that the Eucharist is "a repeated projection of the last judgment." Each celebration fulfills in part, and makes stronger, the promise of both judgment and pardon that we first received in baptism. *Maranatha* thus becomes a salvific cry of both mercy and judgment, as Christ assumes the role of universal judge at the last day.

In 1 Corinthians 11:27-34, Paul criticizes the Corinthians with language that draws on juridical imagery as he speaks of their offensive table fellowship. In particular, he is disturbed by their divisiveness, by the humiliation of the poor by the rich, who were eating first and leaving nothing. This selfish behavior was both an ecclesiological and Christological affront: they were turning the Lord's Supper into their own supper. Even with their terrible table manners, the power of the Eucharist to issue judgment was still in place: "For all who eat and drink without discerning the body, eat and drink judgment against themselves." We celebrate the Eucharist between baptism and last judgment, so even though we have encountered mercy in our baptism, we still await the complete verdict. In this way, the Eucharist has us moving back and forth between Christ's consoling mercy and his discomforting judgment.

Yet another aspect of Eucharist that raises themes of judgment is found in Matthew 26:28, with its language of covenantal sacrifice, the blood "poured out for many for the remission of sins." Repentance and contrition are part of the Eucharist. I am reminded of the optical illusion in which one sees a young woman or, if focusing differently, an old woman. In a sense, the same thing occurs in the Eucharist: depending on the focus, one looks at the image of Christ as the one who forgives or as the one who judges. Thus in all the liturgies of both East and West, the twin themes of remission of sins and non-condemnation recur in connection with the Eucharist, but they are frequently set in reference to Christ's final coming "to judge both the quick and the dead."

In reviewing the Eastern liturgies, Wainwright points out that in comparison, the Western church less often gives such reference to the second coming of Christ and the ensuing judgment. Even in post-communion prayers, where one most typically finds mention of the future, the line of thought usually moves from present and continuing purification of sin and straight into enjoyment of heavenly blessings. In the West, the emphasis has been on a commemorative sacrifice.

In the Eucharist, we "remember the future." Time and space are layered, and therefore it becomes a wide container with tremendously rich imagery. Christ comes to us out of the past in the incarnation, passion, and resurrection, as well as all the promises made in his first coming: "Where two or three are gathered together in my name, there am I in the midst of them." Christ's advent is part and parcel of the eternal God's final purpose, but it is made accessible to us in the present so we can discern in these "glimpses" what our ultimate hopes and fears might be. And inasmuch as "the Lord comes" into each Eucharistic celebration, we may view the Eucharist as a last judgment in miniature.

The abundance of metaphors and images presented in the Christian tradition holds the power to hearten and encourage people as they confront an emerging future, with all its threats and its possibilities. The caregiver of a parent with Alzheimer's, the lonely software worker wrestling with skewed demands and evolving ethics in hi-tech industry, and the community worker organizing for affordable housing in Silicon Valley all come to the Lord's table and encounter the promise that God is working out *God's future*. God is gathering in the kingdom. Take heart! The images and metaphors resonate in the human mind, come to life, and a new heaven and a new earth appear on the horizon. As the hymn "For All the Saints" proclaims in its final refrain,

> And when the strife is fierce, the warfare long,
> Steals on the ear the distant triumph song,
> And hearts are brave again, and arms are strong.
> Alleluia! Alleluia!

Notes

PART ONE

CHAPTER I

Section 1

1. Michael Polanyi, *The Tacit Dimension* (Garden City: Doubleday, 1966), pp. 82-83.

2. Thomas F. Torrance, *Belief in Science and in Christian Life* (Edinburgh: Hansdel, 1980), pp. 4-5.

3. Richard Gelwick, *The Way of Discovery* (New York: Oxford University Press, 1997), p. 26.

4. Marjorie Greene, ed., *Knowing and Being* (Chicago: University of Chicago Press, 1969), p. 85.

5. Polanyi, *Tacit Dimension,* p. 4.

Section 2

1. William Schweiker, "Time as a Moral Space: Moral Cosmologies, Creation, and Last Judgment," and Donald H. Juel, "Christian Hope and the Denial of Death: Encountering New Testament Eschatology," both in *The End of the World and the Ends of God,* ed. John Polkinghorne and Michael Welker (Harrisburg, PA: Trinity, 2000). See also Ben Witherington III, *Jesus, Paul and the End of the World* (Downers Grove, IL: InterVarsity Press, 1992).

2. This clearly expresses my departure from most current scholarship. Few argue against the apocalyptic character of the chapter. Donald Juel finds the term "Little Apocalypse" to be a bit misleading, but he does see the chapter as eschatological ("Christian Hope," p. 175). Most commentators see the chapter as pointing to some distant future.

3. All biblical quotations from Mark in English are taken from the New Revised

Standard Version Bible. Citations of the Greek New Testament are from Nestle-Aland, *Novum Testamentum Graece,* 25th edition.

4. *Theological Dictionary of the New Testament,* ed. Gerhard Kittel, trans. Geoffrey Bromiley, vol. 2 (Grand Rapids: Eerdmans, 1964); see pp. 832-75 for an extensive discussion of *zōē* and *bios.*

5. Schweiker, "Time as a Moral Space," p. 16. Schweiker, who is not a New Testament scholar, brings to the text a clear set of ideas he intends to "find" there. His work is an excellent example of eisegesis.

6. See, for example: *The New Testament Background, Selected Documents,* ed. and with introductions by C. K. Barrett (New York: Harper, 1961), pp. 227-28.

7. R. H. Lightfoot, *The Gospel of Mark* (London: Oxford University Press, 1950). Lightfoot has a fine chapter in this volume entitled "The Connexion of Chapter Thirteen with the Passion Narrative." It is a helpful but very cautious reading of Mark 13.

8. Donald Juel, *Augsburg Commentary on the New Testament: Mark* (Minneapolis: Augsburg Fortress, 1990). Juel also has additional comments in the paper that I noted above.

9. Schweiker, "Time as a Moral Space," p. 132.

10. Juel, *Augsburg Commentary,* p. 175.

Section 3

1. G. B. Caird, *The Revelation of St. John the Divine* (New York: Harper and Row, 1966), p. 262.

2. In his Gifford Lectures, published as *The Faith of a Physicist* (Princeton: Princeton University Press, 1994), John Polkinghorne observes that one of the differences of the new creation from the old is that the first creation was *ex nihilo,* while the new one will be *ex vetere,* created out of the first (p. 167).

3. This culmination of humanity sources the picture of heaven in Hans Küng, *Eternal Life? Life After Death as a Medical, Philosophical, and Theological Problem,* trans. Edward Quinn (Garden City, NY: Doubleday, 1984), pp. 218ff.

4. Jacques Ellul in his *Apocalypse: The Book of Revelation* (New York: Seabury Press, 1977) argues that the inclusion of the New Jerusalem in heaven symbolizes that "God does not annul history and the work of man but, on the contrary, assumes it" (p. 222).

5. Similar vice lists can be found in 1 Cor. 6:9-10; Gal. 5:19-21; and Eph. 5:3-5.

6. Robert Royalty, Jr., *The Streets of Heaven: The Ideology of Wealth in the Apocalypse of John* (Macon: Mercer University Press, 1998), p. 233.

7. Royalty, *Streets of Heaven,* p. 223.

Section 4

1. Frank Kermode, *The Sense of an Ending: Studies in the Theory of Fiction* (London: Oxford University Press, 1968), pp. 160, 162.

2. Jürgen Moltmann, *God for a Secular Society: The Public Relevance of Theology* (Minneapolis: Fortress Press, 1999), pp. 147-55.

Section 5

1. William Stoeger, "Scientific Accounts of Ultimate Catastrophes in Our Life-Bearing Universe," in Polkinghorne and Welker, eds., *End of the World*, p. 19.

2. Gordon D. Fee, *The First Epistle to the Corinthians* (Grand Rapids: Eerdmans, 1987), p. 776.

3. Clarence T. Craig, *The First Epistle to the Corinthians* (Nashville: Abingdon-Cokesbury Press, 1953), p. 246.

4. Raymond F. Collins, *First Corinthians* (Collegeville, MN: The Liturgical Press, 1999), pp. 42-44; Hans Conzelmann, *1 Corinthians* (Philadelphia: Fortress Press, 1975), p. 283; Gordon D. Fee, *First Epistle to the Corinthians*, p. 786; William Orr and James A. Walther, *1 Corinthians: A New Translation* (Garden City, NY: Doubleday, 1976), p. 347.

5. Fee, *First Epistle to the Corinthians*, p. 786.

6. Conzelmann, *1 Corinthians*, p. 283.

7. Fee, *First Epistle to the Corinthians*, p. 786.

8. Orr and Walther, *1 Corinthians*, p. 346.

9. Christoph Schwöbel, "The Church as a Cultural Space," in Polkinghorne and Welker, eds., *End of the World*, p. 115.

CHAPTER II

Section 6

1. Thomas Aquinas, *Summa Theologica*, 1.12.1.

2. Aquinas, *Summa*, 1.12.1.

3. Aquinas, *Summa*, 1.12.2.

4. Aquinas, *Summa*, 1.12.2.

5. Robert Jenson, *Systematic Theology II* (Oxford: Oxford University Press, 1999), p. 344.

6. Aquinas, *Summa*, 1.12.11.

7. Aquinas, *Summa*, 1.12.2.

8. Aquinas, *Summa*, 1.12.5.

9. Aquinas, *Summa*, 1.12.13.

10. Aquinas, *Summa*, 1.12.7.

11. Herbert McCabe, "Introduction," *Summa Theologica*, vol. 3 (New York: McGraw-Hill, 1964), p. xxiv.

12. Aquinas, *Summa*, 1.12.6.

13. Aquinas, *Summa*, 1.12.6.

14. Aquinas, *Light of Faith: The Compendium of Theology* (Manchester: Sophia Institute Press, 1933), p. 362.

15. Aquinas, *Light of Faith*, p. 362.

16. Aquinas, *Light of Faith*, p. 363.

17. Walter Principe, Foreword to Jean-Pierre Torrell, O.P., *St Thomas Aquinas 1:*

The Person and the Work (Washington: The Catholic University of America Press, 1996), p. xii.

18. Aquinas, *Summa*, 11.11.23.6.

19. The best treatment of active and complacent love in Thomas is found in three articles by Frederick Crowe: "Complacency and Concern in the Thought of St. Thomas Aquinas," *Theological Studies* 20 (1959): 1-39, 198-230, 343-95.

Section 7

1. William R. Stoeger, "Scientific Accounts of Ultimate Catastrophes in Our Life-Bearing Universe," in *The End of the World and the Ends of God,* ed. John Polkinghorne and Michael Welker (Harrisburg: Trinity Press, 2000), p. 19.

2. Jürgen Moltmann, *The Coming of God* (Minneapolis: Fortress Press, 1996), p. 50.

3. George Steiner, *Real Presences* (Chicago: University of Chicago Press, 1989), p. 3.

4. CNN/*USA Today*/Gallup poll, December 24, 1999.

5. Gerhard Forde, *Where God Meets Man* (Minneapolis: Augsburg, 1972), p. 93.

6. Forde, *Where God Meets Man,* pp. 94-95.

7. Georges Bernanos, *Diary of a Country Priest* (New York: Macmillan, 1937), p. 19.

8. Mark Mattes, "Gerhard Forde on Re-envisioning Theology in Light of the Gospel," *Lutheran Quarterly* 13 (1999): 377.

9. Even if the story is apocryphal, as Sauter contends, it nonetheless serves to articulate Luther's eschatology. See Gerhard Sauter, *Eschatological Rationality* (Grand Rapids: Baker Books, 1996), p. 175.

10. Forde, *Where God Meets Man,* p. 97.

11. Johann Anselm Steiger, "The *communicatio idiomatum* as the Axle and Motor of Luther's Theology," *Lutheran Quarterly* 14 (2000): 151.

12. Steiger, "The *communicatio idiomatum*," p. 149.

13. Steiger, "The *communicatio idiomatum*," p. 133.

14. Forde, *Where God Meets Man,* p. 98.

Section 8

1. John Polkinghorne, *Science and Theology: An Introduction* (Minneapolis: Fortress Press, 1998), pp. 20-22.

2. Saul Bellow, *Herzog* (New York: Viking Press, 1964), p. 290.

3. Polkinghorne, *The Faith of a Physicist* (Minneapolis: Fortress Press, 1996), p. 69.

4. Quoted in Hermann Diem, *Kierkegaard: An Introduction* (Richmond: John Knox Press, 1966), p. 15.

5. Quoted in Warren Groff and Donald Miller, *The Shaping of Modern Christian Thought* (Cleveland: World Publishing, 1968), p. 375.

6. Groff and Miller, *The Shaping of Modern Christian Thought,* p. 86.

7. Interestingly, there are several excellent web sites on Kierkegaard and his thought. One of the best is by D. Anthony Storm: www.2xtreme.net/dstorm/sk/.

8. See note 7 above.

9. Justo Gonzalez, *For the Healing of the Nations* (Maryknoll, NY: Orbis, 1999), pp. 100-102.

Section 9

1. Paul Tillich, *Systematic Theology*, vol. 3 (Chicago: The University of Chicago Press, 1957), p. 421.

2. Tillich, *Systematic Theology* 3, p. 298.

3. Tillich, *Systematic Theology* 3, p. 395.

4. Tillich, *Systematic Theology* 3, pp. 108, 333, 357-61.

5. Tillich, *Systematic Theology* 3, pp. 282, 364.

6. Tillich, *Systematic Theology* 3, p. 366.

7. Similarly, in his most recent book, *Genes, Genesis and God* (Cambridge University Press, 1999), Holmes Rolston III speaks of a *signum crucis* being written throughout creation. One sees in evolution that things are born and that they die; but in their death there is a new birth. I am indebted to William Stoeger for this reference.

8. Paul Tillich, *The Eternal Now* (New York: Charles Scribner, 1962), p. 46. Langdon Gilkey serves us well here with the following insight: "Perhaps the truth is that vulnerability, suffering, contingency, and death — nonbeing in all its terror for us as a sacral nothingness — are characteristics of deity, shared in by deity and so themselves revelatory of the sacral nothingness of the deity. The divine being can seemingly only create and sustain finite being by continually negating itself, by uniting being and nothingness in its own self. . . . To redeem our being, the divine must negate its own. And this, we say, is expressive of the inmost nature of God, whose being — and nonbeing — is love." Langdon Gilkey, *Society and the Sacred* (New York: Crossroad, 1981), p. 136. "The question is: Where of all places can and shall we see into the ground of all Being? Who can lead our contemplation into the temple, into the holy itself? . . . He who has seen [Jesus the Christ] has seen the Father. This is true only of the Crucified." Paul Tillich, *The New Being* (New York: Scribner, 1995), pp. 131, 133.

9. Tillich, *Systematic Theology* 3, p. 400.

10. Tillich, *Systematic Theology* 1, p. 245 (emphasis added).

11. Tillich, *Systematic Theology* 1, p. 371.

12. Tillich, "The Importance of New Being for Christian Theology," in *Man and Transformation* (New York: Bollinger Foundation, 1964), pp. 172-73.

13. Tillich, *Systematic Theology* 1, p. 385.

14. Tillich, *The Eternal Now*, p. 90.

15. Paul Tillich, *Theology of Culture*, ed. Robert C. Kimball (New York: Oxford University Press, 1959), p. 7.

16. Paul Tillich, *Systematic Theology* 3, p. 113.

17. Spiritual Presence, according to Tillich, helps humankind overcome the tragic and ambiguous character of life, not by making the finite infinite, or taking

nonbeing away, but by giving us the courage to accept our finite lives as finite and to be open to sacrificing our life for the sake of the One in whom we have the power to be at all — God. For Tillich's discussion of Spiritual Presence, see *Systematic Theology* 3, pp. 111-61, 271, 411.

18. Tillich, *Systematic Theology* 3, p. 140 (emphasis added).

19. Tillich, *Systematic Theology* 3, p. 140.

20. Tillich, *The Protestant Era* (Chicago: The University of Chicago, 1948), p. 67.

21. Tillich, *Systematic Theology* 1, pp. 194-95.

22. Tillich, *Systematic Theology* 3, pp. 157-58.

23. Tillich, *Systematic Theology* 3, p. 16. See also Tillich, *The Interpretation of History* (New York: Scribner, 1936), p. 161.

24. Tillich, *The Socialist Decision,* trans. Sherman Franklin (New York: Harper and Row, 1977), p. 3.

25. Paul Tillich, *A History of Christian Thought* (New York: Harper and Row, 1968), p. 117.

26. We are reminded here of a more adequate notion of the doctrine of *creatio ex nihilo* that was offered by Irenaeus and Tertullian; that is, not to imagine or speak of God's bringing the world into being out of nothing, but rather, as establishing the world *in* Being Itself. Cf. Langdon Gilkey, "Creation: Being and Nonbeing," in Gilkey, *Through the Tempest,* ed. Jeff Pool (Minneapolis: Fortress, 1991), p. 99.

27. Paul Tillich, *The Shaking of the Foundations* (New York: Charles Scribner's Sons, 1948), p. 46. See also Tillich, *The Meaning of Health,* ed. Perry LeFevre (Chicago: Exploration Press), p. 3.

28. Tillich, *Systematic Theology* 1, p. 398.

29. Tillich, *Systematic Theology* 2, p. 119.

30. Tillich, "Importance of New Being," p. 169.

31. Tillich, "Autobiographical Reflections," in *The Theology of Paul Tillich,* ed. Robert Bretall and Charles Kegley (New York: Macmillan, 1959), p. 347.

32. Tillich, *Systematic Theology* 3, p. 253; see also pp. 358, 403.

33. Tillich, *Systematic Theology* 3, p. 255.

34. Tillich, "Being and Love," in *Moral Principles of Action,* ed. Ruth N. Anshen (New York: Harper and Row, 1952), p. 345.

35. See Tillich, *Systematic Theology* 2, p. 162; and 3, p. 31.

36. Tillich, *Political Expectation* (New York: Harper and Row, 1971), p. 153.

37. Tillich, *Systematic Theology* 3, p. 269.

38. Tillich, *Systematic Theology* 3, pp. 403, 405.

39. Tillich, *What Is Religion?* (New York: Harper and Row, 1969), p. 111.

40. Tillich, *The Meaning of Health: Essays in Existentialism, Psychoanalysis, and Religion* (Chicago: Exploration Press, 1984), p. 21.

41. Tillich, *The Shaking of the Foundations* (New York: Charles Scribner's Sons, 1948), pp. 109, 186.

42. Tillich, "Being and Love," p. 334.

43. Tillich, *Systematic Theology* 1, p. 299.

Section 10

1. See Stanley Hauerwas, *Dispatches from the Front: Theological Engagements with the Secular* (Durham: Duke University Press, 1994), pp. 109-10.

2. Though Stringfellow writes of the "second coming" of Christ, I suspect he would appreciate the comment of a pastor friend who reminds me that only once does the New Testament describe the fulfillment of the creation in Christ as a "second coming" of Jesus (Hebrews 9:28). The common use of the word *Parousia* by the New Testament writers to describe the final appearing of Christ functions to indicate that the return of Christ will be discontinuous enough with his coming that we should hesitate to liken one to the other. The least we can say is that the second coming of Christ will be as big a surprise as his first coming.

3. William Stringfellow, *An Ethic for Christians and Other Aliens in a Strange Land* (Waco: Word, 1973), p. 44.

4. Stringfellow, *An Ethic for Christians and Other Aliens*, p. 139.

5. Stringfellow, *An Ethic for Christians and Other Aliens*, p. 153.

6. Bill Kellerman, ed., *A Keeper of the Word* (Grand Rapids: Eerdmans, 1994), p. 11.

7. Stringfellow, *The Politics of Spirituality* (Philadelphia: Westminster Press, 1984), p. 73.

8. William Stringfellow, *An Ethic for Christians and Other Aliens*, p. 51.

9. Revelation 21:24 — "The nations will walk by its light, and the kings of the earth will bring their glory into it."

10. Janet Soskice, "The Ends of Man and the Future of God," in Polkinghorne and Welker, eds., *The End of the World*, pp. 83ff.

11. Stanley Hauerwas, *Dispatches from the Front* (Durham: Duke University Press, 1994), p. 108.

12. William Stringfellow, *An Ethic for Christians and Other Aliens*, p. 78.

CHAPTER III

Section 11

1. James Moorhead, "Mainstream Protestants and the End of the World," *Inspire*, Winter 2000, p. 17. (I read this article after I had written the majority of this paper, but Moorhead's concluding words were too good not to use here. The title of this paper is taken from his article.)

2. Neil Postman, "Science and the Story That We Need," *First Things*, January 1997, p. 30.

3. Donald H. Juel, "Christian Hope and the Denial of Death: Encountering New Testament Eschatology," in *The End of the World and the Ends of God*, ed. John Polkinghorne and Michael Welker (Harrisburg: Trinity Press, 2000), p. 182.

4. Quoted in Tom Long, "'When Half-Spent Was the Night': Preaching Hope in the New Millennium," *Journal for Preachers* 22, no. 3 (Easter 1999): 15.

5. Christoph Schwöbel, "The Church as a Cultural Space: Eschatology and Ecclesiology," in Polkinghorne and Welker, eds., *The End of the World and the Ends of God*, p. 122.

Section 12

1. Schwöbel, "The Church as a Cultural Space," in Polkinghorne and Welker, eds., *The End of the World and the Ends of God*, p. 123.

2. Richard Bauckham, *God Crucified: Monotheism and Christology in the New Testament* (Grand Rapids: Eerdmans, 1999), p. 71.

3. Bauckham, *God Crucified*, p. 71.

4. Bauckham, *God Crucified*, p. 71.

5. Paul M. Van Buren, *According to the Scriptures: The Origins of the Gospel and of the Church's Old Testament* (Grand Rapids: Eerdmans, 1998).

6. Donald E. Gowan, *Eschatology in the Old Testament* (Edinburgh: T&T Clark, 1987), p. 15.

7. Jürgen Moltmann, "The Eschatological Trial of Jesus Christ," in *The Crucified God* (Philadelphia: Fortress, 1974), p. 163.

8. Moltmann, "The Eschatological Trial of Jesus Christ," p. 163.

9. Moltmann, "The Eschatological Trial of Jesus Christ," p. 175.

10. Moltmann, "The Eschatological Trial of Jesus Christ," p. 188.

11. Anthony Thiselton, *New Horizons in Hermeneutics* (Grand Rapids: Zondervan, 1992), p. 7.

12. Thiselton, *New Horizons in Hermeneutics*, p. 446.

Section 13

1. Cf. Bob W. Parrott, *Albert Outler, the Preacher* (Nashville: Abingdon Press, 1988), p. 68.

2. Cf. Albert W. Outler, *Who Trusts in God: Musings on the Meaning of Providence* (New York: Oxford University Press, 1968), p. 33.

3. John Polkinghorne, *The Faith of a Physicist* (Minneapolis: Fortress, 1966), p. 162.

4. Cf. Albert C. Outler, *Psychotherapy and the Christian Message* (New York: Harper and Row, 1954), p. 177.

5. Outler, *Psychotherapy and the Christian Message*, p. 178.

6. Outler, *Psychotherapy and the Christian Message*, pp. 178-79.

Section 14

1. Paul Lehmann, *The Transfiguration of Politics* (New York: Harper & Row, 1975), p. 13.

2. Wolfhart Pannenberg, speaking of Jesus, writes, "On the basis of the eschatologically oriented Israelite understanding of truth, according to which the essence of a thing has not always existed — even though hiddenly — but is decided only by what becomes of it, the predestination of all things toward Jesus, their eschatological sum-

mation through Jesus, is identical with their creation through Jesus." *Jesus — God and Man*, 2nd edition (Philadelphia: Westminster, 1997), p. 391.

3. H. Richard Niebuhr writes, "Monotheistic idealism says: 'Remember God's plan for your life.' Monistic deontology commands: 'Obey God's law in all your obediences to finite rules.' Responsibility affirms: 'God is acting in all actions upon you. So respond to all actions upon you as to respond to his action.'" *The Responsible Self* (San Francisco: Harper & Row, 1978), p. 126.

4. Jürgen Moltmann writes, "It was an error of presentative eschatology to identify the present kairos with the eschatological moment and not perceive the difference." Moltmann, *The Coming of God* (Minneapolis: Fortress, 1996), p. 292. The argument of this paper, in contrast, will show that the end is experienced in the present but not exhausted by it.

5. Niebuhr writes, "One way of describing the incarnate character of radical faith in the life of Israel is to say that for this people all human relations were transformed into covenant relations. Promise-making and promise-keeping were the essential elements in every connection between persons." Niebuhr, *Radical Monotheism and Western Culture* (New York: Harper & Row, 1960), p. 41.

6. Matt. 5:44 and Luke 6:27. See Walter Wink's chapter entitled "The Acid Test: Loving Enemies," in *Engaging the Powers* (Minneapolis: Fortress, 1992), pp. 263-77.

7. Consider in this light the call of Jesus for watchfulness; see Mark 13:33-37, for example.

8. Wink, *Engaging the Powers*, p. 234.

9. Wink, *Engaging the Powers*, p. 234.

10. While the woman makes no specific reference to God, clearly she had, in H. Richard Niebuhr's words, a fundamental trust in being itself. See Niebuhr, *The Responsible Self*, p. 118.

11. Psalm 88 is a good example.

PART TWO

CHAPTER IV

Section 15

1. Gotthold Lessing, *Werke*, Vol. 10, 53.

2. Phillip Frank, *Modern Science and Its Philosophy* (Cambridge: Harvard University Press, 1949), chapter 12: "Why do scientists and philosophers so often disagree about the merits of a new theory?"

3. Ernst Mach, *Readings in Philosophy of Science* (Baltimore, 1953), p. 35.

4. Mach, *Readings in Philosophy of Science*, p. 35.

Section 16

1. John Polkinghorne and Michael Welker, eds., *The End of the World and the Ends of God* (Harrisburg: Trinity, 2000).

2. Polkinghorne and Welker, eds., *The End of the World*, pp. 222-33.

3. Polkinghorne and Welker, eds., *The End of the World*, p. 226.

4. Polkinghorne and Welker, eds., *The End of the World*, p. 48.

5. Polkinghorne and Welker, eds., *The End of the World*, p. 48.

6. Polkinghorne and Welker, eds., *The End of the World*, p. 184.

7. Polkinghorne and Welker, eds., *The End of the World*, p. 184.

8. Transcendence is a substantial sticking point. It is an essential dimension of reality when reality is discerned theologically. Since Darwin, science has strongly resisted even intimations of transcendence as off the empirical radar screen.

9. Ted Peters, ed., *Science and Theology: The New Consonance* (Boulder: Westview Press, 1998). In its milder form, consonance is seeing connections or agreeing to shared understandings. In the strongest sense, consonance implies some kind of convergence.

10. Alasdair MacIntyre, *Whose Justice? Which Rationality?* (Notre Dame: University of Notre Dame Press, 1988), pp. 387-88.

11. Polkinghorne and Welker, eds., *The End of the World*, p. 4.

12. See Michel Foucault, *Les mots et les choses: une archéologie des sciences humaines* (Paris: Gallimard, 1966). The English translation is *The Order of Things: An Archaeology of the Human Sciences* (London: Tavistock, 1970).

13. Janet Soskice calls hope "a readiness to act, a directedness, a commitment, a passionate practicality. If you hope in God's future, you do not just feel rosier about a few things, your life is changed by it." Soskice in Polkinghorne and Welker, eds., *The End of the World*, pp. 86-87.

14. Polkinghorne and Welker, eds., *The End of the World*, p. 78.

15. Polkinghorne and Welker, eds., *The End of the World*, p. 57.

16. I am thinking of science's tendency toward reductionism and positivism and what Jean-François Lyotard described as the postmodern condition of being able to have only little and local narratives locked in combat. See Lyotard, *The Postmodern Condition: A Report on Knowledge* (Minneapolis: University of Minnesota Press, 1984).

17. Polkinghorne and Welker, eds., *The End of the World*, p. 183.

Section 17

1. Hans Weder, "Hope and Creation," in Polkinghorne and Welker, eds., *The End of the World*, p. 191.

2. Matt. 24:35; Mark 13:31; Luke 21:33; cf. Matt. 5:18; Luke 16:17; Isa. 65:17; 66:22; II Pet. 3:13; Rev. 21:1.

3. These remarks are clearly pertinent to the theodicy question, which I do not wish to pursue further here. Suffice it to say that I regard God's power as contingent in the formal sense that it must conform to God's love and in the material sense that di-

vine sovereignty does not mean unconditional freedom from the constraints of actual existence in which the only limitations upon divine action are self-imposed. This is to say at least that the creation that God has brought into being possesses an integrity of being and action that God cannot violate. Thus I cannot agree with Weder when he asserts that "death is . . . the point where God's power can act in an unlimited way" ("Hope and Creation," p. 195), if that is taken categorically and not just as a statement about God's freedom to act without resistance in the context of human relations marked by human death. If the statement is to be taken only in the latter sense, then I find its meaning unclear.

4. Matt. 3:9; Luke 3:8.

5. Cf. Isa. 57:1; Jer. 12:11.

6. Rom. 11:36.

Section 19

1. Emil Brunner, *Dogmatics*, vol. 3: *The Christian Doctrine of the Church, Faith, and Consummation* (Philadelphia: Westminster, 1960), p. 346.

2. Brunner, *Dogmatics*, vol. 3, p. 340.

3. Thomas Torrance, *The Trinitarian Faith* (Edinburgh: T&T Clark, 1988), 183.

4. Brunner, *Dogmatics*, vol. 3, p. 442.

5. Athanasius, *The Incarnation of the Word of God* (New York: Macmillan Co., 1947), p. 95.

6. Brunner, *Dogmatics*, vol. 3, p. 444.

7. Torrance, *Trinitarian Faith*, p. 72.

8. Georges Florovsky, *Creation and Redemption* (Belmont, MA: Nordland, 1976), p. 74.

9. Florovsky, *Creation and Redemption*, p. 44.

10. Torrance, *Trinitarian Faith*, p. 73.

11. Brunner, *Dogmatics*, vol. 3, p. 344.

12. John W. Nevin, "Wilberforce on the Incarnation," *The Mercersburg Review* 2 (1950): 171.

13. Brunner, *Dogmatics*, vol. 3, p. 440.

14. Florovsky, *Creation and Redemption*, p. 61.

15. Florovsky, *Creation and Redemption*, p. 246.

16. Brunner, *Dogmatics*, vol. 3, p. 431.

17. Brunner, *Dogmatics*, vol. 3, p. 439.

18. Florovsky, *Creation and Redemption*, p. 246.

19. Brunner, *Dogmatics*, vol. 3, p. 430.

CHAPTER V

Section 20

1. Walter M. Miller, Jr., *A Canticle for Leibowitz* (New York: Bantam Books, 1976).

2. See Genesis 1:6-8. All biblical references will be to the Revised Standard Version.

3. Jürgen Moltmann, *The Coming of God: Christian Eschatology,* trans. Margaret Kohl (Minneapolis: Fortress Press, 1996), pp. 259-60.

4. Erich von Daniken, *Chariots of the Gods?* trans. Michael Heron (New York: Bantam Books, 1971), pp. 37-39. Also concerning Ezekiel, see Josef F. Blumrich, *The Spaceships of Ezekiel* (New York: Bantam Books, 1974).

5. Clifford Wilson, *Crash Go the Chariots* (New York: Lancer Books, 1972) and *The Chariots Still Crash* (New York: Signet Books, 1975).

6. Matt. 13:24-30.

7. Michael Welker, *God the Spirit,* trans. John F. Hoffmeyer (Minneapolis: Fortress Press, 1994), pp. 7-21.

8. Welker, *God the Spirit,* p. 43.

9. Exod. 31:1-6.

10. Welker, *God the Spirit,* p. 102.

Section 21

1. Quoted in Matt Donnelly, "Is Science Good for the Soul? Then Sings My Psychosomatic Unity!" *Books and Culture,* Jan/Feb 2000, p. 36.

2. M. Scott Peck, *Denial of the Soul* (New York: Harmony Books, 1997), p. 157.

3. Michael Welker, "Resurrection and Eternal Life," in *The End of the World and the Ends of God,* ed. John Polkinghorne and Michael Welker (Harrisburg: Trinity, 2000), p. 282.

4. Hans Weder, "Hope and Creation," in Polkinghorne and Welker, eds., *The End of the World,* p. 194.

5. Jürgen Moltmann, *The Coming of God* (Minneapolis: Fortress, 1998), p. 65.

6. Nancey Murphy, *Beyond Liberalism and Fundamentalism* (Harrisburg: Trinity, 1996), p. 98.

7. Quoted in Herbert Benson, *Timeless Healing: The Power and Biology of Belief* (New York: Scribner, 1996), p. 106.

8. Miroslav Volf in Polkinghorne and Welker, eds., *The End of the World,* p. 269.

9. Miroslav Volf in Polkinghorne and Welker, eds., *The End of the World,* p. 268.

10. Carolyn Myss, *Why People Don't Heal and How They Can* (New York: Three Rivers, 1997), p. 84.

11. Andrew Weil, *Spontaneous Healing: How to Discover and Enhance Your Body's Natural Ability to Maintain and Heal Itself* (New York: Knopf, 1995), p. 19.

Section 22

1. Francis Collins and Karin Jegalian, "Deciphering the Code of Life," *Scientific American,* December, 1999, p. 86. Collins, the director of the National Human Genome Research Institute, identifies himself as a practicing Christian "who is particularly interested in the ethical implications of human genetics research" (p. 91).

2. Francis Collins et al., "New Goals for the U.S. Human Genome Project: 1998-2003," *Science,* October 23, 1998. See also www.nhgri.nih.gov.

3. Robyn Leary, "Surviving His Own Bad Habits" (previously unpublished interview with Walker Percy), *Doubletake,* Winter, 2000, p. 71.

4. Collins and Jegalian, "Deciphering the Code of Life," p. 90.

5. John Polkinghorne, *The Faith of a Physicist* (Minneapolis: Fortress, 1996), p. 163.

6. Sondra Ely Wheeler, *Stewards of Life: Bioethics and Pastoral Care* (Nashville: Abingdon, 1996), p. 116.

7. Richard Hays, "Why Do You Stand Looking Toward Heaven?" *Modern Theology* 16, no. 1 (January 2000): 130-31.

8. Donald H. Juel, "Christian Hope and the Denial of Death," in Polkinghorne and Welker, eds., *The End of the World,* p. 174.

9. Francis Collins and David Galas, "A New Five-Year Plan for the U.S. Human Genome Program," *Science,* October 1, 1993, p. 46.

10. Carl Braaten, "The Last Things," *Christian Century,* December 1, 1999, p. 1175.

11. Lewis A. Lawson and Victor A. Kramer, eds., *More Conversations with Walker Percy* (Jackson: University Press of Mississippi, 1993), p. 242.

12. The best discussion of this tendency among non-scientist Christian leaders is found in Ted Peters, *Playing God* (New York: Routledge, 1997).

13. Gnosticism was a dualistic heresy among early Christians that held that flesh was evil and spirit was good (see John 1; 1 John 1). In commenting on our need for the apocalyptic, Richard Hays writes in "Why Do You Stand Looking Toward Heaven?": "where Christian theology has remained most closely in touch with its Jewish apocalyptic roots, it has most firmly insisted on the value and importance of embodied existence, in contrast to forms of Hellenized piety that regard the material realm as evil or inferior. The gospel proclaims the resurrection of the body, not the immortality of the soul. . . . The alternative to the apocalyptic vision, then, is some form of Gnosticism that denies God's redemptive intention for creation and the body" (p. 129).

14. See Jürgen Moltmann, *The Coming of God* (Minneapolis: Fortress, 1996), pp. 324ff; and Geoffrey Wainwright, *Doxology: The Worship of God in Praise, Doctrine and Life* (New York: Oxford, 1980).

15. Charles Wesley, "Love Divine, All Loves Excelling," *The United Methodist Hymnal* (Nashville: United Methodist Publishing House, 1989), p. 384.

Section 23

1. John Shea, *Stories of God* (Allen, TX: Thomas More Publishing, 1978), p. 22.

2. Paul Ricoeur, *The Symbolism of Evil* (Boston: Beacon Press, 1967), p. 351.

3. Sara Maitland, *A Big Enough God: A Feminist's Search for a Joyful Theology* (New York: Henry Holt & Co., 1995), pp. 186, 189.

4. Walter Brueggemann, *Texts Under Negotiation* (Minneapolis: Fortress Press, 1993), pp. 19-20.

5. Walter Brueggemann, *Finally Comes the Poet* (Minneapolis: Fortress Press, 1989), p. 6.

6. Brueggemann, *Finally Comes the Poet*, p. 27.

7. Brueggemann, *Finally Comes the Poet*, p. 9.

8. Brueggemann, *Texts Under Negotiation*, p. 18.

9. Quoted in Barbara Brown Taylor, *The Luminous Web: Essays on Science and Religion* (Boston: Cowley Publications, 2000), p. 23.

Section 24

1. Karl Barth, *Wolfgang Amadeus Mozart* (Grand Rapids: Eerdmans, 1986), p. 16.

2. Barth, *Wolfgang Amadeus Mozart*, p. 56.

3. Barth, *Wolfgang Amadeus Mozart*, p. 47.

4. Hans Küng, *Mozart: Traces of Transcendence* (Grand Rapids: Eerdmans, 1991), p. 34.

5. Küng, *Mozart*, p. 34.

6. George Steiner, *Real Presences* (New York: Faber & Faber, 1989), p. 218.

7. Ralph Vaughan Williams, *The Making of Music* (Ithaca: Cornell University Press, 1955), p. 3.

8. Vaughan Williams, *The Making of Music*, p. 4.

9. Deems Taylor, *Of Men and Music* (New York: Simon and Schuster, 1942), p. 25.

10. Elder Olson, "A Recital by Rudolf Serkin," *The American Scholar* 51 (Spring 1982): 218.

11. Opal Wheeler, *Handel at the Court of Kings* (New York: E. P. Dutton, 1943), p. 53.

12. Quoted from liner notes of "Tamboura," a recording produced by the SYDA Foundation, South Fallsburg, NY, in 1990.

13. Leonard B. Meyer, *Emotion and Meaning in Music* (Chicago: University of Chicago Press, 1956).

14. Lewis Thomas, *The Lives of a Cell: Notes of a Biology Watcher* (New York: Penguin Books, 1978), p. 24.

15. Lewis Thomas, *Et Cetera, Et Cetera: Notes of a Word-Watcher* (Boston: Little, Brown and Company, 1990), p. 146.

16. Thomas, *Et Cetera, Et Cetera*, p. 147.

17. Thomas, *Et Cetera, Et Cetera*, p. 147.

18. Thomas, *Et Cetera, Et Cetera*, p. 147.

19. Thomas, *The Lives of a Cell*, p. 24. These words were selected from Milton's "At a Solemn Music" by Hubert Parry for his composition for chorus and orchestra, "Blest Pair of Sirens."

20. Polkinghorne, *The Faith of a Physicist,* p. 46.

21. Polkinghorne, *The Faith of a Physicist,* p. 45.

22. Polkinghorne, *The Faith of a Physicist,* p. 45.

23. Polkinghorne, *The Faith of a Physicist,* pp. 45-46.

CHAPTER VI

Section 25

1. Ben Witherington III, *Jesus, Paul and the End of the World* (Downers Grove, IL: InterVarsity Press, 1992), pp. 82-83.

2. Walter Brueggemann, "Faith at the Nullpunkt," in John Polkinghorne and Michael Welker, eds., *The End of the World and the Ends of God* (Harrisburg: Trinity Press International, 2000), p. 154.

3. Dietrich Bonhoeffer, *Creation and Fall* (New York: Macmillan, 1959), pp. 67-70.

4. The distinction between primary and secondary theology is developed fully in Aidan Kavanaugh, *On Liturgical Theology* (New York: Pueblo Publishing Company, 1984).

5. See Polkinghorne, *Science and Theology* (London: SPCK, 1998), p. 118: "The scientist-theologians all reject a 'two-languages,' non-interactive account of the two disciplines. There remains the question of where, within the spectrum of relationship bounded by absorption at one end and total independence at the other, a balanced account of the interaction between science and theology is to be located."

Section 26

1. Verses 4 and 5 of the hymn "O Morning Star, How Fair and Bright," Epiphany hymn, *Lutheran Book of Worship.* Nicolai was a pastor in Germany and did much of his work in a town ravaged by plague.

2. In speaking of Christian worship, I am thinking of the historical *ordo* of the church catholic. In its essence this is a gathering of word *and* sacrament. It is a gathering that hears a broad lection of the scriptures read and proclaimed, and offers intercession on behalf of the world as it receives gifts of bath and meal. There are communities of Christians where these factors might not all be present weekly but yet are implied. There are others of course where, in their pandering to culture and class, eschatology has been covered over.

3. While there may be other gatherings where this is the case, I am not aware of any that do it with such density as Christian worship (except perhaps some seminars in physics).

4. "Christ has died, Christ has risen, Christ shall come again," and "He will come again to judge the living and the dead" are two phrases spoken weekly in most gatherings. We are those who confess that at the table we gather with those of "every time and every place."

5. This despite historical antagonisms and insecurities. See Janet Martin Soskice, "The Ends of Man and the Future of God," in Polkinghorne and Welker, eds., *The End of the World*. Her essay concerns some of the nineteenth-century issues. Similarly, see Christoph Schwöbel, "The Church as a Cultural Space," in the same volume, esp. pp. 113-14.

6. See especially Alexander Schmemann, *For the Life of the World* (New York: St. Vladimir's Seminary Press, 1973), p. 119: "the very notion of worship implies a certain idea of man's relationship not only to God, but also to the world."

7. We are just not well practiced at it — nor are we well informed concerning the resources that science offers.

8. Given much of what passes for worship in many congregations, one might wonder if what I have written thus far is simply some idealized romanticism. But even in a time when the "word of the Lord is rare in the land," when so much of the church seems to have caved in to the ways of Babylon, it is also true that as long as that word is read and prayed there will be "hearing" that breaks forth at odd times into action. See Schwöbel, "The Church as a Cultural Space," in Polkinghorne and Welker, eds., *The End of the World*, p. 112: "Going back to the origin has always meant for Christianity to be confronted again with the original eschatological drive of its beginnings."

9. This year's CTI theme heightened my hearing and singing as we moved through the powerful eschatological texts in November and in Advent this past year.

10. Note the attempt of James B. Miller in his article "From the Garden to Gauss: Mathematics as Theological Metaphor" to provide a mathematical metaphor for the Christian doctrine of sin.

11. This will include a process of experimentation; of seeing what does and does not "work."

12. Polkinghorne in *The End of the World*, p. 39, and in his public lecture at Princeton University sponsored by the Center of Theological Inquiry, March 25, 2000.

13. Evident in the liturgical calendar, in the honoring of saints who have never led a nation or made much money, and in the proclamation of a new creation that is both now and coming in the future.

14. See *The End of the World and the Ends of God*, p. 8: "While the physical sciences press us to expand our consciousness of time, recent cultural developments collapse time-consciousness back into the immediate present."

15. Luke 24:36ff.

16. Victor Turner, *Ritual Process: Structure and Anti-Structure* (Ithaca: Cornell University Press, 1977), and *Worship* magazine, Sept.-Oct. 1971.

17. The use of the word "liminal" here is similar to the Celtic use of "thin places" used in the recent work of Peter Gomes, but it also has a time quality about it as well: an in-between time, an in-between place between our regular, ordinary life experiences. For Turner and others, cultures experience *communitas* in rituals that are marginal to the daily status-structures of society and yet utterly necessary for keeping those status-structures penultimate and malleable to change. Cf. Gordon Lathrop, *Holy Things* (Minneapolis: Fortress Press, 1993).

18. *Communitas* is a state of horizontal equality in society. It is imaged well at the Eucharistic table, where all are welcome and all receive the same.

19. Jürgen Moltmann, *The Coming of God: Christian Eschatology*, trans. Margaret Kohl (Minneapolis: Fortress Press, 1996) pp. 291, 282, 295; footnoted in Miroslav Volf, "Enter into Joy," in Polkinghorne and Welker, eds., *The End of the World*, p. 272.

20. Volf, "Enter into Joy," p. 272.

21. William Schweiker in Polkinghorne and Welker, eds., *The End of the World*, p. 133.

22. See Polkinghorne and Welker, eds., *The End of the World*, pp. 8-9.

23. Schmemann, *For the Life of the World*, p. 123.

24. See Schwöbel, "The Church as a Cultural Space," in Polkinghorne and Welker, eds., *The End of the World*, p. 110: "Religious beliefs are integrative beliefs, offering ways of integrating the different dimensions of reality by relating them to one focus that is not part of reality but transcends it."

25. Schweiker in Polkinghorne and Welker, eds., *The End of the World*, p. 126.

26. Polkinghorne and Welker, eds., *The End of the World*, p. 11.

27. Schmemann, *For the Life of the World*, p. 121.

28. Schwöbel, "The Church as a Cultural Space," in Polkinghorne and Welker, pp. 107-23.

Section 28

1. *A Brief Explanation on What to Look For and Expect in the Gospels*, in *Luther's Works*, Vol. 35 (Philadelphia: Fortress, 1986), p. 117.

2. Indented quotations are from my sermons. Each citation indicates (1) the date on the church calendar and (2) the text of the sermon.

Section 29

1. Geoffrey Wainwright, *Eucharist and Eschatology* (London: Epworth Press, 1971), p. 2.

2. Proverbs 9:1-6, which ends, "Come, eat of my bread and drink of the wine I have mixed. Leave simpleness, and live, and walk in the way of insight."

3. Patrick Miller, "Judgment and Joy," in Polkinghorne and Welker, eds., *The End of the World*, p. 166.

4. Wainwright, *Eucharist and Eschatology*, p. 23.

5. Wainwright, *Eucharist and Eschatology*, p. 58.

6. Wainwright, *Eucharist and Eschatology*, p. 59.

7. Wainwright, *Eucharist and Eschatology*, p. 79.

1999-2000 Pastor-Theologian Program

Center of Theological Inquiry
Princeton, New Jersey

Resource Theologians (in addition to members of the CTI Eschatology Project listed in the Preface)

Robert Jenson
Center of Theological Inquiry
Princeton, New Jersey

James Mays
Union Theological Seminary
Richmond, Virginia

Alexander McKelway
Davidson College
Davidson, North Carolina

Dennis Olson
Princeton Theological Seminary
Princeton, New Jersey

Regional Seminar Conveners

Cynthia Jarvis — Northeast
The Presbyterian Church of Chestnut Hill
Philadelphia, Pennsylvania

James Miller — South Central
First Presbyterian Church
Tulsa, Oklahoma

Bruce Rigdon — North Central
Grosse Pointe Memorial Church
Grosse Pointe Farms, Michigan

John Stapleton — Southeast
St. John's United Methodist Church
Aiken, South Carolina

Virgil Thompson — West
Bethlehem Lutheran Church
Spokane, Washington

Pastor-Theologians

Barbara J. Archer
First Christian Church
Church in the Valley
Butte, Montana

Byron Bangert
Presbytery of Ohio Valley
Bloomington, Indiana

Joseph Bassett
The First Church in Chestnut Hill
Chestnut Hill, Massachusetts

Joseph Carle
Chapel Hill Presbyterian Church
Blue Springs, Missouri

Kenneth H. Carter, Jr.
Mount Tabor United Methodist Church
Winston-Salem, North Carolina

John Christopherson
Lutheran Campus Pastor
Montana State University
Bozeman, Montana

Deborah Clemens
Frieden's United Church of Christ
Sumneytown, Pennsylvania

Richard Coleman
First Congregational Church
Plympton, Massachusetts

Randy Cooper
First and Trinity United Methodist Church
Henderson, Tennessee

Richard Crocker
Central Presbyterian Church
Montclair, New Jersey

Thomas Currie
First Presbyterian Church
Kerrville, Texas

Robert Dahlen
Goodridge Area Lutheran Parish
Goodridge, Minnesota

F. Harry Daniel
Second Presbyterian Church
Little Rock, Arkansas

Joseph H. DeRoulhac, Jr.
First Baptist Church of Redlands
Redlands, California

Douglas Dobson
Holy Cross Lutheran Church
Salem, Oregon

Barry H. Downing
Northminster Presbyterian Church
Endwell, New York

Jeffrey Eaton
Emanuel Evangelical Lutheran Church
New Brunswick, New Jersey

Mateen A. Elass
Immanuel Presbyterian Church
Warrenville, Illinois

Barry Ensign-George
Springville Presbyterian Church
Springville, Iowa
Lynn Grove Presbyterian Church
Mt. Vernon, Iowa

Pamela Fickenscher
The Spirit Garage
Minneapolis, Minnesota

Douglas Fletcher
Westlake Hills Presbyterian Church
Austin, Texas

Richard L. Floyd
First Church of Christ in Pittsfield, Congregational
Pittsfield, Massachusetts

Shirley Funk
Lake Edge Lutheran Church
Madison, Wisconsin

James Gilchrist
Second Presbyterian Church
Carlisle, Pennsylvania

Dale Gregoriew
Christ the Servant Lutheran Church
Allen, Texas

Sonja Hagander
Augsburg College Campus Ministry
Minneapolis, Minnesota

Robert Hausman
Lutheran Church of the Resurrection
St. Paul, Minnesota

David Henderson
St. Paul's Episcopal Church
Steamboat Springs, Colorado

Scott Hoezee
Calvin Christian Reformed Church
Grand Rapids, Michigan

Jonathan Jenkins
Holy Spirit Lutheran Church
Lancaster, Pennsylvania

John Mark Jones
Bethlehem United Methodist Church
Bishopville, South Carolina

Albert Keller
Circular Church (UCC, PCUSA)
Charleston, South Carolina

Adelia Kelso
Northminster Presbyterian Church
Pearl River, Louisiana

James Kitchens
Davis Community Church
Davis, California

Joel Kok
Trinity Christian Reformed Church
Broomall, Pennsylvania

Rebecca Kuiken
Stone Church of Willow Glen
San Jose, California

Rebecca L. Lucky
Zion Lutheran Church
Kent, Washington

Donald Mackenzie
University Congregational (UCC)
Seattle, Washington

Paul Matheny
First Christian Church
Conroe, Texas

Harold McKeithen
Hidenwood Presbyterian Church
Newport News, Virginia

Thomas McKnight
St. John's Presbyterian Church
Berkeley, California

Allen McSween
Fourth Presbyterian Church
Greenville, South Carolina

David Miles
Austin Presbyterian Theological Seminary
Austin, Texas

Bruce Modahl
Grace Lutheran Church
River Forest, Illinois

Rush Otey
First Presbyterian Church
Pensacola, Florida

Brenda M. Pelc-Faszcza
First Church of Christ, Congregational (UCC)
Suffield, Connecticut

Thomas Renquist
Lord of the Hills Lutheran Church
Aurora, Colorado

Robert Rice
First Presbyterian Church
Norman, Oklahoma

John Rogers
Covenant Presbyterian Church
Charlotte, North Carolina

John Rollefson
Lord of Light Lutheran Church
Ann Arbor, Michigan

Charles Rush
Christ Church
Summit, New Jersey

Charles Smith
Rocky Mount District Superintendent
United Methodist Church
Rocky Mount, North Carolina

Erik Strand
Edina Community Lutheran Church
Edina, Minnesota

Laird Stuart
Calvary Presbyterian Church
San Francisco, California

Hamilton Throckmorton
Barrington Congregational Church (UCC)
Barrington, Rhode Island

Charles Valenti-Hein
Memorial Presbyterian Church
Appleton, Wisconsin

Douglas Vaughan
First Presbyterian Church
Wilmington, North Carolina

Barry Vaughn
St. Peter's Episcopal Church
Philadelphia, Pennsylvania

F. Joseph Wahlin
Holy Shepherd Lutheran Church
Lakewood, Colorado

Anita Warner
Advent Lutheran Church
Morgan Hill, California

Paul Wee
Church Consultant
Alexandria, Virginia

Ken Williams
Rockland Community Church
Golden, Colorado

DATE DUE

			Printed in USA